Comparative Philosophy and Religion in Times of Terror

STUDIES IN COMPARATIVE PHILOSOPHY AND RELIGION

Series Editor: Douglas Allen, University of Maine

This series is based on the view that significant and creative future studies in philosophy and religious studies will be informed by comparative research. These studies will emphasize aspects of contemporary and classical Asian philosophy and religion, and their relationship to Western thought. This series will feature works of specialized scholarship by new and upcoming scholars in Asia and the West, as well as works by more established scholars and books with a wider readership. The editor welcomes a wide variety of manuscript submissions, especially works exhibiting highly focused research and theoretical innovation.

Varieties of Ethical Reflection: New Directions for Ethics in a Global Context, edited by Michael Barnhart

Mysticism and Morality: A New Look at Old Questions, by Richard H. Jones

Gandhi's Experiments with Truth: Essential Writings by and about Mahatma Gandhi, edited by Richard L. Johnson

To Broaden the Way: A Confucian-Jewish Dialogue, by Galia Patt-Shamir

Comparative Philosophy and Religion in Times of Terror, edited by Douglas Allen

Comparative Philosophy and Religion in Times of Terror

Edited by Douglas Allen

LEXINGTON BOOKS

A Division of
ROWMAN & LITTLEFIELD PUBLISHERS, INC.
Lanham • Boulder • New York • Toronto • Oxford

LEXINGTON BOOKS

A division of Rowman & Littlefield Publishers, Inc.
A wholly owned subsidary of The Rowman & Littlefield Publishing Group, Inc.
4501 Forbes Boulevard, Suite 200
Lanham, MD 20706

PO Box 317
Oxford
OX2 9RU, UK

British Library Cataloguing in Publication Information Available

Library of Congress Cataloging-in-Publication Data

Comparative philosophy and religion in times of terror / edited by Douglas Allen.
   p. cm.
 Includes bibliographical references and index.
 ISBN-13: 978-0-7391-0996-0 (cloth : alk. paper)
 ISBN-10: 0-7391-0996-0 (cloth : alk. paper)
 ISBN-13: 978-0-7391-1617-3 (pbk. : alk. paper)
 ISBN-10: 0-7391-1617-7 (pbk. : alk. paper)
 1. Terrorism—Philosophy. 2. Terrorism—Religious aspects. 3. Violence—Philosophy.
 4. Violence—Religious aspects. I. Allen, Douglas, 1941- II. Title.
HV6431.C652 2006
303.6'2501—dc22   2006010214

Printed in the United States of America

⊖™ The paper used in this publication meets the minimum requirements of American
National Standard for Information Sciences—Permanence of Paper for Printed Library
Materials, ANSI/NISO Z39.48–1992.

Contents

Introduction

Douglas Allen

Ever since the terrorist attacks of September 11, 2001, terms such as "terror," "terrorists," and "terrorism" have been endlessly repeated by politicians, media figures, and others with power. I became President of the Society for Asian and Comparative Philosophy in January 2001, and I took the leadership in organizing the remarkable SACP conference, "Comparative Philosophy in Times of Terror," at Asilomar Conference Grounds, Asilomar, California, May 27-30, 2003. Obviously, the title and focus of the conference and this book are related to what happened on 9/11.

What can philosophy contribute to our understanding of the terror, terrorism, violence, and insecurity that increasingly dominate our discourse and our lives psychologically, economically, politically, militarily, culturally, and religiously? Can philosophical analysis shed light on the nature of our violent and insecure situation and suggest alternative approaches leading to greater nonviolence, peace, and justice?

First, especially as a peace and justice scholar and activist, it has struck me, along with millions of others, how the key repetitious terms—such as "terror," "terrorists," and "war on terrorism"—are usually used by those with power in very narrow, vague, self-serving ways. They often function as little more than emotionally charged slogans or sound bites. They are often used as linguistic weapons, stirring up the emotions of citizens, deflecting attention from careful examination of issues, and shutting off debate and consideration of alternative analyses by asserting that "opponents" are unpatriotic, excuse or support terrorists, or are simply evil. By way of contrast, philosophy emphasizes critical examination and reflection. What the philosophers in this volume reveal is that critical reflection leads to the conclusion that violence, terror, and terrorism are highly complex, nuanced, contradictory, multidimensional, contextually situated and defined, and that key dimensions, variables, and meanings are excluded in the uncritical, self-serving, power-defined discourses.

Second, although this book is clearly related to the events of 9/11 and our post-9/11 world of violence, terror, and terrorism, it would be a mistake to restrict it to those specific contexts. What philosophers in this book reveal is that human beings, throughout history, have lived under conditions of terror. Can the insights and wisdom of different philosophical approaches and traditions help us to understand root causes and diverse forms of violence, terror, and terrorism? In this regard, the following chapters show, for example, how Aristotle in ancient Greece, Confucius in ancient China, authors of the *Bhagavad-Gita* in ancient India, later Mahayana Buddhists and Islamic thinkers, and the twentieth-century Dewey and Gandhi analyzed and related to violence and terror.

Third, comparative philosophy and religion, central to this volume, may provide new insights, analysis, and approaches for relating to violence and terror. In the diverse chapters, we find the attempt by authors to try to understand the positions of "the other" as fairly and accurately as possible. This is always a complex, dynamic, open-ended, hermeneutical process, involving the fusion of the interpreter's own contextually influenced perspective with the perspective of the other and with the gradual emergence of various points of commonality and differences. However, in addition to the obvious value of trying to understand the perspective of the other as accurately as possible, there are unique benefits emerging from a comparative approach. When different traditions, approaches, and perspectives are brought into relation, something new emerges. The other, for example, can serve as a catalyst, causing me to rethink some of my own assumptions, bursting open my previously closed ethical, philosophical, and religious horizons, and allowing me to conceptualize new ways of relating to violence and terror.

I shall not attempt to delineate a long list of significant philosophical issues that emerge from a reading of the following chapters. To mention just a few of these issues, these philosophical studies clearly show the dangers of ethnocentrism and uncritical generalizations. What emerges is the sense that major Asian traditions, for example, are extremely diverse, complex, contradictory, contextually shaped, and often interpret and apply their basic teachings and values in ways that contradict common stereotypical understandings. In addition, various chapters bring out tensions between philosophical and religious traditions that are foundational, essentialist, and formulated on a very abstract or universal level and those "same" philosophical and religious positions that have to be understood in terms of the diversity and relativity of the actual, specific, contextual nature of their approaches to violence and terror.

To provide only one other illustration, various chapters focus on how Asian philosophies and religion often emphasize meditative and other psychological and phenomenological techniques and approaches for gaining awareness of the experiential root causes, conditions, and nature of violence and terror within us. They also propose various techniques and practical means for transforming this violence and terror in terms of greater equanimity, nonviolence, peace of mind, and liberation. Does such psychological and phenomenological awareness and inner transformational process help us to understand and deal with "external," "objective" variables and structures of economic, political, military, and other historical forms of violence and terror discussed by various authors or are the Asian approaches more often attempts to transcend or escape from our violent and terrifying world?

Chapter 1, John M. Koller's "Religious Violence: A Philosophical Analysis," presents the broadest introduction to religion and religious violence. John Koller attempts to clarify the nature of religion, violence, and religious violence, and their complex relations found within different religious traditions. He provides a series of case studies of religious violence and terrorism, including the 9/11 terrorist attacks in the name of Islam and violence in the name of Christianity. One finds the common ideology of violent Divine Warfare that is given religious justification as part of a cosmic war in which the forces of good must use violence to defeat the forces of evil. When it comes to violence and terrorism, is religion then part of the problem or the solution? John Koller submits that the essential nature of all religion reveals shared core features, and he suggests that there are alternatives within religious traditions for resisting religious violence and terrorism.

Chapter 2, Douglas Allen's "Mahatma Gandhi After 9/1: Terrorism and Violence," provides the broadest introduction to the key terms of violence, terror, and terrorism. Doug Allen uses Gandhi, the most famous twentieth-century proponent of nonviolence, as a catalyst providing a critique of our normal dominant assumptions and views and allowing us to rethink our approaches to violence and terrorism. Of special significance is Gandhi's attempt to broaden and deepen our understanding of violence and terror by insisting on the complex, multidimensional, interactive nature of psychological, economic, linguistic, political, cultural, religious, and other forms of violence and his emphasis on the "normal" violence of the status quo. Especially valuable are Gandhi's preventative approach to violence, his analysis of means-ends relations, and his complex dynamic relations of the absolute and the relative in relating to violence and terrorism.

Chapter 3, Anna Lännström's "Responding to Terror: An Aristotelian Approach," presents an analysis of responding to fear and terror that is very relevant today. For Aristotle, unlike many Eastern and Western philosophical and religious approaches, fear and terror often express an accurate understanding of and a natural and appropriate response to our human condition and aspects of reality that are frightening and terrifying. How do we best live with the reality of fear and terror? For Aristotle, courage is the best way of responding to fear and terror. Courage, which is best expressed through courageous action and especially in showing bravery in facing death in battle, means standing firm in the face of frightening conditions, especially death. Anna Lännström goes on to apply this Aristotelian analysis to contemporary concerns, especially our response to threats of terrorism, and she makes some effort to go beyond Aristotle in his model of exemplary courage.

Chapter 4, Sor-hoon Tan's "Pragmatic Lessons in Times of Terror," focuses on John Dewey's pragmatism and on several of his Chinese and American students. What can pragmatism teach us about our basic approach to war, revolution, and particular contemporary issues and crises such as those associated with the U.S. war on terror and the U.S. war in Iraq? Sor-hoon Tan submits that pragmatism has the advantage of refraining from starting with absolute moral principle, from abstract essentialized dichotomies such as good versus evil, and from predetermined, biased, and partisan goals. With its open-ended critical attitude and approach, its attempt to deal with real contextualized situations without predetermined answers, and its commitment to consider evidence, engage in discussion, and come up with the most intelligent solutions, pragmatism is critical of dominant U.S. political approaches and offers valuable alternatives for dealing with war and terror.

Chapter 5, Peter S. Groff's "Wisdom and Violence: The Legacy of Platonic Political Philosophy in Al-Farabi and Nietzsche," presents surprising commonalities in the creative attempts by al-Farabi, the medieval Islamic thinker, and Nietzsche, the late modern, anti-religious, and anti-metaphysical thinker, to reappropriate some of the project of Plato's political philosophy. In this regard, Peter Groff focuses on strengths and disturbing features of Plato's idea of the philosopher king. He then submits that this Platonic ideal of the exemplary individual as ruler, the transfiguration and perfection of humanity, and the necessary use of deception and coercion, appears in different forms in al-Farabi and Nietzsche. In a challenging and controversial conclusion, he submits that such a philosophical approach at times seems to require and justify terror and that we are all "good Platonists" or least sympathetic to much of this Platonic approach.

Chapter 6, Jim Highland's "*Jihad* as Right Effort: A Buddhist Justification of *Jihad* in the Life of Abdul Ghaffar Khan," is primarily a study of the Muslim Pashtun leader, Abdul Ghaffar Khan, also known as Badshah Khan and often described as the Pashtun Gandhi. Especially fascinating is the fact that Abdul Ghaffar Khan was from the very region of Taliban, Al-Quada, and Osama bin Laden support, but he provided alternatives to much of contemporary, dominant, political Islam and terrorism. Jim Highland recognizes that there are different, often contradictory formulations of *jihad*, and he then focuses on Khan's nonviolent and tolerant version, with its peaceful and compassionate striving for justice and good will. He compares some of the Buddhist path, especially right effort and the *paramita* of right exertion, and Islamic *jihad*, especially in terms of Khan's peaceful, tolerant, and compassionate path of nonviolent resistance that is compatible with a Buddhist perspective.

Chapter 7, Christopher W. Gowans's "Standing Up to Terrorists: Buddhism, Human Rights, and Self-Respect," is the first of four chapters focusing on Buddhism. By focusing on teachings of the Buddha, foundational texts of the Pali Canon, the Theravada model of the *arahant*, and contributions of engaged Buddhism, Christopher Gowans analyzes contrasting Buddhist approaches with regard to the relations of rights and duties and conceptions of human rights; the nature of self versus Buddhist non-self and process-self; and the politics of confrontation versus Buddhist politics of reconciliation. In submitting that the Buddha's outlook implies a different approach to violations of human rights and threats of terrorism, Chris Gowans claims that the *arahant* ideal cautions us to avoid usual assertive confrontational force, aim at compassionate politics of reconciliation, and strongly emphasize nonviolence while recognizing that there may be cases in which minimal violent force is required.

Chapter 8, Wendy Donner's "The Bodhisattva Code and Compassion: Mahayana Buddhist Perspective on Violence and Nonviolence," presents a Mahayana Buddhist perspective on violence and nonviolence by focusing on the Bodhisattva ethics emphasizing compassion. In challenging stereotypes of Buddhism as absolutely and inherently nonviolent, Wendy Donner submits that that Bodhisattva ethics allows for, and even justifies, compassionate force, violence, and even killing in exceptional circumstances. The Mahayana ethic is complex, incorporating motivations and intentions, consequences, and a form of virtue ethics. In the Bodhisattva ethics, in which we use compassion and wisdom in our approach to complex ethical circumstances, inaction and nonviolence are not inherently safer or superior to action. In extraordinary circumstances of violence and suffering, there is a Buddhist justification for the use of compassionate force, even killing, in acting without hatred or malice to alleviate greater suffering.

Chapter 9, Michael G. Barnhart's "Rootlessness and Terror: Violence and Morality from a Zen Perspective," explores the complex troubled relationship of Zen Buddhism with ethics and morality. Can Buddhism in general and Zen in particular deal adequately with issues of moral responsibility, violence, and terrorism? Michael Barnhart formulates many excellent challenges, especially ethical challenges, to Buddhism as a whole and primarily to the specific forms of Zen Buddhism. Is there any integral connection between the ideal of *Nirvana* and this worldly *Samsara*? Is there any integral Buddhist connection between

wisdom and compassion and between enlightenment and nonviolence? Does
Zen, in particular, undermine the very possibilities of foundationalism, of
rationality, of ethics, and of continuity in spiritual development that could
provide some meaningful connection?

Chapter 10, Jeffrey D. Long's "Eliminating the Root of All Evil:
Interdependence and the De-Reification of the Self," primarily uses a Buddhist
approach, but also influences from Jainism, Hinduism, and Amin Maalouf. With
an emphasis on intentions and choice, Jeffrey Long submits that the root cause
of violence is a false reified sense of the self. This is analyzed in two
complementary ways: the Buddhist analysis of the construction of the false
reified self driven by desire for separate self as independent reality, and
Maalouf's analysis of how the self identifies with only one allegiance in a
dichotomized self-other construction. In both cases, such false self-constructions
lead to violence and undermine our real sense of interconnectedness and
interdependency. After conceding the possibility of some compassionate
violence, Jeff Long concludes that it is necessary to emphasize nonviolence and
the elimination of suffering based on an adequate understanding of self-
awareness and reality.

Chapter 11, Vance Cope-Kasten's "Loneliness: A Common Fate for
Philosophy and Terrorism?" presents connections between loneliness and
philosophy, on the one hand, and loneliness and terror, on the other. Although
these are not necessary connections, philosophy provides an opening to
loneliness, and leading characteristics of loneliness are evident throughout the
history of philosophy and in leading conceptions of philosophy. In addition,
loneliness is often connected with terror both in terms of the objects of terror
and the agents of terror. While distinguishing philosophy from terror, Vance
Cope-Kasten suggests ways that they share relations with loneliness. Finally, he
suggests that the success of philosophy, as seen especially in certain Confucian
conceptions, can lead to philosophical reconciliation and diminishment of
antagonistic relations, and this can lead to a reduction of loneliness. Terrorism,
by contrast, cannot produce such harmonious relations and the lasting
diminishment of loneliness.

Chapter 12, Joanne D. Birdwhistell's "Gender, Violence, and the Other," by
examining the gender code assumed by Mencian thinking, relates gender to
violence and terror directed at "the other." In contrast to many recent approaches
to Confucianism, Joanne Birwhistell analyzes Confucian hierarchical,
oppressive, violent structures of domination toward women and diverse others.
She interprets *yinyang* as coercive system, not as harmonious nonoppression,
and she submits that the Confucian approach views nature as negative other.
This study emphasizes the complexity, diversity, variability, and
multidimensionality of social and cultural, gendered constructions and

codifications. Even societies revealing structures of hierarchical, violent, male domination are far more nuanced and complex than systems of essentialized male-female dichotomies and oppositions.

Chapter 13, Kirill O. Thompson's "Confucian Perspectives on War and Terrorism," provides a survey and historical background on different Confucian and Neo-Confucian perspectives on war. Although Confucian thinkers were concerned with war and military acts, there was not a focus on the use of force of arms to impose Confucian beliefs and traditions on others. Instead, in clear contrast with many modern perspectives, Confucians emphasized civilized noble rule with wise leaders who understood the roots of true power. Confucian leadership ideals stressed a ritual ethical orientation; education and the cultivation of character development, including effective communication skills; and the flexibility and insights of the sage emperor that allowed for alternative conflict resolutions without war and military conquest. Kirill Thompson concludes by attempting to apply such a Confucian perspective to the contemporary world of violence and terrorism.

Chapter 14, C. Wesley DeMarco's "Great Teacher and Great Soul: Ueshiba and Gandhi on Personal Violence," compares Ueshiba, founder of Aikido, and his approach to the martial arts with Gandhi and his approach to *satyagraha*. The major focus is on Ueshiba's Aikido, remarkable among the martial arts in emphasizing nonviolence, love, and the art of peace, and unique in its central ethical intent. While bringing out many differences, Wes DeMarco submits that an Aikidoist may be Gandhian and a Gandhian may practice Aikido. Each offers potential ways of addressing issues where the other may be undeveloped or deficient. In particular, Wes DeMarco recommends that Gandhians consider Ueshiba's Aikido techniques for situations of personal violence in which Gandhi's responses are deficient, and Aikidoists consider Gandhi's more comprehensive vision, especially his analysis of causes of violence and preventative measures, in which Aikido tends to be undeveloped.

Chapter 15, Judy D. Saltzman's "*Himsa* and *Ahimsa* in the Martial Arts," presents a second unusual study focusing on the martial arts, violence, and terror. Using personal stories from her own background, Judy Saltzman proposes that the martial arts can be a way to peace, harmony, and inner tranquility; an active way of using *ahimsa* to resist terrorism and other forms of *himsa*. In presenting the martial arts as a path of development and empowerment, she emphasizes the importance of mental attitude in changing self-image, refusing to be defenseless victim, and dealing with fear, terror, and threats. Crucial in this approach is the development of alertness for pre-emptive self-defense. She ends by focusing on a Bodhisattva path in which one develops *mushin*, a place of "No Mind" or no ego, of calm alertness beyond terror.

I began this Introduction by indicating that the 2003 SACP conference and this volume are clearly related to the events of September 11, 2001, although these chapters in their breadth and depth go far beyond an analysis of 9/11. Many of the abovementioned essays are significantly different from what authors presented at the Asilomar conference and even what they initially submitted in their revised manuscripts. An editor can assume different roles and function in different ways. I chose to be an active editor and to engage potential authors throughout the process leading to publication. I provided each scholar, even those whose manuscripts I did not accept for publications, with very lengthy feedback and numerous critical observations and suggestions for revisions. What struck me as remarkable in terms of my past experiences is that every author in this volume took a very open, cooperative, and positive attitude. Many authors engaged me in ongoing interaction and dialogue, and many authors did new research and radically revised their manuscripts. Repeatedly authors expressed their views that their final manuscripts were a vast improvement over their initial submissions.

My own feeling is that this unusually positive, cooperative, collegial approach has been motivated by my view, shared by other authors, that our book concerns philosophical and religious issues that are extremely urgent and of the greatest significance. This is combined with the belief that our subject matter and our philosophical approaches allow us to do some very innovative and creative scholarship. Finally, I strongly believe that our motivation has been shaped not only by the possibility of new significant scholarship dealing with significant issues, but also by our personal concerns and engagement with these issues. Both in terms of theoretical philosophical analysis and practical action, we hope that this volume will contribute in a small way to the transformative process in which billions of ordinary human beings, who are often quite extraordinary human beings, can live their lives free from the present contexts of humanly-created and maintained violence, terror, and terrorism.

1

Religious Violence: A Philosophical Analysis

John M. Koller

Why is there so much religious violence in the world today? TV, radio, internet and newspaper stories point to the increase of terrorism and violence around the world committed in the name of religion. Christians killing Muslims in Bosnia; Christians killing other Christians in Ireland and the U.S.; Hindus killing Muslim and Sikhs in India and Buddhists in Sri Lanka; Muslims killing Jews, Hindus and Christians and other Muslims; Jews killing Muslims; Buddhists in Japan spreading poisonous gas in the Tokyo subway system; the list could go on for pages. In all of these cases and many others, it is not merely that someone who happened to be Christian, Hindu, Buddhist, Jewish or Muslim resorted to violence, often extreme violence, but rather that they did this because their religion motivated them and, in their minds, justified their violence.

Of course, religious violence, including the violence of religious terrorism is not a new phenomenon in history.[1] Indeed, if the psychologist, James Hillman, is correct in his claim that religion itself is war, then the violence of war is co-terminus with the practice of religion.[2] In any event, the history of religions is filled with examples of terrible violence, from battles recalled in the Mahabharata and the Ramayana, to the Christian crusades, to the attacks of 9/11.[3]

My concern is with the violence perpetrated by persons who identify themselves with one of the major religious traditions of the world and whose violent acts are thought to be required by the religion itself. Much violence has been perpetrated in the name of ideologies, such as Fascism, Communism, Maoism, etc. Quasi religious cults, often associated with ideological movements, such as the cults of Lenin, Hitler, Mao, etc. have also contributed significant horrors to the world through their violent efforts to change the world. But these cults and ideological movements, although they share some of the characteristics of religion, are not religions in the full sense of the term and can be ignored for the purposes of this analysis.

Violence is, of course, a much-studied and controversial subject. Without entering into the details and subtleties of the discussion I think that we can say, following Miller's analysis,[4] that an act is violent if it 1) involves great force; 2) is capable of killing or injuring persons or damaging or destroying things; 3) the act is intended to kill or injure or damage or destroy. Religious violence includes those violent acts that are intended to achieve religious objectives and that are typically thought by the actors or their leaders to be justified by religion.

Although some of the religious violence that I examine in this paper is the violence of religious terrorism, some is not, and I do not wish to limit my analysis exclusively to religious terrorism. Religious terrorism is always violent, but not all religious violence is terrorism. Terrorism, like violence, is also a controversial subject on which there is a significant literature. In his recent book on terrorism, J. Angelo Corlett, after a careful analysis of the major historical and recent attempts at definition, offers the following useful definition[5]:

> Terrorism is the attempt to achieve (or prevent) political, social, economic, or religious change by the actual or threatened use of violence against other persons or other persons' property; the violence (or threat thereof) employed therein is aimed partly at destabilizing (or maintaining) an existing political or social order, but mainly at publicizing the goals or causes espoused by the agents or by those on whose behalf the agents act; often, though not always, terrorism is aimed at provoking extreme counter-measures which will win public support for the terrorists and their goals or causes...

This broad definition includes various kinds of terrorism, including religious terrorism. The crucial distinction between political terrorism and religious terrorism is that religious terrorism, while it typically also involves political objectives, is carried out in the interests of achieving religious goals. Typically, religious terrorists are so zealously committed to a religious idea or group that their adversaries are dehumanized, frequently demonized, to such an extent that their killing appears justified. As Jessica Stern points out, religious terrorists "begin with an intention to purify the world of some evil, but end up committing evil acts." [6]

Often the perpetrators of religiously inspired violence think that their violence is justified because they see themselves as following a "higher calling" to do good. They see themselves as part of "an army of God," or "doing the will of God," or "ridding the world of evil so that goodness may reign." Where should the blame for religious violence be placed? On misguided individuals or groups who in their rage and misunderstanding subvert religion to their political agendas? Or on religion itself, on each religion's claim to be the only truth and the only way and on religion's inherent insistence that humans submit to a higher power, that human judgment must be subordinated to divine judgment?

How can religion, usually thought of as a source of morality and a way of peace, give rise to violence and terrorism? Is there something within religion itself that is conducive to its violent uses? Or is it the case that religious violence is the result of political forces that are powerful enough to overcome the moral and peaceful agendas of religion? Or is religion not separable from social and political forces and agendas?

Usually when we say that a violent act is an act of religious violence we mean that it was performed in the name of religion and justified by appeal to religious beliefs and practices. But this presumes that we already know both what religion is, and what violence is, and that a simple combination of violence and religion constitutes religious violence. It is not clear, however, that we know either what religion is or what violence is; both concepts are used in a bewildering variety of ways, often inconsistent with each other. Our first task, therefore, is to clarify the concepts of violence and religion in order to inquire into religious violence. My approach to this task of clarification is to analyze a number of examples, beginning with what seems to me a clear and unambiguous example, indeed, a paradigm, of religious violence, namely, the 9/11 attacks.

Violence in the Name of Islam

Bruce Lincoln, in the first chapter of his new book, *Holy Terrors*,[7] provides an excellent analysis of the religious nature of these attacks, using the *"Final Instructions"* found in the luggage of Muhammad Atta as a key document. Although Lincoln's definition of religion differs from mine in important aspects, there is sufficient commonality within our definitions to allow his analysis of the 9/11 violence to work for my definition as well as his. I see religion, at its core, as a way of transforming what is perceived to be a radically defective life into a perfected life. Religious transformation is effected through sets of practices held to be grounded in the salvific power issuing from an ultimate sacred reality that is regarded as the highest authority. The authority of the sacred is known, in the final analysis, through faith. But religion has an inherent political dimension because religious faith and practice take place in, shaping and being shaped by, communities governed by institutions that regulate the communities of the faithful. It is these communities that provide leadership to guide the faithful and to interpret and defend orthodoxy of belief and practice.

Because religious faith and practice is, above all, a means of overcoming or transforming life, it is essentially a struggle, a struggle which requires the greatest possible effort because salvation is at stake. And because the power to succeed in this struggle, to win salvation, comes from the ultimate sacred reality, a power believed to be far greater, indeed, infinitely greater, than the individual, it behooves the individual to accept and submit to the higher authority of the sacred reality.

The *Final Instructions*, a brief text of only 38 paragraphs, with no claimed authorship, was most likely read by the attackers as a true declaration by representatives of God Himself (in this case the representatives were probably understood to be the Al Qaeda leadership), thereby having the ultimate authority of God, as invested in sacred scripture and Islamic tradition. The instructions begin with the usual formal Islamic invocation, "In the name of God, the most merciful, the most compassionate," placing it in the tradition of sacred texts. All but 8 of the 38 paragraphs refer to God, who is mentioned a total of 89 times. The prophet Muhammad and the first generation of Muslims are referred to 25 times, as the Final Instructions attempt to place the attacks squarely within Islamic tradition, going back to the time of the Prophet and the first Muslim community. The frequent calls to prayer, devotion, and recitation of the Quran represent an attempt to connect everything required by the project to God through the practices that tradition has ordained as religious duty.

The first four pages of the document obtained by *The Washington Post* are handwritten on large paper and recite some basic Islamic history about the Prophet fighting infidels with 100 men against 1,000. They also include prayers such as, "I pray to you God to forgive me from all my sins, to allow me to glorify you in every possible way."[8] In the text Muhammad and his group are reminded that "In this night you will face many challenges. But you have to face them. Obey God, his messenger, and don't fight among yourself where you become weak. God will stand with those who stood fast."

"You should pray, you should fast," the text continues. "You should ask God for guidance, you should ask God for help. . . . Continue to pray throughout this night. Continue to recite the Koran." "Purify your heart. . . the few hours that are left you in your life are very few. From there you will begin to live the happy life, the infinite paradise."

A recurring theme is the promise of eternal life. "Keep a very open mind, keep a very open heart of what you are to face," the document says. "You will be entering paradise. You will be entering the happiest life, everlasting life."

The attackers are instructed to "Remember God frequently, and the best way to do it is to read the Holy Qur'an, according to all scholars, as far as I know. It is enough for us that it is the words of the Creator of the Earth and the plants, the One that you will meet [on Judgment Day]." The *Final Instructions* also invests the present project with the sanctity of paradigmatic heroic acts of the first generations of devout Muslims. Those first generations are regarded as fervently committed to overcoming their enemies, seen simultaneously as God's enemies, through the use of force in accord with the Prophet's call. Those early victories against numerous and powerful enemies, and by extension, the anticipated current victory, were seen as the result of God's support to those faithful to Him. As a result, as Lincoln notes "power is redefined as a function of piety rather than wealth, arms, or numbers."[9]

Finally it should be noted that the *Final Instructions* construes the project as a battle against the enemy of Islam that is part of a larger religious war against the forces of evil that threaten the way of God. The text calls these enemies infidels, nonbelievers, and allies of Satan, whom the armies of the believers, the faithful, allies of God, and God's faithful servants must, as a matter of religious duty, defeat and overcome.

Reading these *Final Instructions* makes clear that the attackers thought that their religion required, as a matter of religious duty, that they perform the violent acts of 9/11. The phrase, repeated four times, "Be happy, optimistic, calm, because you are heading for a deed that God loves and will accept," summarizes, as Lincoln says, "the text's persuasive project: definition of the entire undertaking—theft of the planes, murder of their crews, and the final paroxysm of death and destruction—as something religiously sanctioned: "a deed that God loves and will accept."[10]

The document concludes by saying: "God, I trust in you. God, I lay myself in your hands," closing with the words, "There is no God but God, I being a sinner. We are of God, and to God we return."

But the 9/11 violence, clearly seen by Muhammad Atta as a mission carried out as a service to God, was only the latest in a long series of violent actions carried out by Muslims in the name of religion. Mahmud Abouhalima, convicted for the 1993 bombing of the World Trade Center and widely considered to have masterminded the attack, described his reason for engaging in this and other violent actions as "being my job as a Muslim," saying that he had a mission "to go wherever there is oppression and injustice and fight it."[11]

This raises the question: What is the theological justification in Islam for violence? It would seem that Islam, as its very name suggests, is, at its core, a way of peace with a vision of spiritual development that includes social harmony and justice. Because one of its central principles is that one "should not slay the life that God has made sacred" [6.152], it would appear to be extremely difficult for a Muslim to justify the violence of terrorism. Historically, perhaps the main justification of violence in Islam is its use in self-defense, a rather elastic notion in the minds of contemporary militant Muslims. For example, Abd al-Salam Faraj, a recent Egyptian thinker, claims that justification of Islamic violence is grounded in the Qur'an and the Hadith. Jihad, meaning "to fight," he says is meant literally from the very beginning of Islam, and has always meant the duty to fight for Islam, a duty that calls for "fighting, which meant confrontation and blood." Against whom is one required to fight? According to Faraj, and other militant Muslims, against whoever deviates from the moral and social requirements of Islam, both the apostates within Islam and its enemies outside.[12]

Faraj's thinking in turn was shaped by the teachings of Sayyid Qutb and Mawdudi [Maulana Abu al-Ala Mawdudi]. It is from these three modern radical Muslim thinkers that many militant Muslim individuals and groups draw their justification for the use of violence to fight against the enemies of Islam. In waging religious war to defend the faith practically all means are justified, including the use of violence and terrorism. Indeed, the reward for doing so is a guaranteed place in paradise.

Qutb, in his last and most radical work, insists that the fight against the corruption and ignorance called jahiliyyah requires jihad to overcome the entrenched political and military powers that support the jahili systems. He says, "When the purpose is to abolish the existing system and to replace it with a new system which in its characteristic principles and all its general and particular aspects is different from the controlling jahili system, then it stands to reason that this new system should also come into the battlefield as an organized movement and a viable group. It should come into the battlefield with a determination that its strategy, its social organization, and the relationship between its individuals should be firmer and more powerful than the existing jahili system."[13]

This call for warfare against the enemies of Islam reminds us that throughout its history, Islam has understood jihad in two different ways, corresponding to its division of the world into two quite different realms. The realm of peace (dar al-Islam), is the realm governed by the principles of Islam. The realm of war (dar al-harb), is the world not governed by the principles of Islam. Within the realm of peace, jihad is the constant internal struggle to achieve self-perfection as understood within Islam. But in the realm of war, jihad is militant, involving military campaigns and tactics to overcome corruption and ignorance and to convince these outsiders to submit to God, bringing them into the fold of Islam.

Just as clear as that the attacks of 9/11 carried out in the name of religion is the fact that the attacks were acts of violence. The Final Instructions, as well as Osama bin Laden's videotaped address of 10/7/2001, show clearly that the attackers intended to destroy and damage property and to kill and injure persons, using sufficient force to achieve their objectives.

Violence in the Name of Christianity

Let me turn now to examples of violence carried out in the name of God by Christians in America, violence that the perpetrators attempt to justify by appealing to Christian teachings. There are, unfortunately, many examples to choose from, ranging from the shootings at a Jewish day care center in California by a member of the Christian Identity group to the 1996 bombing of the Atlanta Olympic Games to the murders/suicide of nearly one thousand people carried out by the Rev. Jim Jones People's Temple group to attacks on abortion clinics and murder of doctors, to name just a few.[14] I will focus primarily on the violent attack on clinics and clinic staff and doctors, in part because of the articulateness of its perpetrators and supporters.

The Rev. Michael Bray, convicted in 1985 of destroying seven abortion facilities in Delaware, Maryland, Virginia and D.C., wrote what has been called the definitive book on the moral and religious justification of violence. In his book, *A Time to Kill*, he defended murder and attempted murder by others, notably the Rev. Paul Hill who murdered Dr. John Britton and his volunteer escort, James Barrett, as they drove up to a clinic in Pensacola in 1994, and Rachel Shannon, who confessed to a series of abortion clinic bombings and who was convicted of attempted murder for shooting Dr. George Tiller in front of his clinic in Wichita. He justified these acts, as well as his own terrorist acts, because they were committed in order to destroy evil and evil-doers. He views American society as hopelessly corrupt, controlled by satanic forces, and the federal government as a satanic power working to undermine personal freedoms, religion and Christian morality.

Bray's views are aligned with the theological positions of Reconstruction and Dominion thinkers who claim that Christianity must reassert the dominion of God over all things, including politics and every aspect of society. This is a position articulated by widely influential religious spokespersons such as Pat Robertson and Jerry Falwell and embraced by large numbers of religious conservatives in American society.

Seeing himself and other Christian activists as defending God's plan for humankind to live according to the biblical code, a plan that they regard as being attacked by atheists, secularists and Jews, Bray argues that the war they are engaged in justifies the use of violence when necessary. Bray saw it as the duty of Christians to join the army of God (which, by the way, is the title of an underground manual containing detailed instructions for various forms of terrorism). As a soldier for Christ, it is necessary to fight against the evil forces of Satan that have corrupted American government and the major institutions of American society. Utilizing the theological explanations of Reconstruction and Christian Identity writers, this Christian subculture sees itself justified in its violent responses to what it sees as a vast and violent repression waged by the secular (and, in some versions of this vision, Jewish) agents of a satanic force.

Drawing on traditional Christian just-war theory and the mainstream 20th century theologian Reinhold Niebuhr, these Christian activists and activist writers argue that the use of force is sometimes required to overcome evil. Niebuhr's argument, based on Augustine's teachings concerning original sin, is that righteous force is sometimes necessary to correct injustices and overcome evil in a sinful world, and that occasionally strategic violent acts are necessary to prevent large-scale violence and injustice. This argument is expanded by some fundamentalist writers into a claim that any means thought necessary to achieve their ends are justified. The Christian activists' claim that their use of violence is justified because "God wills it" echoes the battle cry of Christian crusaders, "Deus Volt" ("God wills it"). The crusaders, who, in the course of nine bloody crusades, over the course of three centuries, killed tens of thousands of innocent Muslims and Jews, also claimed that "Deus Volt" justified their violence.

But the reconstructionist theologians, the most radically conservative wing of the dominionists, do not turn to the historic example of the crusades to justify their use of violence. Instead, they look to the ideas of Cornelius Van Til, a 20th century Presbyterian theologian at Princeton Seminary, who agreed with John Calvin that Christians must act in the world with the presupposition of God's authority. As understood by Gary North, the most prolific reconstructionist writer, this means that it is the "duty of Christians to recapture every social institution for Jesus Christ,"[15] and that they are authorized by Jesus Christ to use whatever means are necessary. Furthermore, there is an urgency about performing this duty, because reconstructionists believe that Christ will return to earth for the millennium only after Christians have paved the way by providing a thousand years of religious rule through the creation of the necessary social and political conditions. The use of violence is regarded as justified if it is seen as bringing about the fulfillment of God's law and establishes his kingdom on earth.

Divine Warfare

One of the dominant motifs in both Christian and Muslim militant activist attempts to justify their use of violence is that of war, specifically, war between the forces of good and evil. Indeed, images of divine warfare are persistent features of religious militant activism in Hindu, Buddhist, Jewish, and Sikh traditions as well. As Mark Juergensmeyer points out in his book, Terror in the Mind of God, "What makes religious violence particularly savage and relentless is that its perpetrators have placed such religious images of divine struggle—

cosmic war—in the service of worldly political battles. For this reason, acts of religious terror serve not only as tactics in a political strategy but also as evocations of a much larger spiritual confrontation."[16] As we saw before, Michael Bray envisions a world caught in an imminent and almost eschatological confrontation between the forces of good and evil arrayed on the battlefield of politics. We also saw how Muslim militant thinkers couched their justification of violence in terms of defensive warfare against evil. It turns out that this worldview is remarkably similar to the worldview of militant Hindus and Sikhs in India, the Aum Shinrikyo in Japan, Rabbi Kahane's Kach party in Israel, Sheik Omar Abdul Rahman's following in Egypt and New Jersey, and other groups associated with recent acts of terrorism. Theirs have been acts of desperation in response to what they perceive as a desperate situation: a world gone terribly wrong, a world at war in which the forces of evil are threatening to overcome the forces of good.

Dr. Abdul Aziz Rantisi, assassinated in 2004, was one of the founders of the radical organization Hamas. He described the young Hamas suicide bombers as soldiers in a great war who diligently and reverently gave up their lives for the sake of their community and their religion. The videotapes taken of some of these young men—so-called "self-chosen martyrs"—the night before their deaths indicated that they thought of themselves in just that way. They were trying not to avoid life, but to fulfill it in what they considered to be an act of both personal and social redemption, an act of service to Islam and to God.

The conviction of being engaged in warfare involves a view of oneself in the world in a certain way. To live in a state of war is to live in a world in which individuals know who they are, why they have suffered, by whose hand they have been humiliated, and at what expense they have persevered. The concept of war, particularly a cosmic war with political objectives, provides cosmology, history, and eschatology and offers participants the hope of eventual political control. Perhaps most important, it holds out the hope of victory and the means to achieve it. In the images of cosmic war this victorious triumph is a grand moment of social and personal transformation, transcending all worldly limitations. One does not easily abandon such expectations. For those whose lives are otherwise empty, who feel left out and demeaned, who feel marginalized by society, to be participants in a cosmic battle, on the side of good, performing one's God-given duty creates a powerful sense of religious identity.

The analysis of the reasons for violence involved in the 9/11 attacks given by Mansoor al-Jamri, editor of Bahrain newspaper Al Wasat, speaks of loss of respect and dignity and of anger that grows out of hopelessness and the importance of a sense of identity gained through participation in a religious cause. He says:

> We have six people from Bahrain in Guantanamo Bay. One is
> a member of the ruling family. The other five are . . . from the
> upper class. And for a young man from the ruling family, who
> receives a monthly salary, who is 23 years old, to go to
> Afghanistan to fight, there must be some sort of explanation.
> You fill him with money, you fill him with material things, but
> that does not fulfill his aspirations as a human being. There is
> a vacumn; He is not fulfilled. And all of a sudden someone
> comes and tells him that the cause of all this emptiness and
> meaninglessness is this global power [America], which has
> insulated us, which continues to look at us as a bunch of
> nothings, who are basically eating and sleeping and going
> after women. And all of a sudden he directs his anger at what
> he thinks is the reason why doesn't have what he wants—his
> sense of being a true human able to express himself and
> having influence on his society and being respected locally
> and internationally. This lack of respect as a dignified person
> has resulted in a bin Laden phenomenon. [17]

The bin Laden phenomenon referred to here is the powerful appeal of a religious
identity gained through joining a religious cause that promises to do God's work
in fighting a war to overcome evil in the world.

While the sense of engaging in cosmic religious war provides powerful
motivation for engaging in religious violence, obviously not all
religious/political confrontations take on the character of cosmic war.
Juergensmeyer suggests that confrontation is likely to take on the character of a
cosmic war only under the following conditions: (1) If the cosmic struggle is
understood to be occurring in this world rather than in a mythical setting. (2) If
believers identify personally with the struggle. (3) If the struggle is at a point of
crisis in which individual action can make all the difference. (4) If the struggle
is perceived as a defense of basic identity and dignity. If the struggle is thought
to be of ultimate significance—a defense not only of lives but of entire cultures,
such as Christian America, Judaism, or Islam—then it is more likely that it will
be seen as a cultural war with spiritual implications. (5) If losing the struggle
would be unthinkable. If a negative outcome to the struggle is perceived as
beyond human conception, the struggle may be viewed as taking place on a
transhistorical plane. (6) If the struggle is blocked and cannot be won in real
time or in real terms. Perhaps most important, if the struggle is seen as hopeless
in human terms, it is likely that it may be reconceived on a sacred plane, where
the possibilities of victory are in God's hands.[18] All of these conditions are met,
for example, in both Michael Bray's defense of the use of violence and in
Osama bin Laden's defense of terrorism.

War is a very ancient and basic human activity that figures largely in the images and stories that are part of most religious traditions.[19] Warfare organizes people into a "we" and a "they," and it organizes social history into a storyline of persecution, conflict, and the hope of redemption, liberation, and conquest. It gives the warrior a sense of mission and importance, especially if the mission is commissioned by God.

The image of participating in a cosmic, spiritual war, defending one's faith, one's integrity, and goodness itself, gives the religious warrior a powerful identity and a special status in his own eyes and in the eyes of the supporting community. When these warriors succeed, they are heroes; if they die performing their mission they are even greater heroes, for now they are martyrs.

Part of the reason the image of sacred war is so powerful and so terrible is that participants are thereby able to turn the other into an enemy that is automatically demonized. This, of course, legitimizes the violence directed against the enemy in the minds of the perpetrators. In his booklet, Jihad Is an Individual Duty, Osama bin Laden declares that America deserves to be targeted for violence because it is the biggest terrorist in the world. Among the reasons he gave were a list of America's crimes, which included "occupying the lands of Islam in the holiest of places, the Arabian Peninsula, plundering its riches, dictating to its rulers, humiliating its people, terrorizing its neighbors and turnings its bases in the peninsula into a spearhead through which to fight the neighboring Muslim peoples" Having labeled America the aggressor in waging war on Islam and the Muslim people, Osama issued his fatwa calling on every Muslim, as an individual duty, to join in a righteous war against America, "to kill the Americans and their allies." "He sealed his fatwa with the reassurance that 'this is in accordance with the words of Almighty God' and that 'every Muslim who believes in God and wishes to be rewarded' should 'comply with God's order'."[20]

Religion: Problem or Solution?

Given this analysis of religious violence, the question arises, can the correctives and antidotes to violence be found within religion itself? Or is religion inherently conducive to violence? As we have seen, in the minds of the perpetrators and defenders of violence in the name of religion, the violence is justified by their understanding of religious duty. They see themselves engaged in war, a cosmic war, in which they are arrayed against the forces of evil, commissioned by God to fight in his army. They see their actions as required by their religion and commanded by the highest authority, God himself, or his spokespersons on earth.

Clearly, not all religious people condone or turn to violence; indeed most Christians condemn the violence of Christian terrorism, most Muslims condemn the violence of Islamic terrorism, most Hindus condemn the violence of Hindu terrorism, etc. On the other hand, many advocates of religious violence view the non-militant persons in their religious traditions as apostates who have lost or corrupted the faith, as enemies to be attacked. How are we to explain these radically opposing views of their religion by members of the same faith? Have the militant extremists lost sight of the true religion? Have they corrupted the ideals and teachings of their own traditions? Or have the non-militant people in the mainstream lost sight of their true duties to fight evil and carry out the commands of God? To address these questions we need to look at the core features of religion as manifested in the great religious traditions of the world over the centuries.

The Nature of Religion

Religion can be looked at in many ways, in terms of practices, teachings, scriptures, from psychological, or political, or sociological perspectives, etc. In what follows I look at religion from the perspective of the fundamental ideas that constitute the world views of the major religious traditions, expanding on the definition of religion I gave at the beginning of this paper. In order to talk across the various religious traditions it is imperative that we use categories that fit all of the traditions and that don't favor some at the expense of others. For example, if we talked about religion only in terms of relationship to God, we would exclude all the non-theist traditions, such as Buddhism, Jainism, Taoism and Confucianism. If we talked about religion only in terms of the soul and afterlife we would exclude those traditions that reject the notion of soul and for whom salvation or liberation takes place in this life in this world.

What comparative study of the world's major religious traditions shows is that from a broad philosophical perspective each of them finds its basic organization in four distinct, but related, categories. In each tradition the religious person accepts that human life, as it is usually experienced, is defective in a fundamental way, but is convinced, usually through faith, that this defectiveness can be overcome and a perfect, or more perfect life can be achieved—either in this lifetime or in a future lifetime. The transformation of this defective life into a perfect life is made possible by means of sacred powers made available through a relationship with the ultimate sacred reality.

When we look at the different religions in terms of these four categories we find that each has a concept of an ultimate sacred reality, of a perfected life as the goal of religious activity, of a fundamental defectiveness, and of special means, empowered by the ultimate sacred reality, of transforming defective into perfected life. We also see that the concepts of ultimate reality, fundamental defectiveness, means of transformation and the perfection to be attained differ from religion to religion. For example, the Abrahamic religions see a one, only personal God as the ultimate sacred reality, whereas Buddhists and Taoists do not conceive of the Ultimate as a personal God, but as an impersonal reality. Buddhists, unlike Christians, do not conceive of the perfected life occurring after death in a heavenly realm, but right here in this very lifetime. Hindus see the radical defect as ignorance, whereas Jews see it as sinfulness. For Muslims the key to transforming defectiveness into perfection is faith in God, whereas for Taoists the key is keeping to the Tao.

Every religion incorporates the imperative to struggle, to make a great effort, to overcome the powerful forces that render this life and this world radically defective. As indicated above, this defectiveness is viewed in different ways in different religions. The Abrahamic religions of Judaism, Christianity and Islam see this defectiveness in terms of sin; a willful turning away from goodness, the goodness symbolized by God. These religious traditions emphasize the need to strive to overcome sinfulness, to struggle to overcome the inherent inclination to sin. These religions assure their adherents that there is a supreme power, an ultimate reality in the form of a personal God, who will show them the way to overcome the defectiveness of sin and assist them in the effort required to overcome evil. Frequently the struggle is cast in terms of cosmic warfare, in terms of a battle between the forces of good and evil, with the forces of good under the command of God and the forces of evil under the command of Satan, prince of demons. The main difference between militant and non-militant interpretations of this battle of good vs. evil is that non-militants see it primarily as a spiritual battle, and indeed, a spiritual battle waged within one's own heart, whereas militants see it in terms of social and political warfare.

The Indian religions, Jainism, Hinduism and Buddhism, see the fundamental defectiveness in terms of ignorance, a failure to know the perfection of being that is the ultimate ground of all existence. These religions emphasize the efforts that are needed to overcome the darkness of ignorance that is the root cause of all the defectiveness that is experienced in this life, that prevents a person from experiencing the perfect bliss that true knowledge brings. Because knowledge and action are related, these religions emphasize the importance of moral action as well as meditative insight in the effort to free the light of knowledge from the bondage of the forces of darkness. Although typically in these traditions the struggle to overcome ignorance is viewed as a spiritual effort that occurs within the individual, enlightened individuals are expected to be morally exemplary and to work for the betterment of society. Hindu and Buddhist militants view the requirement to transform action in accord with knowledge as justifying violence when necessary.

In all of the religious traditions the various means of transforming defective into perfected existence are seen as empowered by the ultimate sacred reality. That is why, at the heart of every religion, what is most important is being in the right relationship with the sacred. In theistic religions the ultimate reality is symbolized in personal terms as God, and though of course God is no ordinary person, the pattern for relatedness is human relatedness, emphasizing love, respect, loyalty, obedience, etc. In Hinduism, where the ultimate, Brahman is seen to be beyond all possible description, the human need of relatedness has led to the development of the concept of finite appearances [avatars] of Brahman in the form of various Gods and Goddesses, who mediate between the strictly human and the ultimate. These personalized forms of the ultimate are frequently the objects of intense personal relationships, and sometimes, as in the case of Rama, depicted as leading armies in victory over the forces of evil.

In Buddhism, where the ultimate sacred reality is just this ordinary reality, seen as it truly is, with the enlightened mind, the need of ordinary people to relate to the ultimate was satisfied by elevating Buddhas and Bodhisattvas to almost deity status, a development that has made it possible for some militant Buddhist to justify their engagement in violent activities by seeing it as "what the Buddha requires to protect the Dharma."

The perfection that religious persons in all traditions seek is typically seen as spiritual perfection, and when envisioned as a Heaven or Paradise, located beyond this world. This perfection is typically the mirror image of the defectiveness seen in this life and this world. Thus, although descriptions vary from religion to religion, generally it is held that ignorance and sin are overcome, virtue rather than vice reigns, happiness rather than suffering prevails, and love, kindness, generosity and justice characterize the perfected condition. Most religions have codified the perfected state as some sort of heaven or paradise, and its opposite, the completely defective state, as some sort of hell. In many traditions, Hindu and Buddhist as well as Christian and Muslim, heavens and hells are depicted very graphically and colorfully, and provide significant motivation for adhering to the teachings. Following the teachings brings the bliss of heaven; failure to follow the teachings brings the terrible suffering of hell.

But most religions also have a strong ethical component, which insists on observing fundamental ethical principles in interactions with other persons and in working for justice in society. It is here, in the sphere of religious duties to strive to achieve the ideal community in this life, in this world, that the required effort can easily take militant forms.

Is There a Religious Solution?

With this basic understanding of religion in mind, let us look at some of the key features of religious violence and ask if these features can be addressed by religion itself. As we have seen, the perpetrators of religious violence tend to see it as their religious duty to seek the perfection of this world by fighting a cosmic war against the injustices and evils of human society and in this they see themselves following the true teachings of their religion and thereby assured of reaching heaven, and avoiding hell, because of their efforts.

One of key features of the violence of religious terrorism is that its perpetrators are convinced that absolute truth is on their side, that God has spoken to them directly or that the teachings of their religion leave no doubt that it is their religious duty to engage in violence. Because they view their truth as absolute, no compromise with the other is possible. And because they are at war with the other, the only outcome they can envision is a victory that destroys their enemy.

A second feature of the violence of religious terrorism is its insistence on blind obedience. At the center of many acts of religious violence stands a charismatic leader claiming to have the truth and demanding total obedience. This is true, for example, in the case of Asahara Shoku, founder and leader of the Buddhist sect, Aum Shinrikyo, that poisoned the Tokyo subway. It is true in the case of Jim Jones of the People's Temple, responsible for the death of a thousand of his followers. It is true of Osama bin Laden and the Al Qaeda network, and true of many religious cults that have resorted to violence to achieve their objectives. What happens when followers blindly follow their leaders is that they then surrender their own sense of responsibility and judgment. It would seem that moderate religious voices could attack the insistence on blind obedience as a corruption that negates the power of conscience.

A third feature of the violence of religious terrorism is its insistence on literalist interpretations of scriptural or traditional teachings. Moderates might argue that literalist interpretations should be rejected because they assume that the meaning a person happens to read into a text is what the author intended. But in fact it is only what the reader finds in his or her own mind, which he or she now equates with the authority and absoluteness of the Divine mind. Opponents of literalist and absolutist interpretations might argue that because the ultimate is infinite it can never be known literally and absolutely by human minds. Therefore the ultimate must be understood through symbols and myths, an understanding that must be embraced tentatively and with humility because of the limitations of the human mind. As Charles Kimball says, "A human view of truth, one that is dynamic and relational, enables religious people to embrace and affirm foundational truths without necessarily solidifying the word into static, absolute, propositional statements."[21]

Can moderate, non-militant voices in the tradition convince the extremists that the absolutism that underlies their use of violence is a mistaken and dangerous interpretation of core religious teachings? Or are the arguments against absolutism and blind obedience, although important, hard for religious adherents to make? Are they hard to make because it is essential to religion to have faith in a higher reality or power, which precisely because it is higher, is authoritative? The appropriate posture toward the higher is one of acknowledgement, acceptance, and submission. To ignore or reject the authority of God is incompatible with having faith in God. The critical, but difficult, task for any religious person is to place complete faith and trust in God, to accept God as the ultimate authority, and at the same time take total and complete responsibility for one's own actions and life.

I have argued that, to a significant extent, the religious violence of the militant extremist is rooted in an absolutist understanding of God's will and God's teaching. If this is correct, then one way to decrease religious violence might be to show that a deeper religious understanding of truth is non-absolutist. This deeper understanding is grounded in a more humble epistemology that recognizes the limitations of human understanding of the infinite. A deeper understanding of the epistemic limitations of human knowledge of the divine can, in turn, provide a basis for tolerance, and perhaps even for dialog.

It might be instructive, in this respect, to look at the understanding of truth that helped keep the Jain tradition relatively free of violence throughout its more than 3,000 year history. According to Jainism, the very nature of reality is so rich and manifold that no single perspective or interpretation can ever grasp it perfectly. The use of multiple perspectives and the insistence on the conditional nature of human knowledge has imbued this tradition with an epistemological humility and a deep tolerance for differences.[22] The non-absolutism of knowledge embraced by Jainism does not allow an epistemological exclusivism that rejects all other views as false and mine alone as true. It opens the door to the recognition of the Indian sage voiced 3,000 years ago, in the Ṛg Veda, that "Ekam sat, viprah bahuta vadanti" ("reality is one, but is spoken of in various ways").[23]

Notes

1. Many scholars have inquired into the relation between violence and religion and the role of violence in religion, especially the violence of religious sacrifice, which appears to be at the heart of many religions. Of the following authors, Girard is especially interesting, especially in his attempt to argue that by ritualizing violence religion "tames"

it and transforms it from a divisive and destructive force into a constructive, socially cohesive force. Principal works of some of the important scholars of violence and religion include: Maurice Bloch, *Prey Into Hunter* (Cambridge: Cambridge University Press, 1992); René Girard, *Violence and the Sacred*, trans. Patrick Gregory (Baltimore: Johns Hopkins University Press, 1977); Walter Burhert, Girard, *Violent Origins: Ritual Killing and Cultural Formation* (Stanford: Stanford University Press, 1987); Eli Sagan, *Cannibalism: Human Aggression and Cultural Form*, foreword by Robert N. Bellah (New York: Harper and Row, Harper Torchbooks, 1974); Eli Sagan, *The Lust to Annihilate: A Psychoanalytic Study of Violence in Ancient Greek Culture* (New York: Psychohistory Press, 1979); and Mark Juergensmeyer, ed., *Violence and the Sacred in the Modern World* (London: Frank Kass, 1991).

2. See Chapter 4, "Religion is War," in James Hillman, *A Terrible Love of War* (New York: The Penguin Press, 2004), 178–217. Hillman regards war as more fundamental feature than sacrifice.

3. For a brief account of the violence of religious terrorism in Judaism, Christianity and Islam see David C. Rapoport, "Fear and Trembling: Terrorism in Three Religious Traditions," *American Political Science Review* 78, no. 3 (September 1984): 658–76. For an in-depth study of violence in the major monotheistic traditions see Regina M. Schwartz, *The Curse of Cain: The Violent Legacy of Monotheism* (Chicago: The University of Chicago Press, 1997). For a study of the radical Islamic sect, the Assassins (Ismailis-Nizari), that terrorized Muslim lands from 1090 to 1275 in its efforts to "purify" Islam, see Bernard Lewis, *The Assassins: A Radical Sect in Islam* (Oxford: Oxford University Press, 1987). For comparisons with contemporary Islamist terrorism see also this author's recent work, Bernard Lewis, *The Crisis of Islam: Holy War and Unholy Terror* (New York: Modern Library, 2003).

4. Ronald B. Miller, "Violence, Force and Coercion," in *Violence: Award-Winning Essays in the Council for Philosophical Studies Competition* (New York: David McKay, 1971), 25–26.

5. J. Angelo Corlett, *Terrorism: A Philosophical Analysis* (Dordrecht: Kluwer Academic Publishers, 2003), 119-200.

6. Jessica Stern, Terror in the Name of God: Why Religious Militants Kill (New York: HarperCollins Publishers, 2003), xx.

7. Bruce Lincoln, Holy Terrors: Thinking About Religion After September 11 (Chicago: The University of Chicago Press, 2003).

8. The full text of the *Final Instructions* is reprinted in Lincoln, *Thinking About Religion*, Appendix A, pp. 93-98. All quotations are from this appendix.

9. Lincoln, Thinking About Religion, 12.

10. Lincoln, *Thinking About Religion*, 11.

11. Quoted by Mark Juergensmeyer, in *Terror in the Mind of God: The Global Rise of Religious Violence* (Berkeley, Calif..: University of California Press, 2001), 66.

12. Juergensmeyer, *Terror in the Mind of God*, 81.

13. As quoted by Lincoln, 15.

14. Charles Kimball, in *When Religion Becomes Evil* (San Francisco: HarperCollins, 2002), 75-91.

15. Gary North, *Backward Christian Soldiers? An Action Manual for Christian Reconstruction* (Tyler, Texas: Institue for Christian Economic, 1984), 267.

16. Juergensmeyer, *Terror in the Mind of God*, 146.

17. *www.alwasatnews.com.* March 7, 2004. Translated by Mansour al-Badwi.

18. Juergensmeyer, *Terror in the Mind of God*, 161-63.

19. Among the more useful studies of war, especially in relation to religion, in addition to Hillman, *A Terrible Love of War* (New York: Doubleday, 1958); Barbara Ehrenreich, *Blood Rites: Origins and History of the Passions of War* (New York: Henry Holt, 1997); Chris Hedges, *War is a Force That Gives Us Meaning* (New York: Public Affairs, 2002); Donald Kagan, *On the Origins of War and the Preservation of Peace* (New York: Doubleday, 1995); and Howard Zinn, *Terrorism and War*, ed. Anthony Arnove (Toronto: Seven Stories, 2002).

20. Quoted by Juergensmeyer, *Terror in the Mind of God*, 178. See also http://rjgeib.com/thoughts/burning/africia-bombings.html.

21. Kimball, *When Religion Becomes Evil*, 72.

22. See John M. Koller, "Why is *Anekantavada* Important?" in *Ahimsa, Anekanta and Jainism,* ed. Tara Sethia. (Delhi, India: Motilal Banarsidass, 20204), 85-98.

23. See John M. Koller, "*Ekam Sat:* A Principle for Religious Pluralism," *Indian Philosophical Annual.* Vol. 23, no. Fall, 2002 (2002): 61-84.

2

Mahatma Gandhi after 9/11: Terrorism and Violence

Douglas Allen

Ever since the tragedy of 11 September 2001, terrorism and security have been at the center of U.S. political and military policies, media coverage, and public concerns. On 9/11, approximately 3,000 people were killed as civilian airliners were transformed into weapons of mass destruction and two planes were crashed into the World Trade Center in New York, another plane was crashed into the Pentagon in Washington, D.C., and a fourth plane was crashed in rural Pennsylvania. Key U.S. political figures repeatedly justify violent policies and the curtailment of civil liberties by maintaining "everything changed with 9/11."

Since 9/11, I've given many lectures in the United States, India, and other parts of the world focusing on Gandhi's analysis of violence and nonviolence, terror and terrorism. Audiences always seem curious, fascinated, and even sympathetic. When it comes time for the question and answer period, the first question is usually some variation of the following: What would Gandhi have done about the 9/11 terrorists? What would he do to stop the suicide bomber? The questioner usually seems confident that Gandhi has nothing relevant to offer the contemporary world when it comes to certain kinds of violence, terror, and terrorism. At best, Gandhi, in his extreme commitment to nonviolence and pacifism, is naïve and completely irrelevant. At worst, Gandhi is complicit in furthering terror and terrorism and is culpable since he opposes the very violent measures necessary to deal with post-9/11 crises that threaten to destroy us.

My position is that Gandhi is very insightful and relevant in serving as a gadfly and a catalyst challenging dominant immoral and unsuccessful positions. He challenges us to rethink our views of violence and nonviolence, terror and terrorism, insecurity and real security. When interpreted and applied selectively and creatively, Gandhi provides a radical critique of dominant, contemporary, political, economic, social, cultural, and religious priorities and policies. He

19

provides invaluable insights and positive directions allowing us to reformulate our views about terrorism, violence, and our relations to others. Gandhi does not have all of the solutions, but Gandhian analysis, when integrated with other complementary approaches, offers real hope for dealing with contemporary terrorism and with the billions of human beings now being defined, devalued, and destroyed as "the other."[1]

What is Terrorism?

"Terrorism" is a difficult term to define. A "terrorist" to some is often a "freedom fighter" to others. From perspectives of British colonialists, many eighteenth-century American or twentieth-century Indian revolutionary "freedom fighters" could be classified as terrorists. In the 1980s, Dick Cheney, later Vice-President under George W. Bush, and other key policymakers in Washington, repeatedly described the anti-apartheid African National Congress as a terrorist organization and its leader, Nelson Mandela, as a terrorist who should not be freed from imprisonment on South Africa's Robbin Island.

Terrorism always involves explicit violence or the threat of violence. As defined by *Webster's Revised Unabridged Dictionary* and other standard dictionaries, violence has two major meanings. Many definitions emphasize that violence is a quality or force that is intense, immoderate, fierce, and rough. In addition, most definitions emphasize that violence is a negative force that involves aggression, infringement, assault, oppression, and injustice. Most violence does not involve terrorism. Terrorism is a specific kind of violence.

Terrorism always involves the infliction or threat of terror, a specific kind of violence. Terror involves extreme fear and anxiety and the experience of violent dread. Perpetrators of terrorism certainly intend to create great fear in the victims of their terror. In addition, conditions of terror breed certain kinds of terrorists. People who live under daily conditions of terror, who experience humiliation, domination, and hopelessness, sometimes find messages of terrorists appealing or at least they see no alternatives.

Nevertheless, terror can be distinguished from terrorism. Most terror does not involve terrorism. Human beings, who experience terror, when confronting their own mortality or other existential crises, rarely transform their sense of terror into any form of terrorism. Even most people living under humanly caused, socioeconomic, and political forms of terror, do not turn to terrorism. Their sense of hopelessness and despair resulting from such terror frequently leads to withdrawal and passivity in which they accept oppressive conditions as overwhelming, natural, inevitable, or eternal. Human beings often turn their feelings of hopelessness and powerlessness on themselves, turning to alcohol and drugs. They may turn their repressed rage against family members and others most vulnerable who are not the real causes of their oppressive conditions and consequent feelings of terror. They may engage in imaginary escapist fantasies that do nothing to change the objective conditions that oppress and terrorize them. They may turn to religious messages of divine or supernatural retribution and of a better life in the next world. Only under certain conditions do a minority of people, who are terrorized and living under conditions of terror, turn to terrorism as a means for expressing their sense of humiliation and rage.

What then is this specific form of violence utilizing terror that can be considered "terrorism"? My definition of terrorism, consistent with Gandhi's approach to violence, is the following: "Terrorism" consists of intentional policies and actions that use explicit violence or implicit forms of violence and threats of violence—economically, militarily, psychologically, politically, culturally, religiously—primarily directed against civilian populations in order to terrorize or inflict extreme fear and insecurity as the means to achieving political and other objectives. Discussions of terrorism are invariably linked with demands for "real security." I use the term "security" as freedom from danger and risk and involving a well-founded confidence.

As is evident in the above definitions, I (and Gandhi) use such terms as terror and terrorism, violence, and insecurity and real security, in much broader ways than one finds expressed by politicians, business leaders, and media figures. I find that the usual, much narrower uses are oversimplified, inadequate, self-serving, and used to obfuscate and justify ideologically questionable policies and actions of dominant power interests. Consistent with my definition, 9/11 highjackers, suicide bombers, and small terrorist organizations certainly perpetuate terrorism. However, U.S. and other military and economic forces can also be seen as actively creating, funding, supporting, and benefiting from policies and actions of terror and terrorism. In addition, my definition also points to much of terrorism as rooted in the violence of the status quo. One can speak of corporate and state terror and terrorism and of policies of terror and terrorism formulated by dominant, "respectable," powerful, economic, political and military forces.

Terrorism and Intentionality

Critics have mainly challenged the component of my definition claiming that terrorism is "intentional." It may be true that individual terrorists and small groups usually calculate and intend the devastating consequences of their actions, but this cannot be said of dominant economic, political, and military interests and the violence of the status quo. Critics submit that the devastating terrorism of such corporate, state, and military policies and actions is usually unintended.

Although this criticism has merit, it seems important to retain the intentional component of terrorism, and there are several possible responses to such criticism. First, I would submit that justifications for dominant polices and actions are too apologetic. Multinational corporate chief executive officers, military officers, and political leaders are not so naïve or uninformed about the likely terrorism resulting from their priorities and decisions. They usually are very aware of such destructive consequences but they don't care or they have other priorities that overrule such concerns. One thinks, for example, of political and military leaders who employ weapons of mass destruction with the predictable death and suffering inflicted on innocent civilians and then cover this up or rationalize this as unintended "collateral damage." Similarly, one thinks of war profiteers and other corporate leaders who do best when selling profitable weapons of mass destruction and when exploiting conditions of insecurity, fear, violence, war, and terrorism.

Second, there certainly are cases in which those perpetuating terrorism may be completely unaware of the consequences of their policies and actions. Even Gandhi, who did not perpetuate terrorism and focused on the nonviolent moral will and good intentions, often wrote of how he had been uninformed or misjudged situations, and how his actions then produced unintended violence and other negative results. Much of this he learned from unintended consequences, from failed experiments in truth. For example, he realized that much of his earlier faith in noble British intentions and in British law had been uninformed; that he had underestimated the violent nature of British colonialism and modern civilization. In his *satyagraha* campaigns in India, the well-intentioned Gandhi later realized that he had sometimes misjudged the moral and spiritual preparation and commitment of other *satyagrahis*. In these failed nonviolent experiments, some Indians revealed that they were not sufficiently committed to nonviolence or lacked the courage necessary to submit to brutal violence and self-suffering. In short, in numerous examples, Gandhi later acknowledges that the violence was not intentional, desired, or even willingly undertaken in terms of conscious awareness and choice.

Returning to those cases in which the perpetrator of terrorism is unaware of terrorist consequences, in which there is no intentional terrorist structure of consciousness, we may respond as follows. It is usually possible to reconstruct the intentionality of a rationally informed consciousness with the reasonable requirement that one will attempt to understand the objective situation and likely consequences resulting from one's policies and actions. In such cases, ignorance is no excuse. If one sells powerful weapons to brutal dictators, who have known records of repression and human rights violations, one cannot rationalize that the resulting predictable terror and terrorism were completely unintended. If corporate leaders, in their exclusive focus on fiduciary responsibility and maximizing profits, maintain high prices and thus deny supplies of medicine to poor people, they cannot rationalize that the resulting predictable terror, suffering, and death of millions of human beings were completely unintended.

Third, in some examples seemingly lacking a human intentional component, there is, indeed, devastating terror but not terrorism. One thinks of human beings being terrorized as a result of natural disasters, of terrifying experiences with animals, or of many relations with others with power and authority to make life and death decisions effecting one's survival. In such cases, there is often terror but usually no sense of terrorism.

In such cases of terror when relating to those with power and authority, structures of terrorism are not in fact sometimes present. For example, in the Abu Ghraib prisoner scandal in Baghdad revealed in 2004, U.S. authorities granted that Iraqi prisoners were subjected to all kinds of abuses involving terror, including degrading sexual practices and defenselessness before vicious dogs. The defense was that these were isolated acts of terror inflicted by a few soldiers and civilian contractors. However, it seems more likely that these acts of terror were part of policy of terrorism in which prisoners were intentionally terrorized in order to obtain information and achieve certain objectives as part of the Iraq war and the war on terrorism. This possibility of terrorism is evident in many cases of economic, political, and military power relations, but it also extends to illustrations such as educational relations. A teacher, for example, may intentionally use grades and other hierarchical power relations to inflict terror on students in ways that satisfy all of the conditions in our definition of terrorism.

Finally, and perhaps most seriously challenging my inclusive formulation, there are economic and other impersonal structures of power domination that seem to function completely independent of any human agency with its intentional structure of consciousness. Marx tells us that capitalism, as a structural system of economic relations, consists of foundational principles—such as the centrality of exchange value, the extraction of surplus value, and laws of capital accumulation—that function regardless of the intentional consciousness of individual human beings. Structuralists are also correct in maintaining that one cannot understand objective reality, including contemporary terrorism, by reducing it to the functioning of intentional consciousness of subjects with intended consequences.

My response is to grant that such structures, including those of the violence of the status quo that can result in terrorism, do, to some extent, assume a life of their own independent of intentional consciousness with its intended consequences. There is a real world of objective structures and relations that exists independent of what I intend and that determines, to a great extent, the limits and possibilities of my human existence. Nevertheless, it is a mistake to analyze such structures in completely impersonal terms as if they are totally detached from human agency. Human beings have constituted, continue to reconstitute, and maintain and develop these structures, such as those disclosed in the dynamics of terrorism. What may seem to be completely impersonal is in fact an intentional structure that is disclosed as being for human consciousness, and one that is contingent and open to our dynamic reconstitution.

Gandhi's Different Approach to Violence and Terrorism

Gandhi's most important contribution toward understanding terrorism is seen in his lifelong attempt to redefine, broaden, and deepen our understanding of violence. In radically transforming our understanding of violence, both quantitatively and qualitatively, Gandhi transforms our approach to those forms of violence classified as terror and terrorism.

In most discussions of violence, including contemporary violent terrorism, contexts and meanings of "violence" are restricted to expressions of overt physical violence. Gandhi also devotes a lot of attention to such physical violence as seen in the wartime acts of death and destruction, killings and acts of domestic physical abuse directed at family members and those of oppressed classes and castes, acts of religious communal violence, and so forth.

However, for Gandhi, such important acts of overt physical violence are only a small part of overall violence. In his attempt to broaden and deepen our sensitivity and awareness of violence, Gandhi claims that most of us who profess to stand for peace and nonviolence are actually very violent. For example, Gandhi always emphasizes internal violence as well as external violence. Love, often identified as *ahimsa*, is nonviolent, whereas hatred is violent. I may not kill you or inflict direct violence on you, but if I have a violent will, if I am full of hatred, then I am a violent person and my violence will be manifested in violent relations toward myself and toward others.

Gandhi broadens and deepens our approach to violence, and hence to terror and terrorism, in two significant ways. First, he emphasizes the diversity, multidimensionality, complexity, and interactional nature of overt and subtle forms of violence. Second, his approach to such complex multidimensionality of expressions of violence is especially insightful in emphasizing the usually neglected structures of the violence of the status quo. Such violence of the status quo is part of our "normal" everyday life, part of business as usual, and it is usually not even recognized as violent. For example, from the Gandhian point of view, much of seemingly nonviolent therapy and conflict resolution consists of identifying "dysfunctional" acts of individual overt conflict or violence and then attempting to transform the "antisocial" person so that she or he is harmoniously integrated into the structures of the violence of the status quo.

In addition to acts of overt physical violence, Gandhi primarily emphasizes multidimensional foundational structures and diverse kinds of violence: economic violence, psychological violence, linguistic violence, social violence, cultural violence, religious violence, educational violence, and so forth. It is inadequate to restrict our attention and approach to overt acts of suicide bombers and other individual terrorists. We must primarily focus on the many dimensions of violence that get at the foundations, root causes, and key determinants of such terrorism and that continue to fuel terrorism. Not only must we come to terms with these diverse kinds and structures of violence, but we must also recognize that they cannot be understood and approached as separate isolated expressions of violence. They mutually interact and reinforce each other as integral parts of a violent whole.

For example, the 9/11 terrorists and Al Qaeda use violent language, often presented in violent jihadist formulations. To understand such holy war language, with its classification of others as infidels and its language of victimhood and martyrdom, one has to understand the underlying historical, economic, psychological, cultural, and religious conditions that both fuel such violent language and provide it with an ideological appeal and justification for millions of human beings. To the extent that it takes hold, such violent language has a profound effect on redefining and reinforcing interconnected economic, cultural, religious, national, gender, and other relations.

From Gandhi's perspective, the very same observations can be made with respect to the Bush Administration's violent language often presented in formulations of the war on terrorism. To understand these dominant versions of this holy war language, in which God is on "our" side and the others are evil, one has to understand the underlying historical, economic, political, cultural, religious, racial, and other conditions that provide the contexts and ideological appeal and justifications for such a violent worldview. Such violent language then reinforces and furthers the relations of the permanent world economy, justifies doctrines of might makes right and the need for preemptive war, and promotes relations with "friendly" dictators who act in the U.S. interest, as defined by certain power interests, even if they terrorize their own populations.

Economic Violence: An Illustration

Gandhi's different approach to violence and terrorism can be seen in one of his major concerns: economic violence. It is easy to recognize Gandhi's emphasis on some other kinds of violence, such as psychological violence with his focus on ego-driven feelings and thoughts, selfishness, greed, hatred, and other motives and inner states of consciousness. However, it is also easy to devalue the emphasis of the "spiritual" Gandhi on economic conditions and economic violence. Such violence, primarily manifested through the "normal" structures and relations of the status quo, is normally overlooked or deemphasized by others in their approaches to violence and terrorism.

Unlike many others who share Gandhi's emphasis on the need for a spiritual and ethical approach, he emphasizes the importance of economic and material causes and conditions in shaping our lives. Gandhi tells us that it is only when one has focused on basic material necessities of life and dealt with basic human needs necessary for survival dominating the lives of starving and impoverished human beings that one can address *swaraj*, freedom, and "higher" ethical and spiritual values.[2] Gandhi sometimes writes about poverty as the worst form of violence. In most of his uses, violence is synonymous with exploitation. Although Gandhi resists personalizing the struggle against violent oppression, thus keeping open the possibilities for personal reconciliation, he repeatedly identifies with the plight of peasants, workers, and others who are disempowered. In his approach to violence, Gandhi is always attentive to unequal, asymmetrical, violent power relations in which some, who possess wealth, capital, and other material resources, are able to exploit and dominate those lacking such economic power.

A Gandhian approach to violence, terror, and terrorism today emphasizes the following kinds of economic violence. The economic violence of the status quo is expressed domestically and globally through the concentration of wealth and power defined by the domination of the ruling class, multinational corporations, and the military-industrial complex. True nonviolence, security, and democratic empowerment are only possible under economic conditions and structures of a more decentralized, more equitable distribution and control of economic resources and power.

The economic violence of the status quo is expressed through the permanent war economy which removes vital resources that could be used to meet human needs and which flourishes most under conditions of terror, insecurity, violence, and war. The economic violence of the status quo is also expressed through dominant economic power relations, both globally and domestically, in which indigenous and local self-sustaining economic relations are destroyed, and food, medicine, and other commodities are produced on the basis of profit for the least needy and more privileged and powerful who can afford them.

The main concern for Gandhi, in all such economic violence, is that it involves humanly-caused exploitation, domination, and suffering. Gandhi goes so far as to tell us that if my neighbor is impoverished or suffering in other ways and if I could change the conditions and help alleviate the suffering, but I choose not to get involved, then I am complicit in the violence of the status quo. As

Gandhi learned from the *Bhagavad-Gita*, inaction is a kind of action. If I do nothing about economic exploitation and refuse to serve the needs of other suffering human beings, I perpetuate and am responsible for the economic violence of the status quo.

If we want to understand and confront contemporary terrorism, Gandhi challenges us to examine economic violence. Otherwise our understanding is limited and our approach inadequate, self-defeating, and dangerous. Providing such an explanation, trying to understand terrorism, in no way justifies terrorism. As Gandhi repeatedly emphasized, if we want to combat and overcome the threat of violence and terrorism, we must understand and then eliminate the root causes and oppressive conditions. Otherwise short-term actions will do little to overcome long-term insecurity and repetition of tragedies at home and abroad. Only by understanding such economic violence can we understand the suffering, humiliation, hopelessness, rage, terror, and violence of those committing overt violent acts of terrorism and of those supporting or not opposing terrorism. And it is only by understanding such economic violence that we understand how those with dominant economic power, as expressed through the violence of the status quo, create and maintain conditions of exploitation, domination, and terror and exercise their own forms of terrorism.

A common refutation to such an economic analysis of 9/11, especially by those representing dominant U.S. power interests, is the obvious objection that Osama bin Laden is extremely wealthy and therefore his Al Qaeda terrorism has nothing to do with any experience of suffering economic violence. This objection misses the strength of Gandhi's analysis. First, in focusing on economic violence, Gandhi is not a simple, deterministic, economic reductionist. Violence is multidimensional, has multiple causes, and religious and other causal factors sometimes become major determinants. Second, the fact that bin Laden is personally wealthy does not mean that he has not been motivated by claims about economic exploitation, oppression, and humiliation of Islamic societies. Third, and most important for our analysis, Gandhi's analysis of economic violence is very significant for understanding why so many millions of human being are receptive to bin Laden and other terrorist messages.

Gandhi and Terrorists

Gandhi was very aware of terrorists, their arguments, and their refutations of his position. Indeed, throughout his life, he attempted to engage in dialogue with terrorists in order to understand their positions and to attempt to persuade them of the greater morality and effectiveness of nonviolence. *The Collected Works of Mahatma Gandhi* contains numerous writings on terrorism and terrorists, often addressed to extremists, anarchists, and revolutionaries.[3]

Gandhi's *Hind Swaraj*, written in only ten days in November 1909 while on a ship returning from England to South Africa, may be his most important single work for grasping the fundamental principles of his life and his philosophy.[4] Gandhi formulated *Hind Swaraj* as a dialogue between a newspaper Editor, representing Gandhi's views, and a Reader, representing the contrasting views of "modern" Indians, including expatriates he had met in London. These Indian expatriates included those who accepted violence and terrorism as legitimate means in the struggle for independence from British colonial rule.

Particular mention may be made of V.D. Savarkar (1883-1966), who lived in London during 1906-1910 and was an influential figure among the Indian expatriates. The revolutionary Madan Lal Dhingra (1887-1909), who came under Savarkar's influence, assassinated Sir William Curzon-Wyllie, the aide-de-camp to Lord Morley, the Secretary of State for India, on July 1, 1909, a few days before Gandhi arrived in London.[5] The same Savarkar also had a great influence on the assassination of Gandhi on January 30, 1948. The assassin, Nathuran Godse, was a Savarkar follower.[6] Many passages expressing Gandhi's views on Krishnavarma Shyamji, Savarkar, Dhingra, and terrorists or those justifying violence and terrorism can be found throughout *The Collected Works of Mahatma Gandhi*.

Although Gandhi sometimes asserts that Madam Lal Dhingra and other terrorists act in a cowardly manner, since they are willing to inflict violence on others without suffering the violence themselves, such a simple impression can be misleading. Gandhi's approach is very different from that of President George Bush and his administration after 9/11. Unlike Bush, who repeatedly described the terrorists as cowards who simply envy and resent our freedom, Gandhi acknowledges that terrorists are often patriots who act with courage and are willing to die for their cause.

In this regard, Gandhi's position on terrorism is similar to a position on violence that he expressed in numerous passages.[7] Some soldiers and other perpetrators of violence have high ideals, are brave, and are more courageous than the cowardly response of so-called nonviolent people who are passive and refuse to get involved in resisting oppression and injustice. Gandhi prefers courageous violence to cowardice. However, he usually adds a third alternative, that of the *satyagrahi*, the nonviolent peace and justice activist, who expresses the most moral and spiritual position; this is the bravest position that requires the greatest courage in voluntarily accepting self-sacrifice and self-suffering without inflicting violence on others.[8]

Gandhi strongly refutes the terrorist position. First, although some terrorists are brave, there is a morally and spiritually superior position that requires far more courage: that of nonviolent resistance in which I refuse to inflict violence and suffering on others. Second, Gandhi repeatedly claims that Indian expatriate terrorists and other proponents of "modern civilization" actually imitate the worst features of colonial and other oppressors. Indians, as victims who accept the legitimacy of terrorism, are linked with the violence and terrorism of the modern civilization of the British oppressor. Violence and terror, if successful in driving out the British, will lead to a false independence, not real *swaraj*, in which Indian violent oppressors simply replace British oppressors. Third and most importantly, expanding the second objection, Gandhi repeatedly introduces his famous analysis of the integral relation of means and ends.

Gandhi's Means-Ends Analysis

Gandhi rejects utilitarianism and many other contemporary positions, including various justifications of terrorism, which maintain that the ends justify the means. We must emphasize both means and ends and their integral, mutually reinforcing relations. On the whole, Gandhi places even more emphasis on means because he tells us that we often have much greater control over our means, whereas noble ends may be unattainable because of unintended consequences or because they express ideals that are beyond our power of realization.

Regardless of short-term benefits, Gandhi repeatedly emphasizes that we cannot use violence to overcome violence and achieve nonviolence. We cannot use terror and terrorism to overcome terrorism and achieve real security free from terror. If we use violent and impure means, these will shape violent and impure ends regardless of our moralistic self-justifying slogans and ideology.

In language similar to formulations of the law of *karma*, Gandhi repeatedly warns us that violence leads to more violence, terror leads to more terror, and we become entrapped in endless vicious cycles of escalating violence. For Gandhi, as it was for the Buddha, most of violence has a moral character and involves intention and choice. It is this moral character of volitional *karmic* intention and choice that binds us to the vicious cycles of violence and suffering. The only way to move toward more nonviolent ends, free from terror and terrorism, is to introduce nonviolent causal factors through the adoption of nonviolent means. Such nonviolent factors will begin to weaken the causal factors that produce violent chain reactions and will undermine the mutually reinforcing causal relations that keep us trapped in destructive cycles of violence.

Gandhi's warning and critique can be illustrated by any of the contemporary sites of overt terrorism. In the Middle East, more powerful Israeli governments and their military forces have spent decades inflicting terror and terrorism on Palestinians in order to break the Palestinian will of resistance and achieve security for Israel. And for decades, Palestinians have attempted to inflict terror and terrorism on Israelis in order to break the Israeli will and achieve Palestinian objectives. The result has been mutually reinforcing, escalating cycles of violence and terrorism with no real security for either Palestinians or Israelis.

The most obvious illustration, at the center of the Bush Administration's post-9/11 war on terrorism, is the U.S. war in Iraq that began in March 2003. Through preemptive war and the overwhelming use of means of terror, including actions and policies of terrorism that involved larger regional and global objectives, the U.S. would overcome terrorist threats and be more secure. Instead, the U.S. has found itself drained economically and militarily, trapped in a quagmire of escalating violence and war without end. Before March 2003, Iraqis had been terrorized by the brutal Saddam Hussein dictatorship, but there was no evidence of Al Qaeda or other terrorist links or weapons of mass destruction threatening U.S. security. Following Gandhi's approach, we can better understand how U.S. terror and terrorism has not only trapped the U.S. in destructive cycles of violence; it has created and conditioned new form of anti-U.S. terror so that today Iraq is indeed a center of terrorism. Such massive U.S. violence has made the U.S. much more vulnerable to terrorism and much less secure.

In many respects, Gandhi's means-ends analysis is similar to the Buddha's formulation of this Doctrine of Dependent Origination (*pratitya-samutpada*).[9] Through his formulation of the 12 links or factors, Buddha analyzes how we become imprisoned in this cyclical world of existence (*samsara*), the world of suffering (*dukkha*). *Samsara* is the world of dynamic, impermanent, interdependent relatively. There is not one, independent, absolute cause to our entrapment in this world of suffering. Each relative and contingent factor is conditioned as well as conditioning; caused by antecedent causal conditions and is itself a causal factor shaping future conditions. The Buddhist path involves identifying these causal factors and gradually weakening the causal links that keep us trapped in cycles of ignorance and suffering by introducing more ethical and spiritual causal factors.

Gandhi's means-ends approach to violence, terror, and terrorism shares much with this particular Buddhist orientation and other Indian orientations. Violence, terror, and terrorism are not independent, inevitable, eternal, or absolute. They exist within a violent phenomenal world of impermanent, interdependent relativity. Terrorism and other forms of violence are caused and conditioned, and they themselves become causes and condition other violent consequences that then become new violent causal factors. The path and goal for Gandhi involves focusing on the means that allow you to decondition such violent causal factors and conditions, to introduce nonviolent causes and conditions; that will lead to more nonviolent results that will then become new causal factors moving you closer to your nonviolent ends. The means-ends relation involves mutual interaction, since the adoption of nonviolent ideals as ends will also have a causal influence on shaping appropriate means.

In this way one aims at transforming the causally connected, means-ends, interdependent whole, of which you are an integral part, from one constituted through ignorance, violence, and suffering to a more moral and spiritual relational whole. This very process of means-ends causal transformation, by which one transforms relations with others in order to serve their needs, is the very process by which one transforms one's own self toward greater freedom and self-realization.[10]

Gandhi's Preventative Approach and Short-term Violence

The tremendous contribution of Gandhi's approach to 9/11, terrorism, and violence lies not in any insights about how to respond when the terrorist is about to strike, but rather about what to do beforehand. Gandhi's major focus is always on preventative measures that we must take in order to transform and remove the violent conditions and causes before they reach the point of exploding into terror and terrorism.

This emphasis by Gandhi on the larger picture and the need for preventative approaches should be evident from previous sections, especially formulations of Gandhi's deeper and broader analysis of violence and terror, including economic violence, and his analysis of means-ends relations in terms of a larger framework for getting at roots causes and conditions underlying violence and terrorism. As Gandhi repeatedly warns us, if we do not understand and respond to the larger framework of complex, multidimensional, interrelated structures and relations of violence, if we do not address the roots causes, conditions, and dynamics of violence, then our short-term responses will not be sufficient for dealing with escalating violence and future terrorism.

This is why Gandhi, in his approach to violence and nonviolence, devotes so much time and effort to a radically different model of education with emphasis on character building and moral and spiritual development.[11] This is why he is preoccupied with expanding our psychological awareness and analysis of how we constitute and must decondition ego-driven selfishness and greed, defense mechanisms responding to fear and insecurity, hatred, aggression, and other violent intentions and inner states of consciousness. This is why Gandhi is so attentive to political, cultural, social, economic, linguistic, religious, and other aspects of our overall socialization that contribute to, tolerate, and justify violence, terror, and terrorism.

A frequent response to such a Gandhian nonviolent approach is that it may have value for long-term preventative measures, but what do we do about the short-term threat of terrorism? Unfortunately, we cannot wait for long-term educational and other preventative measures gradually to reconstitute our human

relations in more nonviolent, ethical, and truthful ways. We live in a contemporary world of terrorists who are intent on inflicting terrorism on us right now.

In this regard, it is important to emphasize that Gandhi's preventative
measures are intended not only for the gradual long-term changes that are most
important for dealing with violence, terror, and terrorism. His preventative approach also has profound short-term benefits.

If I am relating to someone intent on inflicting short-term violence, there are
many Gandhian responses that may be effective in preventing the violence and
terrorism. If I manage to limit my own ego, achieve a larger perspective, and
empathize with feelings of the terrorist, even if I find them inadequate and dangerous, this may allow for dialogue and for creating nonthreatening relations
with the other. In addition, as Gandhi repeatedly emphasizes, while intellectual
approaches with rational analysis often have no real transformative effect on the
other, approaches of the heart involving deep personal emotions and feelings
often have profound, relational, transformative effects. If I refuse to strike back
and am willing to embrace self-sacrifice and self-suffering, this can disrupt the
expectations of the violent other, lead to a decentering and reorienting of an extremely violent situation, and touch the heart of the other. Throughout his writings on *satyagraha* and other methods for resisting and transforming violence,
Gandhi proposes numerous ways for relating to short-term violence and moving
toward conflict resolution and reconciliation grounded in truth and nonviolence.

Nevertheless, I acknowledge that Gandhi's nonviolent proposals are sometimes completely ineffective in preventing certain kinds of short-time violence. I
would submit that non-Gandhian proposals are also ineffective in preventing
such violence. What does one do about the suicide terrorist about to explode a
bomb? What does one do about the madman about to shoot innocent people?
What does one do about the pilot about to drop napalm on innocent civilians?
What does one do about the determined rapist as the victim is being raped?

The major difficulty with these and related examples, often presented as
refutations of Gandhi's approach, is that there is no opportunity for empathy,
communication, changing causes and conditions and human relations, or any of
the other preventative measures that are the strength of Gandhi's orientation.
The terrorism and other forms of violence are at the explosive stage and beyond
our nonviolent preventative interventions. They are also often expressed through
completely impersonal structures and relations in which there is no possibility
for constructive, personal, nonviolent interaction.

It may surprise some readers to learn that Mahatma Gandhi, the best-known
twentieth-century proponent of peace and nonviolence, sometimes concludes
that violence is a necessary response. To understand on what grounds Gandhi
allows for violent preventative intervention in certain extreme situations, we
must turn to his key distinction between absolute truth and relative truth.[12]

Absolute Truth, Relative Truth, and Terrorism

In many of his writings, Gandhi conveys the impression of a rather simple, rigid absolutist with respect to violence, nonviolence, and other ethical and spiritual concepts and values. A more comprehensive and adequate examination reveals a Gandhi who is much more nuanced and recognizes the complexity and difficulty of sorting out and resolving conflicts and contradictions in human relations.

It is true that Gandhi is firm in upholding ideals of absolute truth, love, and nonviolence. In terms of such absolutes, he resists many contemporary views of complete subjectivism or unlimited facile relativism. Gandhi would never agree that the infliction of terror and terrorism may be wrong for him, but it may be right for the terrorist.

What is often overlooked is that Gandhi also repeatedly emphasizes that he and others exist in this world as relative, finite beings of limited embodied consciousness. Our knowledge is conditioned and perspectival. As Gandhi repeatedly tells us, he at most has "glimpses" of absolute truth and nonviolence. Since we have partial truths, we should be tolerant and open to other points of view; others have different relative perspectives and glimpses of truth that we do not have. Our ethical and spiritual path is to move from one relative truth to greater relative truth. As relative finite beings with limited knowledge, we often misjudge situations and even misjudge our motives, and that is why we must learn from our errors in the movement toward greater truth and nonviolence.[13]

One of the most arrogant and dangerous human moves is to make what is relative into an absolute. This is the move of those inflicting terrorism, whether emanating from Al Qaeda and other militant Islamists or from militants in Washington and the military-industrial complex, who act as if they posses the absolute truth and the other is absolutely evil.

Such absolutists pose the greatest challenge to Gandhi's approach to violence, terror, and terrorism: How does one deal with others who reject the relative-absolute distinction and Gandhi's inclusivistic tolerant approach and framework? If you adopt an exclusivistic, rigidly dichotomous approach, in which you claim to possess absolute truth and goodness and regard me as representing pure evil, you may have no interest in dialogue, mutual understanding, and nonviolent reconciliation. If your goal is to establish absolute truth and goodness, your intention and relevant means may be directed at destroying others as evil.

How does the absolute-relative distinction guide Gandhi in approaching the most difficult cases we have cited: those challenges in which the terrorists or perpetrators of violence reject Gandhi's inclusive, tolerant approach, claim that they possess the absolute truth, and are at the explosive point of inflicting terror and extreme violence? Unlike some critical interpreters, I do not think that Gandhi is rendered passive. He is not reduced to inaction and simply allowing terrorist acts to take place.

In extreme cases with no nonviolent options with any possibility of success, Gandhi suggests that we may use necessary violence in the cause of nonviolence. We act, using violent means if necessary, to prevent the terrorism or extreme violence because that is the least violent, effective response possible. Consistent with other responses in his writings, Gandhi would tell us to use violent means if necessary in order, say, to stop the suicide bomber about to kill many innocent human beings.[14]

It is essential that we distinguish such a Gandhian response from the usual, dominant, violent actions and policies endorsed as necessary in the war on terrorism and for dealing with other forms of crime and violence. First, Gandhi would only advocate such violent means as a last resort, when preventative measures have failed and there are no remaining nonviolent alternatives. Gandhi, for example, could never support Bush's "doctrine of preemptive war," used to justify the invasion and war in Iraq. In such a situation—in which there were no Iraqi weapons of mass destruction, no Iraqi links with Al Qaeda or 9/11, and no evidence of an Iraqi imminent threat to the U.S.—Gandhi would view such a doctrine, justifying war in order to prevent some potential future threat, as an early resort, not a last resort. For Gandhi, 99 percent of the time that we resort to violence, there are nonviolent options and means that we have overlooked or are unwilling to consider.

Second, even in those extreme cases in which we have exhausted nonviolent options and in which we are forced to use violent means to avoid much greater violence, Gandhi's approach is radically different from usual proponents of such violent means. Even when we are engaged in relative violence, we must always uphold the absolute truth, the ideal of absolute nonviolence. We must never glorify violence, even when it is necessary and we have no nonviolent relative options. When we use violence, what we do is tragic and is a terrible thing. It may be necessary, but it is not moral. That we live in a world of violence, terror, and terrorism is an indication of human failure. That we are forced to use violence is also an indication of human failure; that we have failed to create preventative nonviolent structures, relations, and conditions and to take nonviolent actions that could have avoided the need for such violence. Rather than extol and celebrate such violence, we should be saddened, seek forgiveness and work toward reconciliation.

Third, by maintaining the absolute ideal of nonviolence, we approach use of necessary violence with an attitude, intentions, and goals informed by a commitment to nonviolence. This means that we severely limit the need for violence and restrict to a minimum the intensity and extent of such relative violence. This means that when we engage in such tragic relative violence, we then do everything possible to change conditions and human relations to avoid the repetition of such violence.

Relating to the Other

Ever since René Descartes's well-known formulation of his process of methodological doubt, resulting in the conclusion that the only thing of which he could be absolutely certain was the existence of his own ego, Western thought has increasingly focused on the primacy of the self.[15] The modern focus on the primacy of the I-me self or ego, with its focus on self-interest and individual realization, is reflected in our socialization, our economic system, our educational system, our legal system, our culture, and all aspects of our life. In this sense, nationalism often appeals to a kind of collective ego; the nation is ideologically presented as embodying and expressing the essence of the individual self of its citizens. As Descartes established, such a focus on the primacy of one's self renders problematic any meaningful relations with the other, and one is constantly confronted with the possibilities of solipsism and various forms of self-alienation.

Gandhi not only disagrees with this focus on the primacy of the ego, but he advocates a radical inversion of the self-other relation.[16] As with the Buddha, Gandhi maintains that the construction and focus on the primacy of one's self leads to illusion, unhappiness, selfishness and greed, violence, war, and lack of ethical and spiritual development. Gandhi, in complete contrast to dominant Western modern orientations, proposes that we focus on the primacy of the other, by striving to reduce our self to a state of egoless consciousness and by directing our attention toward serving the needs of the other.

Ever since 9/11/01, with the overwhelming emphasis on terror and terrorism, there has been an increasing anti-Gandhian focus on the primacy of self with the devaluation of the other as the enemy and as evil. This, of course, is true of those who planned, perpetrated, and supported the terrorism of 9/11, but it is also true of those in charge of the U.S.-led "war on terrorism."[17] Both view the world in rigid, dichotomous, Manichean terms. We are good and the other is evil. You are either with us or you are with the enemy. For Osama bin Laden and Al Qaeda, the U.S. and those aligned with it are infidels, an evil enemy that must be terrorized through policies and acts of terrorism. For the neoconservatives, within the Bush Administration and as part of the Project for a New American Century and other conservative think tanks shaping Washington's policies, militant Islamists and others resisting U.S. truth and goodness are evil, enemies that must be destroyed through violence and terrorism.

In the Gandhian approach I've presented, George Bush and Osama bin Laden are closer to each other than either is to Mahatma Gandhi. From Gandhi's point of view, each is sometimes mirror image of the other. Each serves as evil enemy and the other necessary for the other's self-definition as absolute truth and goodness. And since each refuses to recognize the limited relativity of their partial truths and refuses to privilege the real needs of the other, each becomes trapped in arrogant self-assertions and escalating cycles of ignorance, violence, and terrorism.

There should be no confusion about Gandhi's position on the immediate terrorism of 9/11: He would speak out unequivocally on how such terrorism is unjustified and must be opposed. But he would also maintain that refusal to understand basic conditions, causes, and dynamics of escalating cycles of violence and terror, insistence that ends justify means, and refusal to relate to the needs of the other and the need for a long-term nonviolent preventative approach will guarantee failure in dealing with the real problems of insecurity, violence, terror, and terrorism.

Notes

1. Unlike my previous Gandhi publications, I shall not provide extensive documentation from Gandhi's writings. Most of my analysis from Gandhi, such as his focus on truth (*satya*), violence (*himsa*), and nonviolence (*ahimsa*), is well known and can be found in the 100 volumes of *The Collected Works of Mahatma Gandhi* (*CWMG*. New Delhi: Publications Division, Ministry of Information and Broadcasting, Government of India). For my documentation of major aspects of Gandhi's philosophy, see my "Philosophical Foundations of Gandhi's Legacy, Utopian Experiments, and Peace Struggles," *Gandhi Marg* 16, No. 2 (July-Sept. 1994): 133-60; "Gandhian Perspectives on Self-Other Relations as Relevant to Human Values and Social Change Today," in *Human Values and Social Change*, Vol. I, ed. by Ishwar Modi (Jaipur and New Delhi: Rawat Publications, 2000), pp. 283-309; "Gandhi, Contemporary Political Thinking, and Self-Other Relations," in *Contemporary Political Thinking*, ed. by B. N Ray (New Delhi: Kanishka Publishers, 2000), pp. 129-70.

2. See Ronald J. Terchek, *Gandhi: Struggling for Autonomy* (Lantham, Md.: Rowman & Littlefield Publishers, 1998), pp. 111-12.

3. See, for example, "My Friend, the Revolutionary' (*Young India*, September 4, 1925), in *CWMG* 26: 486-92, with Gandhi's assertion that "I do not regard killing or assassination or terrorism as good in any circumstances whatsoever"; "Letter to Lord Ampthill" (October 30, 1909) in *CWMG* 9: 508-10; "Speech at Plenary Session of Round Table Conference" (London, December 1, 1931), in which Gandhi addresses how "the page of history is soiled red with the blood of those who have fought for freedom" and "I hold ho brief for the terrorists" or those who "would encourage terrorism" (*CWMG* 48: 356-68, especially. 358-59).

4. *Swaraj* means "self-rule" and "independence." In *Hind Swaraj*, Gandhi gives *swaraj* two interconnected meanings: "Indian Home Rule," Gandhi's title for his English translation of the work, and individual self-rule. Highly recommended is the edition, M.K. Gandhi, *Hind Swaraj and Other Writings*, edited by Anthony J. Parel (Cambridge: Cambridge University Press, 1997) with Parel's excellent introduction.

5. See Parel's edition of *Hind Swaraj*, pp. xiv-xviii, 77-78, 95n, 118.

6. In his *Rediscovering Gandhi* (London: Century, 1997), Yogesh Chadha devotes considerable time to reconstructing the hatching of the plot and the assassination of Gandhi and the debate over whether Savarkar was directly responsible for Godse's killing of Gandhi.

7. There is a crucial difference in Gandhi's attitude toward violence and violent terrorism. Gandhi grants that some people perpetrating violence and some violent terrorists may have high ideals and show courage. In passages in which the only choice is between cowardice and courageous violence, Gandhi advocates the latter. However, he never advocates terrorism. With regard to war, where there is often a lot of bravery, Gandhi seemed to change his view about just war. Although he supported the British war efforts against both the Boers and the Zulus in South Africa, he later rejected any view of a just war.

8. There are numerous formulations throughout Gandhi's writings on the relations of cowardice, violence, and nonviolence. See, for example, "The Doctrine of the Sword' (*Young India*, August 11, 1920) in *CWMG* 18:131-34; "Hindu-Muslim Tension: Its Cause and Cure' (*Young India*, May 29, 1924) in *CWMG* 24:140-42;"Has Non-Violence Limits?" (*Young India*, August 1, 1926) in *CWMG* 31:292; "Non-Violence v. Cowardice" (*Young India*, October 10. 1929) in *CWMG* 42:73. Although one can appreciate Gandhi's reaction against cowards who pretend to be nonviolent and can understand why he thinks that the brave proponents of violence are closer to his courageous *satyagrahis*, some of his advice is troubling. In some cases, I'd prefer the inactive and perhaps even cowardly person to the brave person, incapable of courageous nonviolence, who is advised by Gandhi to exert violent force, especially when this may result in the death and suffering of many innocent human beings. My only defense of Gandhi in such passages is that he certainly knows that history is full of brave violent people who have caused great suffering and that he must be assuming an unacknowledged moral and spiritual approach and framework. In other words, the brave violent person, while not at the ethical and spiritual level of the truly nonviolent person, will only use violent force consistent with ethical and social *dharma* (duty) and other positive values.

9. The Doctrine of Dependent Origination (*pratitya-samutpada*, Pali *paticca-samuppada*), also known as Conditioned Genesis, found in *Samyutta-nikaya* xxii.90, appears in many translations, including Sarvepalli Radhhakrishnan and Charles A. Moore, eds., *A Source Book in Indian Philosophy* (Princeton: Princeton University Press. 1957), pp. 278-79. See also the translation of Dependent Origination, found in *Visuddhi-magga* xvii, in Radhhakrishnan and Moore, eds., *A Source Book in Indian Philosophy*, pp. 279-80.

10. Here and in so many other ways, it is important to note that Gandhi, while deeply influenced by Hindu, Buddhist, and Jain approaches and analysis, is not a "tradi-

tional" Hindu or Indian. He is an original, creative thinker who often rejects dominant, traditional, Indian approaches and reconstitutes positions in new ways. To use the present illustration, Gandhi accepts the rather traditional Indian approach of viewing the *karmic* world of illusion in terms of causally-connected relations of ignorance, violence, bondage, and suffering. However, unlike traditional Indian philosophy that views worldly existence as imprisonment in vicious causal cycles and has the spiritual goal of freeing oneself from such worldly involvement, Gandhi places a much higher value on our human relations in this world. An essential part of his moral and spiritual path is the transformation rather than the transcendence of such violent human relations.

11. I develop this analysis at length in Douglas Allen, "Peace Education and Mahatma Gandhi," *Peace Education for Contemporary Concerns*, ed. Naresh Dadhich (Jaipur, India, forthcoming).

12. Although Gandhi's distinction of relative and absolute truth resembles classical formulations of the "doctrine of two truths" found in Indian philosophy, Gandhi's approach is significantly different from that found in Shankara's Advaita Vedanta or Nagarjuna's Madhyamika Buddhism. For the difference in Gandhi's approach to relative and absolute truth, see Allen, "Gandhi, Contemporary Political Thinking, and Self-Other Relations," pp. 163-65.

13. I previously emphasized Gandhi's focus on intentions as essential to the good will and his rejection of utilitarianism and consequentialism. It is also an error to classify Gandhi's approach as Kantian or purely deontological. One must focus on both intentions and results, as seen in Gandhi's emphasis on both means and ends. Gandhi is very practical and there is something very pragmatic about his approach to violence and terrorism. Even with the best of intentions, our experiments in truth may be failures because of unintended violent consequences. Sometime Gandhi assesses and reconsiders his own motives and intentions based on later negative consequences. In short, Gandhi's approach includes the importance of both intentions and consequences and how they are often dialectically and integrally connected.

14. In several previous publications listed in note 1, I formulate such an interpretation of Gandhi's approach, consistent with his description of himself as a "practical idealist." In such an interpretation, Gandhi recognizes and struggles with the specificity and complexity of relative contextual situations, and he is much more nuanced, flexible, and relevant than some uncompromising, rigid, "pure," absolute Mahatma. For a very creative interpretation, see the chapter "Gandhi's Challenge to the Paradigm of Justifiable Violence," pp. 13-26, in Bart Gruzalski, *On Gandhi* (Belmont, Calif.: Wadsworth, 2001).

15. See René Descartes, *Meditations on First Philosophy* (Cambridge and New York: Cambridge University Press, 1986). For a more developed formulation of Descartes's orientation, as well as alternative non-Cartesian perspectives, see Douglas Allen, "Social Constructions of Self: Some Asian, Marxist, and Feminist Critiques of Dominant Western Views of Self," in *Culture and Self: Philosophical and Religious Perspectives, East and West*, edited by Douglas Allen (Boulder, Colo.: Westview Press/Harper Collins, 1997), pp. 3-26.

16. For a much more detailed treatment of Gandhi's analysis of self and self-other relations, see Allen, "Gandhi, Contemporary Political Thinking, and Self-Other Relations," pp. 129-70, especially "Self-Other Relations: A Radical Inversion," pp. 152-57, and "Key Questions Regarding the Self and Self-Other Relations," pp. 157-65. Gandhi usually endorses a dynamic, social, relational view of self in which there is no ethical and

spiritual self without the other, and the other is an integral part of who I am as self. However, there are other writings in which Gandhi emphasizes "the inner voice" of an autonomous, nonsocial, individual self that is distinguished from and contrasted with any relational other. Finally, there are still other writings in which Gandhi accepts a deeper, ultimate, metaphysical, spiritual self (or Self), often identified with the Hindu, Upanishadic, nondualistic *Atman* but also capable of other formulations in Gandhi's inclusivistic approach. These self and self-other formulations are often complementary, but they also express ambiguities, tensions, contradictions, and unresolved philosophical problems and issues.

17. This may at first seem to be a surprising claim. It is certainly true of certain militant Islamists directly involved in the terrorism of 9/11, but what about the neoconservatives ("neocons") in charge of Washington's "war on terrorism"? If one reads the policy positions of those identified with the Project for a New American Century and other neoconservative policymakers, the same pattern emerges. We are in possession of truth and goodness, and as the world's only superpower, we have both the capacity and the moral duty to ensure that our absolute values are applied globally. Iraq comes first as we use our power, including extreme shock and awe violence, to remake Iraq in ways consistent with our model of truth and goodness. Then Iranians, Syrians, Lebanese, Palestinians, and others, in awe of our determination and capacity to use terrifying violence, will be receptive to such radical restructuring according to our values and interests. In our attempt to remake the region and the world, you can join us and be part of the coalition of truth and goodness, or you can oppose us or refuse to join us, in which case you support or tolerate terrorism and forces of evil. If you do not follow our position, you are of no consequence and you will become dysfunctional and eventually extinct since our position defines truth, goodness, and the future.

3

Responding to Terror: An Aristotelian Approach

Anna Lännström

Aristotle is not known for fear and existential angst. Rather, he appears placid and sometimes even complacent. The world is a pretty good place and no radical changes are called for. Indeed, he argues against radical changes, suggesting that it is usually better to keep the status quo. Still, as Martha Nussbaum has shown, a close reading of the *Nicomachean Ethics* reveals Aristotle's acute awareness of human fragility and vulnerability and of the inescapability of such vulnerability (Nussbaum 1986, see especially pp. 318-372). Building upon Nussbaum's reading of the *Ethics*, I will argue that Aristotle views fear and even terror as natural and appropriate responses to the human condition. (Terror, as I understand it, always involves the experience of extreme fear, but most fear does not extend to the level of terror.) Because fear and terror are unavoidable, courage means handling them properly rather than eliminating them. In this essay, I will first examine Aristotle's view of the human condition and his account of courage. Then, I will turn to contemporary concerns, asking how an Aristotelian might respond to the threat of terrorism and how she might view the role of comparative religion in combating this threat.

The *Ethics* focuses upon *eudaimonia* ("happiness"). It asks what constitutes living and doing well for human beings and what is required for us to actually attain this *eudaimonia*. To what extent is the good life up to us and to what extent is it vulnerable to circumstances entirely or partly beyond our control?

Plato's Socrates affirmed that the good life and the good man are entirely invulnerable. On trial for impiety and corruption of the youth, he insisted that a good man cannot be harmed (*Apology*). Similar statements can be found in the *Gorgias*, and the *Republic*: "A good man cannot be harmed either in life or in

41

death, and [. . .] his affairs are not neglected by the gods" (*Apology* 41d); "Injustice is never more profitable than justice" (*Rep.* 354a); "A good and honorable man or woman, I say, is happy, and an unjust and wicked one is wretched" (*Gorgias* 470e); "Anyone, as it seems, who desires to be happy must ensue and practice temperance " (*Gorgias* 507d).

Socrates makes sense of this position by defining harm as 'damage to one's soul,' and he argues that such harm can only be self-imposed. Other kinds of harm, the sort that others can cause, are unimportant and insignificant. Thus, while others can and sometimes do kill the good man, they cannot harm him. Indeed, nothing bad can happen to him. (Of course, while Socrates might have been able to believe this, his students and followers in the *Phaedo* have a much harder time—possibly reflecting a hesitation on the part of Plato?)

The Stoics as well as many Indian philosophers express similar views. The goal, they argue, is to get to a standpoint where the flux of the world does not bother us. We must aim to attain true detachment and come to recognize that our inner core remains unharmed by whatever life throws at us and we stop worrying about what is beyond our control. Thus, Krishna's advice to Arjuna who is bristling with fear is to stop being a coward and to fulfill his *dharma* (duty) by fighting in the battle. He will not harm anything that matters.

Like Plato, then, these thinkers seem to believe that we can reach a stage where fear is understood to be an inappropriate reaction. Fear ends not because we remove frightening things but because we stop fearing them, and we stop fearing them by recognizing that they cannot harm anything that matters.

Aristotle dismisses this view as silly. Frightening things are and remain frightening precisely because they can harm what matters most. Nobody, he says pointedly, would say that somebody who suffers "the worst evils and misfortunes" is happy, unless he is trying to defend "a philosopher's paradox" (1096a2-3). Events outside our control really can damage our very essence.

It is unrealistic, Aristotle proclaims, to believe that we can live a good life in the midst of chaos and distress. The recognition of the detrimental effect of chaos and disorder on virtually all human enterprises is, I think, what underlies Aristotle's preference for social stability and his conservatism. Part of his point is rather simple. If we have to live in constant fear and struggle for necessities, we are not going to be able to live a good life. Fear is disruptive; terror is even more so.

But Aristotle also argues that external circumstances can damage the soul. He agrees with Plato that the good man will be less vulnerable to external mishaps and disasters than the rest of us. His stable character will make him better able to deal with whatever bad things may come along: "[T]he happy person has the [stability] we are looking for and keeps the character he has throughout his life" (1100b17-18); "a truly good and prudent person, we suppose, will bear strokes of fortune suitably . . ." (1101a1-2). Consequently, by becoming as good as possible, by acquiring a good and stable disposition, we lessen the destructive force that bad luck will have upon our lives. However, we can never eliminate it, and we cannot even make it insignificant.

The good life for human beings is different from that of gods because of its vulnerability. The gods do not need to engage in just or temperate actions but can spend eternity suspended in thought. They do not need money, friends, or lovers (1178b9-20). In contrast, the good human life requires sufficient financial resources, and it is usually (but not always) aided by physical health and good looks (1178b33-36, 1099a30-1099b5). It requires friendships and family as well as the opportunity to engage in virtuous activity. All human goods, then— external goods, goods of the body, and goods of the soul—are in varying degrees vulnerable to circumstances outside our control.

This bears repeating. The soul itself is and remains vulnerable to what happens outside it. Not even virtue can deliver us from pain and unhappiness because imprisonment or lack of resources can prevent us from engaging in virtuous activity (1099a1-3). Furthermore, external circumstances and misfortunes eat away our very virtue. The happy person will not be easily shaken from virtuous activity, but many serious misfortunes will do it (1100b30-35). Recovery from them, Aristotle says, will take "no short time" and will require "great and fine successes" (1101a7-12). In less optimistic terms, recovery is long and arduous and it is possible only if circumstances cooperate. But, of course, they might not cooperate. If circumstances are bad enough for long enough, our very virtue, the core of our being, will be seriously damaged as well.

A happy person is not in pain, and he is not suffering. However, this does not mean that pain always should be avoided; Aristotle is not a hedonist. It also does not mean that the best way of becoming happy is by doing whatever I can to avoid pain and suffering. Indeed, making pain-avoidance into my main goal is probably the quickest way to profound unhappiness because happiness consists in virtuous activity, and virtuous activity is painful in the beginning and perhaps even for a long time.[1] Aristotle holds out hope that if we keep doing the fine, we will habituate our desires so that the formerly painful action will stop being painful and even become pleasant. Some virtuous activity, like courageous activity, will never become pleasurable but will at best no longer be painful.

Finally, Aristotle argues, we are more closely related to and connected with other people than Socrates recognizes. Most importantly, perhaps, our happiness is tied up with the lives of other people because we are interdependent with, at the very least, our family and our friends, but also with our fellow citizens. As he says in the famous line from Book 10, nobody would choose to live without friends, even if he had all the other goods: "It would seem absurd, however, to award the happy person all the goods, without giving him friends; for having friends seems to be the greatest external good. . . . No one would choose to have all [other] goods and yet be alone, since a human being is a political [animal], tending by nature to live together with others" (1169b9-20). And this means that we are dependent not only upon our own fragile beings but also upon other equally fragile beings. What happens to them affects us and if it is bad, it hurts us. When they suffer, I suffer with them. When they are in danger, I fear for their safety. (Witness Aristotle's discussion of whether the dead person's happiness is affected by what happens to his friends and family after he dies, 1100a10-30.)

At this point, one might respond by agreeing that people generally feel in this way, but that the goal is to get beyond this merely human viewpoint. In other words, Aristotle believes that his happiness is tied up with the well-being of his body and of other people and that his very core can be affected by what happens to them, but this belief is a sign of his spiritual immaturity. Thus, we return to a metaphysical disagreement: What kind of thing is the soul really? Can it be independent of the body? Should we view the life here as a mere preparation for immortality? Is philosophy properly described as preparation for death? And if the soul exists after death, is it a better existence?

For Aristotle, the answer to those questions seems to be 'no.' Our bodies are not mere vessels which carry the soul for a short time. Rather, they are an essential (albeit inferior) part of us. Soul and body are not separate substances, as Descartes would have it, but two sides of the same coin: form and its matter, matter and its form.[2] In *De Anima* 2.1 Aristotle writes: "Those have the right conception who believe that the soul does not exist without a body but is not itself a kind of body" (DA 414a19-21).[3] If the body is suffering, so is the human being. If the body is killed, the human being and the soul die with it: "[Death] is a boundary [*peras*], and when someone is dead nothing beyond it seems either good or bad for him anymore" (NE 1115a27-28).

Now, I need to acknowledge that there are passages in *De Anima* which on some interpretations contradict the thesis I am attributing to Aristotle. In the chapter immediately preceding the one quoted above, Aristotle writes: "[T]hat, therefore, the soul or certain parts of it, if it is divisible, cannot be separated from the body is quite clear . . ." (413a3). So far, this is what one would expect. However, he goes on to say that nothing prevents "at any rate *some* parts from being separable" and that "it is not clear whether the soul is the actuality of the body in the way that the sailor is of the ship" (413a4-11). Here, then, he introduces the possibility of the soul surviving the death of the body. This passage seems to foreshadow 3.5 where Aristotle draws a notorious distinction between the active and the passive intellect, and where he seems to suggest that the active intellect will survive the death of the body: "When isolated it is its true self and nothing more, and this alone is immortal and everlasting" (430a25).

The interpretation of 3.5 has been much discussed. Alexander of Aphrodisias suggested that Aristotle is here referring to the divine mind, while St. Thomas Aquinas argued that he is introducing personal immortality rather similar to the Platonic (and Christian) variety.[4] Others disagree with both positions. Hamlyn for example argues that "Aristotle provides no ground here for any kind of belief in personal immortality" (Hamlyn 1993 rpt. 141, n. 430a18).[5]

Since the scope of this paper does not allow a discussion of this issue, I will just state briefly that I agree with Hamlyn. In addition, it seems to me, even if we were to accept that Aristotle argues for personal immortality in *De Anima* 3.5 and that he raises the possibility that the soul might exist separately earlier in the book, these passages do not have sufficient weight to overthrow Aristotle's often repeated view that the soul is the form of the body which, given his hylomorphism, means that it cannot be separable from it. I reiterate, then: It is Aristotle's considered view that when the body dies, the human soul dies with it. Death does not come as a savior; death is a terrifying thing and a boundary which marks the end of our existence (1115a10-27).

If this is the human condition, we have plenty of reasons to be frightened. The good is not securely in our hands but it is affected and bruised by external circumstances. Gods are never frightened and certainly never terrified because they have no reason to be. But they escape fear because they are immortal and because they do not care for anything mortal. Humans can escape fear only by giving up such care. But in Aristotle's view, that means giving up care for human beings, both oneself and others, refusing to care for what is in fact good (or at least what can become good). It means pretending that we are other than what we are, that we are souls that live in a body for a while and then move on to a better existence, unencumbered by the body. It means being fundamentally deceived about human nature.

Human beings are often frightened and sometimes terrified, and they should be. Fear and terror are appropriate reactions in the face of our reality; they express an understanding of the human condition. If we did not experience them, we would be displaying our lack of understanding.[6] We cannot become invulnerable to them unless we learn to ignore what is by nature frightening or terrifying. Unless we opt to live a lie, then, we have to live with fear, terror, and uncertainty.

So how do we live with fear and terror in the best possible manner? Aristotle responds that courage is required. However, even if we are very courageous, fear will remain and sometimes it will overpower even the most courageous among us: "Some things are too frightening for a human being to resist" (1115b8). There are conditions that "overstrain human nature and that no one would endure" (1110a25-26). Thus, the brave person is not fearless, but he is "unperturbed, as far as a human being can be" and he will stand firm against the sort of thing that is not irresistible (1115b12-14).

Aristotle discusses courage in Book 3 of the *Nicomachean Ethics* (and Book 3 of the *Eudemian Ethics*). Like other virtues of character, courage deals with feelings (*pathê*). To have courage is to have appropriate feelings with respect to fear and confidence (1115a7), that is, to feel fear in the face of what is in fact frightening, and then to act appropriately. And, finally, courage must not be just a disposition; it must be realized in courageous action.

Aristotle focuses upon the primary case of courage where courage is most fully and nobly expressed. This is a familiar Aristotelian procedure. His view seems to be that if we want to understand a kind of thing, we should look at the perfect exemplar, at the flourishing individual or the healthiest tree. In the case of courage, he will focus upon the cases in which courage is most required and where it is most useful. Courage concerns standing firm against frightening conditions and this means especially death since death is the most frightening thing for mortal beings (1115a27).[7] But Aristotle narrows the focus still further. The primary case of courage is facing death in battle and the corresponding cowardice throwing down one's shield and running. The brave person is not primarily concerned with death in sickness or on the sea (1115a28). I take it that Aristotle's point is that if we want to understand courage, it is better to study how brave people act in battle than how they act in sickness or at sea because courage is somehow better expressed in battle than in the other two situations. Why is that? There seem to be two basic reasons. Aristotle writes: "We act like brave men on occasions when we can use our strength, or when it is fine to be killed; and neither of these is true when we perish on the sea" (1115b5)

First, Aristotle believes that courage, at least in the purest sense, requires that there is something we can *do*. Our courageous disposition must not remain merely potential but it must be actualized through activity in which we face our fears and act in spite of them. When we are facing an army, we can fight. In sickness or on the sea, however, there is nothing we can do. Aristotle does not deny that the courageous and the cowardly person would face these forms of death in very different ways; he writes: "[C]ertainly the brave person is also intrepid [*adeês*] on the sea and in sickness . . . " (1115b1). But it would not be a perfect case of courage because he can't act.[8] Aristotle's remarks reflects his view that, at its best, virtue is not just an attitude or disposition but it is exhibited in action. Here too, we can see how dependent our goodness is on circumstances. We can end up in situations in which through no fault of our own we can do little or nothing. In such a situation, we might still have a courageous character, but we will not be able to actualize that character; we will not be able to express our courage in action. And, as already noted, Aristotle suggests that if such a situation endures for long enough, it might destroy our character.

Second, courage in the primary sense is possible only in a situation when there is something noble to be done, when we are facing a fine [*kalon*] rather than a meaningless death: "[S]omeone is called fully brave if he is intrepid in facing a fine death and the immediate dangers that bring death" (1115a34-35). "The brave person aims at the fine" (1115b23). If I am not aiming at the fine, I am not courageous, even if I do exactly what the courageous person does; my motivation is deficient. This point is illustrated in Aristotle's discussion of the five states that resemble courage. In order for the character to be truly virtuous, he argues, it is not enough to do the fine thing; one must be doing it for the sake of the fine. Thus, the so-called courage of the citizen, for instance, is not really courage because they do not stand firm against dangers for the sake of the fine but "with the aim of avoiding reproaches and legal penalties and of winning honors" (1116a20). Others do the courageous thing but they do it due to compulsion, experience which shows them that there is nothing to fear, or anger. In contrast, "the brave people act because of the fine" (1116b32). If my motivation is faulty, then, my action is not truly courageous.

The importance of acting for the sake of the fine enables Aristotle to draw a distinction between battle on one hand and sickness and sea travel on the other. Risking one's life in a battle for the sake of the fine is Aristotle's most important example of meaningful action in the face of grave danger. Dying at sea or in sickness, on the other hand, is without purpose. One is not sick and dying for the sake of the fine, one is sick for no good reason. This means that dying in battle is not the important thing. If the battle is not for a worthwhile cause, then the death would be without purpose, just like the death at sea. And if we could act when facing a death at sea or in sickness, imbuing the death with meaning (as I am convinced that it can), then it could count as courageous.

On the Aristotelian picture, we will have to face fear and terror in two basic types of situations: First, when the threat cannot be avoided or stopped but only ignored (human mortality first and foremost) and when it perhaps can be (human action). In practice, of course, the two are often combined. In battle, we are facing our own mortality, but the agent of our death is a human being.

The two seem to call for different responses. For the first, we have to live with the recognition that we are mortal fragile beings and, if we are Aristotelians, that our souls will not survive the death of these fragile bodies. We must also recognize that our happiness is interwoven with that of other equally fragile beings. That is, we have to accept that we are mortal beings outside the garden of Eden. In some cases, brave people will go beyond fear here. In describing brave people in danger at sea, Aristotle uses *adeês*, which means 'without fear.' They are without fear, it seems, because they have given up hope of being saved, and they have accepted that there is nothing they can do to save themselves. In the *Rhetoric*, Aristotle describes those "who are being beaten to death" in this way (1383a12). In certain situations, action is not called for; indeed, action is futile. Consequently, courage cannot express itself through in the best way, i.e., through courageous action. When we face danger that we can do nothing about, the quiet dignity of calm and fearless resignation is the best reaction open to us.

Still, to think that we can or should transcend fear in general is both unrealistic and foolish. After embracing the Socratic fearless resignation just described, Aristotle immediately pulls back. Having just said that the brave man would be *adeês* as he perishes at sea, Aristotle reminds the reader that some things "are frightening for everyone, at least for everyone with any sense" (1115b7). Resignation and fearlessness when we face such things is possible only if we lack the sense to understand how frightening they are.

Appropriate reactions to the second type of situation—threats created by humans—are very different because there should be something we can do. Quietism is not the best option available. Rather, the courageous response seems to inch close to Aristotle's focal meaning of courage; namely we act in a meaningful cause. The constant background fear that most of us have felt since September 11 seems to fall in the second category: that which, at least in principle, can be removed by eliminating the reason to fear. So what is the appropriate answer to it?

Here, it seems to me, it is crucial that we go beyond Aristotle. First, we need to make clear that courage often is called for even when we do not face men with swords. But that point is not so relevant here for the obvious reason that we are facing men armed with the contemporary equivalent of swords. Second, throwing down our shield and running does indeed appear to be a sign of cowardice, but refusing to pick up the shield and sword in the first place might not be. Gandhi was no coward and I am inclined to think that he was right to argue that refusing to fight often requires more courage than does fighting. Aristotle's focus upon battle obscures this point. We should agree with Aristotle, I think, in stressing that courage is ideally displayed in action. However, it seems mistaken and even dangerous to assume that the best action must be to display courage in battle, that a courageous solution to a problem is necessarily a violent or forceful solution, that the actualization of courage requires conflict.[9] If we follow Aristotle in this direction, our very definition of courage gives priority to confrontation over dialogue. The opposite seems to be desirable.

Removing the threat in this neo-Aristotelian way calls for courage combined with practical reason (*phronêsis*), another favorite notion among Aristotelians. Aristotle stresses that correct action requires practical reason, the ability to figure out what would be the right thing to do under the circumstances. In the case of threats, then, practical reason is thought about how we might be able to remove or lessen the threat in the best way, what actions ought to be taken and which ones avoided, and so on. It is practical reason that might caution us, saying that picking up weapons may not be the best solution available. It is sometimes tempting to think that what counts is that we are trying to do the right thing. It might be what counts when our moral value is calculated (although I personally doubt that). However, well-intended action uninformed by practical reason and knowledge about the other side may cause more harm than good. I remember school cafeteria staff in my home town assuring the first Muslim kids in town that there was no pork in the spaghetti sauce, even though there was. Their intentions were good; they were just trying to make sure that the kids had a well-rounded meal instead of just spaghetti. However, their practical reason and knowledge of the alien kids' culture was, to put it mildly, deficient.

This example indicates that practical reason does not operate in a vacuum. It must be strongly contextualized. That is, it must include knowledge and understanding of the relevant people and their cultures and religions. And here, the study of religion and of the religions of others in particular becomes crucial. Part of our fear and dislike of the other side seems to stem from ignorance and misconceptions about the others. But it also seems to be part of human nature to fear what is strange and different. We fear death in part because it is, as Aristotle says, a boundary, beyond which lies we know not what. We fear strangers because we do not understand their beliefs, their motivations, and their anger, and because we do not know what they might do. Through knowledge, strangers may become familiar (even though they may remain different). Their motives and the sources of their anger will become clearer to us and might even seem to be rational responses to a difficult situation. Hopefully, they will become less frightening.

But they might not. Understanding others is not the only task before us because they can kill and maim even if we understand them. Aristotle's emphasis on action is useful, I think, because it emphasizes that mere study is not enough; action is required. Strangers are frightening because they are strangers and because we do not understand them, but they are also frightening because they are angry. Consequently, understanding who they are, what they believe, and why they are angry is an important beginning, but it is not enough. As long as they are still angry, they will be dangerous. This means that we must try to remove their anger. Encouraging them to understand us as we should strive to understand them should help. (The problem, of course, will be getting them to listen.) Still, even that may not be enough because chances are that they have good reasons to be angry and will be angry until we act to correct wrongs and injustices committed. Thus, comparative philosophy must understand both its important role and its significant limitations. Comparative studies are necessary but they are not, by themselves, enough. If we are going to remove the terror springing from terrorism in our lives, comparative philosophy needs to be supplemented by action that promotes social justice.

Notes

1. "[P]leasure causes us to do base actions, and pain causes us to abstain from fine ones. That is why we need to have had the appropriate upbringing—right from early youth, as Plato says—to make us find enjoyment or pain in the right things; for this is the correct education" (NE 1104b10-14). In other words, if we seek pleasure and avoid pain, we will become base. We must force ourselves to do fine things even though it is painful. If we do, we will come to enjoy acting finely, learning to "find enjoyment . . . in the right things."

2. "We speak of one particular kind of existent things as substance, and under this heading we so speak of one thing *qua* matter, which in itself is not a particular, another *qua* shape and form, in virtue of which it is then spoken of as a particular, and a third *qua* the product of these two. And matter is potentiality while form is actuality . . ." (DA 412a6-10). He concludes a few lines later: "The soul must, then, be substance *qua* form of a natural body which has life potentially. Substance is actuality. The soul therefore will be the actuality of a body of this kind" (DA 412a18-21) or in other words, "the soul is the first actuality of a natural body which has life potentially" (DA 412a27).

3. See also DA 412b6-8, 412a16-20, Met. 1045b16-21.

4. For an overview of the most important interpretations, see Hicks (1907 lxiv-lxix)

5. Hamlyn writes: "The part of the soul which is said to be eternal is a rather abstract entity which has only a metaphysical role to play as a necessary condition of the functioning of the soul" (Hamlyn 1993 rpt. 142, n. 430a18). He also points out that the text appears corrupt. Jonathan Barnes also rejects the idea that Aristotle is arguing for personal immortality in the passage in question (Barnes, 1979 rpt., 40).

6. In the *Eudemian Ethics*, Aristotle writes: "The brave man is concerned with fears. . . . The coward . . . [is] more afraid than is proper [*dei*] and less daring than is proper and the daring [rash] man . . . [is] less afraid than is proper" (EE 1228a32-35). "Whereas the cowardly and the daring man are mistaken owing to their characters, since the coward thinks things not formidable formidable and things slightly formidable extremely formidable and the daring man on the contrary thinks formidable things perfectly safe and extremely formidable things only slightly formidable, to the brave man on the other hand see exactly what they are" (EE 1229b22-26).

7. When I read this paper at 2003 SACP conference, Barbara Darling Smith suggested that death is not the most terrifying thing, arguing that facing a debilitating disease like Huntington's disease seems worse. I think this is probably right.

8. It does not affect Aristotle's main point, but it is clear that his view of illness (and of sailing!) is problematic. He seems to think of the ill person as necessarily passive, unable to act. Assuming that we are talking about somebody who is still conscious and mentally aware, we have no reason to follow him here. Surely, different courses of action are open to the sick person. She can pursue different kinds of treatments, she can speak with dignity or without, and so on.

9. Aristotle is, after all, arguing in the *Rhetoric* that "to take vengeance on one's

enemies is nobler than to come to terms with them; for to retaliate is just, and that which is just is noble; and further, a courageous man ought not to allow himself to be beaten" (1367a). On the other hand, later on in the *Rhetoric* Aristotle strikes the opposite note: "It is equitable to pardon human weaknesses and to look, not to the law but to the legislator; not to the letter of the law but to the intention of the legislator; not to the action itself, but to the moral purpose; not to the part, but to the whole; not to what a man is now, but to what he has been, always or generally; to remember good rather than ill treatment, and benefits received rather than those conferred; to bear injury with patience; to be willing to appeal to the judgment of reason rather than to violence; to prefer arbitration to the law court . . ." (1374b).

Works Cited

Aristotle. 1983. *De Anima.* Books II and III with Passages from Book I. Trans. D. W. Hamlyn. Oxford: Clarendon Press.

———. 1995 rpt. *On The Soul.* Trans. W. S. Hett. Loeb edition. Cambridge: Har vard UP.

—. 1984. *Ethica Nicomachea.* Ed. I. Bywater. Oxford, Oxford UP, 1894. 1970 rpt.

———. 1996 rpt. *Eudemian Ethics.* Trans. H. Rackham. Cambridge: Harvard UP.

———. 1999. *Nicomachean Ethics.* Trans. Terence Irwin. 2nd edition. Cambridge: Hackett.

———. 1926. *Rhetoric.* Trans. J. H. Freese. Loeb edition. Cambridge: Harvard UP.

Barnes, Jonathan. 1971-72. "Aristotle's Concept of Mind." *Proceedings of the Aristotelian Society* (72): 101-14. Rpt. in *Articles on Aristotle: Psychology and Aesthetics.* London: Duckworth 1979. 32-41.

Hamlyn, D.W. 1993, first published 1968. Introduction and notes. *Aristotle De Anima Books II and III.* Oxford: Clarendon Press.

Hicks, R. D. 1907. *Aristotle: De Anima.* Cambridge.

Nussbaum, Martha. 1986. *The Fragility of Goodness: Luck and Ethics in Greek Tragedy and Philosophy.* Cambridge: Cambridge UP.

Plato. 1981. *Apology.* In *Five Dialogues: Euthyphro, Apology, Crito, Meno Phaedo.* Trans. G.M.A. Grube. Cambridge/Indianapolis: Hackett.

———. 1991. *Gorgias.* Transl. W. R. M. Lamb. In The Loeb Classical Library, *Plato III.* Ed. G. P. Goold. Cambridge: Harvard UP, 247-533.

———. 1991. *Republic.* Trans. Allan Bloom. 2nd ed. United States: HarperCollins.

4

Pragmatic Lessons in Times of Terror

Sor-hoon Tan

John Dewey's Pragmatism is concerned not with the abstract problems of philosophers but with the problems men and women face in the world they live in, with all its complexities, messiness, and uncertainties. Unlike other philosophers, Pragmatists could not hide in ivory towers during crises; their philosophical commitments require them to reflect and propose Pragmatic solutions to the problems facing their communities during difficult times. What might we learn from Pragmatists during these times of terror?

In this chapter, I compare the views on use of force, violence, and war of John Dewey and his student and follower—prominent Chinese intellectual Hu Shih and American radical Randolf Bourne. Hu Shih is credited with attempting to practice his teacher's Pragmatism in China during the 1920s and 1930s; according to some commentators, the insistence on educational reforms and resistance to revolution doomed the "Dewey experiment" in China (Keenan 1977; cf. Tan 2004). This seems to indicate that Pragmatists hold too idealistic a position on the use of force in politics. Yet Dewey himself, in contrast to Hu Shih's pacifist stance on what should be China's response to Japan's aggression during World War I, had supported America's entry into that war in Europe. For this, he was attacked by his one-time follower, Randolf Bourne, who became disillusioned with Dewey's instrumentalist form of Pragmatism. For Bourne, Pragmatism was insufficiently resistant to the evils of war; it was a philosophy suited only to times of peace. Is there a consistent Pragmatist position on the use of force, violence, and war?

Pragmatists on Force, Violence, and War

Pragmatists are neither absolutely for nor absolutely against war or any use of force, as we can see from the writings of John Dewey and Hu Shih. Both of them lived through the two World Wars and held different and complex views about war that changed over time.

By his own admission, Hu Shih, who was studying in the United States during World War I, was "a zealous pacifist" for a time. His pacifism, based on a cosmopolitan and humanist outlook, was modified from a purely moral view with both eastern and western roots to incorporate a belief, due to Norman Angell's and Dewey's earlier influence (Dewey was initially against American involvement in the war), that war had become economically unprofitable.[1] He argued for "patriotic sanity" against those who favored an immediate declaration of war on Japan in response to the infamous "twenty-one demands" Japan presented to the Chinese government in 1915 (Hu 1915). In 1916, he argued that "The real problem is to seek a more economical and therefore more efficient way of employing force: a substitute for the present crude form and wasteful use of force." As he saw it, World War I, "which is the greatest display of force ever undertaken by mankind, has only resulted in a deadlock"; force had not prevailed because it had been wasted (Hu 2000, 668). However, when peaceful settlement of the Sino-Japanese conflict failed twenty-one years later, Hu Shih actively supported the Nationalist military action to preserve the Chinese state (Grieder 1970, 293). This is not unprincipled opportunism; rather, it manifests flexible decision making based on case by case understanding of each specific situation.

Hu Shih's opposition to student activism and political actions that often ended in violence between the World Wars is related to his pacifism. Deweyan democracy requires us "to take as far as possible every conflict which arises— and they are bound to arise—out of the atmosphere and medium of force, of violence as a means of settlement into that of discussion and intelligence" (L14, 228).[2] It is common belief that democracies do not go to war with one another. Domestically, democratic processes provide mechanisms for changing those in power, and resolving conflicts without revolution or other forms of violence. Although the democratic state, like other states, has to resort to use of force on occasions, any use of force must always be troubling even when judged necessary. Violence is prima facie evidence that a polity is not yet perfectly democratic, since people should be able to resolve their disagreements through debates, deliberation, and compromise in an ideal democracy. It is not surprising that discussing the path China should take in the decade following World War I, Hu Shih was adamantly against any "revolution wrought by violent despotism . . . that use violence to overthrow violence" (Hu 1996, 4:314).

Dewey, writing about the need for liberalism to advocate radical change in order to remain relevant in the 1930s, basically affirmed Hu's earlier rejection of violence: "radicalism also means, in the minds of many, both supporters and opponents, dependence upon the use of violence as the main method of effecting drastic changes. Here the liberal parts company. For he is committed to the organization of intelligent action as the chief method" (L11.45).

In rejecting violence, Hu was a true Deweyan liberal. But one should not equate all wars or use of force (*wuli* 武力) with violence (*baoli* 暴力), though Hu (1996, 4.311-12) did not seem to notice the difference. In Dewey's thinking, force is not always bad: it can be energy, coercion or constraint, or violence (M10.212). In 1916, Dewey commented, "Unless war can be shown to be the most economical method of securing the results which are desirable with a minimum of the undesirable results, it marks waste and loss: it must be adjudged a violence, not a use of force" (M10.214-15).

Dewey believed in 1917 that American intervention in the war was an economic use of force to secure democracy at home and abroad in the prevailing situation. The war did not make the world safer for democracy, the justice of the peace was suspect, and some would argue that the seeds for World War II were sowed at Versailles. Dewey came to play a key role in a movement to outlaw war after World War I. He believed that legalizing war was a fundamental obstacle to creating an international code that would facilitate peaceful resolution of conflicts between nations (M15.123). On the domestic front, the infringements of liberties and various other undemocratic aspects of war (which we are seeing once again in the Patriot Act and homeland security measures) also cast doubt on the viability of war as a means to democracy. The failure to achieve the democratic goals of the United States entry into World War I might not have been incidental, and might have everything to do with the means employed. In Dewey's words, "If there is one conclusion to which human experience unmistakably points, it is that democratic ends demand democratic methods for their realization" (L14.367).

The outbreak of World War II would seem to show that the lessons of World War I had not been learnt. Until Pearl Harbor, Dewey struggled to find a way to oppose totalitarianism without advocating war with the fascist powers; but he did not counsel turning the other cheek, nor did he subscribe to any absolute pacifism. He even aided the Allied war effort in the Far East by writing a "Message to the Chinese People," which was translated into a propaganda leaflet distributed over Chinese cities by the US Army Airforce in 1942. It is significant that he began the message by reiterating the common "peace-loving" character of both China and the US, and spoke of their "common end in this war [they] have been forced to enter in order to preserve [their] independence and freedom. [They] both want to see a world in which nations can devote themselves to the constructive tasks of industry, education, science, and art without fear of molestation by nations that think they can build themselves up by destroying the lives and work of the men, women, and children of other peoples" (Dewey 1973, appendix A, 305). Even though he supported the fight against totalitarianism and imperialism when war became inevitable, Dewey no longer believed that war can be a means for democratic ends (L11.252, 298), and constantly reminded others to aim for a world "in which the war system has no standing" (L15.302).

To some, Dewey's support for the United States' entry into World War I showed how fatally flawed Pragmatism is. While Hu Shih was attacked for insisting on education as the means to democracy when more forceful political action was required, Randolf Bourne (1977, 339) attacked Dewey for supporting the use of force. He argued that "It was education, and almost education alone, that seemed susceptible to the pressure of an 'instrumental' philosophy" (1977, 338). Bourne's complaint was not about Pragmatic method being limited to recommendation of gradualist transformation of society so that it paralyzes needed action during times of international crises, but rather it could not stand up against pressures to use war as a weapon in international disputes. To Bourne, Dewey's philosophy was suited only for peace, where institutions were malleable and there was strong desire for progress; faced with war, "instrumentalism" could do nothing more than describe and justify what was happening. Bourne denounced Dewey's disciples who were "making themselves efficient instruments of the war technique, accepting with little question the ends as announced from above" (1977, 343). To this once ardent, then disillusioned disciple, Dewey's Pragmatism lacked vision and led to a subordination of ends to means.

In fact, subordination of ends to means implies a dualism that would contradict Dewey's philosophy, in which interdependent and relative means and ends must be developed together, each to be modified in view of the actualization of the other. Our actions aim at some ends. To act successfully requires discrimination of means and ends and adjusting them to fit together, so that a series of acts culminate in the fulfillment of a goal (M4.28). Distinction between means and ends is relative rather than absolute. What we aim for at this moment may be a means to a further end. An end to be realized in the future (an end-in-view) operates as a means in determining which actions to take in the more immediate future. We start by selecting the means that would take us towards some desired end. These means often involve not just one simple act, but a series of acts. Along the way, we may find ourselves veering off course. In such circumstances, we usually need to re-examine the means we have selected to detect where we might have gone wrong, and what changes need to be made to earlier plans to get back on track to reach the still desired end. However, the consequences of employing certain means may also reveal information that could affect our views about the end and its desirability; then it may be the end that requires re-adjustment.

Bourne acknowledged that "Dewey calls for a more attentive formulation of war purposes and ideas, but he calls largely to deaf ears" (Bourne 1977, 343). So Dewey himself is not guilty of ignoring the ends of war or allowing them to be determined by others. However, he might be guilty of being too short-sighted and narrow in his view of what is involved in using war as a means. Bourne makes a stronger point: the subordination of ends to means is not merely a subjective error, but is objectively unavoidable when war is the means. "War determines its own ends—victory, and government crushes out automatically all forces that deflect, or threaten to deflect, energy from the path of organization to that end. All governments will act in this way, the most democratic and the most autocratic" (1977, 324).

According to Bourne, war is "inexorable . . . as near an absolute, coercive social situation as it is possible to fall into" (1977, 322). In Bourne's depiction, war comes close to an absolute evil. His absolute certainty that war can never be the means to democracy is incompatible with a Pragmatism committed to fallibilism. There is some justice in charging him with a tendency to "exalt commitment without intelligence" (Tiles 1992, 4). But Robert Westbrook (1991, 202-11) also has a point in praising Bourne for providing the kind of Pragmatic analysis of the concrete situation, inquiry into means and ends, purposes and consequences, required to decide the matter that Westbrook considered missing in Dewey's own writings of that period. Whether or not he considered his support of World War I a mistake, what is more important is that, true to his Pragmatism, Dewey learned from that experience. Among the lessons are "the impotency and harmfulness of any and every ideal that is proclaimed wholesale and in the abstract . . . [and] the tragic need for the more realistic study of forces and consequences, a study conducted in a more scientifically accurate and complete manner than that of the professed *Real-politik*" (M12.154).

Deweyan Inquiry and the Path to War

True to its fallibilism and insistence on solving each specific problem by attending to its particular context, Pragmatism does not have a fixed absolute position on the legitimacy of nation states using force beyond their borders. The criterion for any use of force must be whether it will solve the problem without causing worse problems. This criterion must be applied in a broad context, where the nature of the problem and the likely consequences of actions proposed are analyzed as thoroughly as possible, its ramifications surveyed as comprehensively as possible. To a Pragmatist committed to democracy, war must always be a last resort, and only acquiesced to after a rigorous social inquiry. A democratic public has a responsibility to strive for clear understanding of the goal, of the nature and ramifications of the means, of the likely consequences of proposed actions, and how to deal with them.

A Deweyan social inquiry is certainly not the immediate reaction to the terrorist attack on the World Trade Center in New York. Nor would a Pragmatist expect it to be. Initial reactions are understandably more emotional than anything else, "an outpouring of impulse as a perturbation from clash or failure of habit" (M14.54). People were literally paralyzed with fear and shock at the sight of the two skyscrapers collapsing before their eyes; grief and anger followed at this wanton destruction and slaughter. Not all habits failed. Individuals and organizations, official and voluntary, mobilized quickly, effectively drawing on past habits of dealing with crises in rescue efforts, reestablishing some kind of order, carrying out investigations in order to bring the perpetrators to justice and protect citizens from further attacks.

Is the War on Terror a reaction out of impulse, habit, or intelligence, or a combination of all three? Dewey often warned us against the emotionalism that pervades times of crises. Discussing World War II, he remarked "Intense emotion is an all-or-none affair. It sees things in terms of only blackest black and purest shiny white" (L15.61). Nor will habits, unless they are intelligent, be enough to solve the problems. How intelligent the War on Terror is from a Pragmatist viewpoint depends to a large extent on the consequences. Will it make the world a safer place? A year after United States troops entered Iraq in March 2003, many were doubtful that the war had made the world a safer place. Many asserted that it had made the United States *less* safe. Were the costs of war, to the American people, to Iraq, to the rest of the world, as accurately estimated as they could have been? Has the war turned out to be too costly even if one believed its goals were desirable?

Moreover, effectiveness and minimum negative side effects alone will not assure us that our action is intelligent. *Why* it succeeds is as important, since one could solve or escape a problem by lucky chance, rather than because of a successful exercise of intelligence in a Pragmatist inquiry. There is little reason to see the war with Iraq as an intelligent response on those grounds. There was overwhelming support for the Allied army going into Afghanistan given reliable intelligence that Osama Bin Laden was hiding there and the Taliban regime had been actively aiding the Al Qaeda. Unfortunately, the Allied troops failed to apprehend Osama. There was much less enthusiasm for war with Iraq; the United States proceeded despite worldwide popular protests and the objections of key member states of the United Nations. Although a majority of Americans polled in 2002 may have supported going to war, many, especially the overwhelming majority outside the United States, saw the case for war with Iraq as being built on rather flimsy and unconvincing evidence.[3] Some suspected the Bush administration might be using terrorism as an excuse to get rid of a long-time enemy. There is also the question of who stood to gain financially should the Saddam regime be toppled and to what extent the war might be motivated by the selfish interests of the rich and powerful.[4]

What is troubling to a Pragmatist about the days leading up to the war with Iraq is the nature of public discussions about September 11 and appropriate responses. Was there enough discussion? Were the discussions sufficiently free and open, with sufficient access to relevant information and exploration of possibilities both in terms of actions and consequences? Were participants holding different views listening to their opponents, thinking and re-thinking through the problem(s) with the new facts and value issues revealed in dissenting views? Or was everybody interested only in hearing confirmation of his or her own view, dismissing all other views as absolutely wrong or motivated by sinister affinities? Granted that national security issues may require a certain amount of secrecy, but are those with access to classified information at least following these rules of effective inquiry? One year into the war, evidence began to emerge showing that the people had been misled, even deliberately lied to by those who swore to defend democracy.

Members of the American intelligence community accused the Bush administration of pressuring them to link Iraq with Al Qaeda and manipulating their work to exaggerate the Iraqi threat and drum up support for war (Judis and Ackerman 2003). This accusation was not substantiated by the Senate Intelligence Committee which has issued a report that instead aims most of its scathing criticisms against the Central Intelligence Agency (CIA). The Committee found that allegations about Iraq's possession of weapons of mass destruction were based on faulty analyses and a dynamics of "group think" among the CIA analysts who suffered from a "collective presumption" that Iraq had weapons of mass destruction. Critics continue to believe that the flawed intelligence was further exaggerated and misused to lead the United States into war. Whether or not that turns out to be the case, it seems likely that the White House under the Bush regime was, and probably still is, as afflicted with "group think" as the CIA.

Others besides Pragmatists would also be concerned about rational, open discussion and public debate about something as important as the nation going to war.[5] What distinguishes Deweyan inquiry is eschewing taking positions "on principle," by making absolute distinctions such as opposing two groups as "good" versus "evil." This kind of absolutism leads one easily into the kind of "group think" that resulted in the CIA's "failure of intelligence."

The rhetoric of the War on Terror was riddled with a moralism that obscures the ends that might be successfully pursued with such a war and other alternatives for dealing with terrorism. It distracts from a thorough consideration and comprehensive estimate of its costs and the need to plan for undesirable consequences that the war would undoubtedly have. Finding the genesis of the problem is central to diagnosing and solving a problem. The rhetoric of the War on Terror is based on an overly simplistic view of the problem: reducing it to the evil in some individuals and regimes that support them; this "evil" is then translated into hatred of Americans, of democracy, of the free world, of all that is good and pious. Suggestions that there might be social and political causes such as some United States' foreign policies, Middle East politics, and the way capitalist interests have operated in certain parts of the world have often been met with outrage as attempts to excuse the terrorists. Narrow-minded views of terrorism prevent better understanding of its complex causes and how to reduce support for it and bring it under control.

The spectacular nature of the September 11 attack tempts one to think of the incident as unique; but human atrocities are not new. There is a perception, at least outside America, that the United States did not pay enough attention to terrorism in the past, and then overreacted to September 11. Brushing aside the mass demonstrations against war in so many countries and riding roughshod over other United Nations member states (including some long time allies) did not boost the United States' credibility as a defender of democracy. The moralistic attitude of the Bush regime is also a grave cause of concern for many. It is not the first time in American history that a government went on a "moral crusade" and took the nation into war.

Historian Arthur Schlesinger, who "acknowledged the stimulus of Pragmatism" (Menand 1997, xxvi-xxvii), highlighted a similar moralism in his assessment of the Vietnam War, which he calls "a morality trip and moral absolutism the final stop."[6] In an article provocatively titled "The Necessary Amorality of Foreign Policy," he argued not that morality is totally irrelevant in dealings between nation states, but that "questions such as when a nation is justified in using force beyond its frontiers...cannot be answered by a priori moral principles but only by careful case by case assessment" (Schlesinger 1971, 75). Such assessment of foreign policy is best conducted via the weighing of national interest. "An intelligent regard for one's own national interest joined to unremitting respect for the interest of others seems more likely than the invocation of moral absolutes to bring about greater restraint, justice and peace among nations" (1971, 77).

According to Schlesinger, the initial intervention in Indochina by the United States was justified by its national interest, but turning its involvement into a moral crusade escalated the war beyond its national interest, beyond what is "compatible with the moral values of the national community" (1971, 76). "Enjoined by our leaders as to the sublimity of our mission, we cast ourselves as saviors of human freedom, misconceived the extremely restricted character of our stake in Indochina and, step by step, intensified senseless terror till we stand today as a nation disgraced before the world and before our own posterity" (1971, 77).

In the public discussions leading up to the war in Iraq, analyses of means of removing the global terrorist threat were short-sighted and mechanistic: kill the terrorists and their supporters, destroy their economic resources and military bases. Is the fear of being the next target in the War on Terror sufficient to stop others from joining Bin Laden's call for Jihad? Or will the war harden the resolve of those who already believe that the United States and its allies are imperialistic powers and enemies of Islam? Discussions of alternatives to war that appeared in the major United States media channels accessible to international audience were hampered by jingoism and lacking in imagination. Nor was there sufficient consideration of the consequences of war and how to ensure that it would not cause more long-term problems, such as more instability in the Middle East, increased perception that United States policies are anti-Islam and imperialistic, and a lesson that might makes right. Inadequate analyses went hand-in-hand with less than free and open discussion, compounded by a failure to communicate the reasonableness of the proposed "solution" to all who are likely to be affected, the inchoate world public.

The failure of social inquiry and communication is of course not only the fault of those proposing war. People must first be willing to listen and think for any effort to communicate in a way that could achieve cooperation to succeed. This willingness was all too often sorely lacking on all sides while the pro-war factions beat their war drums and demonstrators in the streets chanted slogans that range from anti-war to anti-Bush, anti-US, anti-imperialism, and anti-capitalism.

Conclusion

Pragmatists must look with dismay at the events of 2003-2004. Neither the American government nor American public appear to have conducted the required social inquiry in a Deweyan democracy. This is not the first time that a self-proclaimed democracy has failed to live up to its ideal; nor will it be the last.

Rather than bemoaning past mistakes, the Pragmatist will reiterate the need to scrutinize what is actually happening, thinking and questioning, trying as far as possible to establish and maintain intelligent control over future events through continued inquiry. Both the means and ends in our fight against terrorism need to be re-examined. Rather than beginning from absolute moral principles, or worse, driven by partisan political goals, the United States government and publics should put more resources in and pay more attention to in-depth impartial studies of terrorism and war. Whatever its gains, there is no doubt that war brings suffering even long after the guns are silent. War threatens our most cherished human values. In war time, even more than peace time, and especially during these times of terror, vigilance and courage are required more than ever to prevent the betrayal of democracy in the service of short-term political goals.

Notes

1. In an entry (12 July 1916) in his *Dairies* regarding winning an Essay Competition organized by the *American Association for International Conciliation*, Hu Shih mentions that the greatest influence on his award-winning essay ("Is There a Substitute for Force in International Relations?") are Dewey and Angell (Hu 2000, 667). Also Hu 1959, 61; Angell 1913, 28-49. All citations from Hu's Chinese works translated by author unless otherwise stated.

2. All citations in the text from Dewey's works give volume and page numbers from Jo Ann Boydston (ed.), *Middle Works* (M) and *Later Works* (L).

3. In August 2002, a Gallup poll showed support for war with Saddam down from previous levels, at a post- September 11 low—although the majority was still in favor, 53% in favor, 41% against (Judis and Ackerman 2003, 2). This support has since eroded as American casualties mounted and evidence emerged that the threat posed by Iraq had been exaggerated. By end of June 2004, CNN reported that a majority of Americans polled thought that the war was a mistake.

4. Some even fingered Bush and his business cronies for benefiting financially to the tune of billions by sending the least advantaged group of Americans to war (see Michael Moore's controversial documentary released in July 2004, *Fahrenheit 911*).

5. This is not surprising since Dewey offers his theory of inquiry as a model of general (good) thinking. It is to be expected that many who do not think of themselves as Pragmatists emphasize the same thing when it comes to solving collective problem. If Dewey is right, it is what intelligent people should do.

6. Schlesinger 1971, 77. Despite his acknowledged debt to Pragmatism, one must point out that not all Pragmatists would agree with Schlesinger's definition of "national interest" or condone his overall position on Vietnam.

Works Cited

Angell, Norman. *The Great Illusion: A Study of the relation of Military Power to National Advantage*. London: Heinemann, 1913.

Bourne, Randolf. *The Radical Will: selected writings, 1911-1918*. Olaf Hansen (ed.). Stanford: University of California Press, 1977.

Dewey, John. *Lectures in China, 1919-1920*. Robert W. Clopton and Tsuin-chen Ou (eds.). Honolulu: University Press of Hawai`i, 1973.

——. *The Middle Works, 1899-1924*, Jo Ann Boydston (ed.), 15 vols. Carbondale: Southern Illinois University Press, 1976-1983.

——. *The Later Works, 1925-1953*. Jo Ann Boydston (ed.), 17 vols. Carbondale: Southern Illinois University Press, 1981-1991.

Gering, Verna (ed.). *War After September 11*. Lanham, Md.: Rowman & Littlefield, 2003.

Grieder, Jerome. *Hu Shih and the Chinese Renaissance*. Cambridge: Harvard University Press, 1970.

Hu Shih. *Diaries During Studies Abroad, 1910 - 1917 (Liuxue riji)*. Changsha: Yuelu shushe, 2000.

——. *Collected Essays of Hu Shih (Hu Shi wencun)*. 4 vols. Hefei: Huangshan shushe, 1996.

——. *Hu Shih's Personal Reminiscences*. Interviewed, compiled, and edited by Tang Degang. Hu Shih (ed.). Columbia University: Oral History Project, 1959.

——. "A Plea for Patriotic Sanity: An Open Letter to All Chinese Students," *The Chinese Student's Monthly* 10.7 (April 1915): 425-26.

Judis, John B. and Spencer Ackerman. "Deception and Democracy—the Selling of the Iraq War. The First Casualty." *The New Republic Online* (30 June 2003).

Keenan, Barry. *The Dewey Experiment in China*. Cambridge: Harvard University Press, 1977.

Levine, Daniel. "Randolf Bourne, John Dewey and the Legacy of Liberalism," *Antioch Review* 29.2 (Summer 1969): 234-44.

Menand, Louis (ed.). *Pragmatism: a Reader*. New York: Random House, 1997.

Schlesinger, Arthur. "The Necessary Amorality of Foreign Policies," *Harper's Magazine* (Aug. 1971): 72-77.

Shusterman, Richard (ed.). *The Range of Pragmatism and the Limits of Philosophy*. Oxford: Blackwell, 2004.

Stuhr, John J.. "Old Ideals Crumble: War, Pragmatist Intellectuals and the Limits of Philosophy," *Metaphilosophy* 35, nos. 1/2 (Jan. 2004): 82-98. Also in Shusterman 2004, 80-95.

Tan, Sor-hoon. "China's Pragmatist Experiment in Democracy: Hu Shih's Pragmatism and John Dewey's Influence in China," *Metaphilosophy* 35, nos. 1/2 (Jan. 2004): 44-64. Also in Shusterman 2004, 43-62.

Tiles, James E. (ed.). *John Dewey: Critical Assessments.* Vol. 2. New York: Routledge,
        1992.
Westbrook, Robert. *John Dewey and American Democracy.* Ithaca: Cornell University
        Press, 1991.

5

Wisdom and Violence: The Legacy of Platonic Political Philosophy in al-Farabi and Nietzsche

Peter S. Groff

> "And now what's left is by no means the easiest to go through."
> "What is it?"
> "How a city can take philosophy in hand without being destroyed.
> For surely all great things carry with them the risk of a fall, and,
> really as the saying goes, fine things are hard."
> Plato, *Republic* 497d[1]

In this paper, I attempt to open up a dialogue between two philosophers who at first sight might seem to have very little in common: Abu Nasr al-Farabi and Friedrich Nietzsche. Al-Farabi, by most accounts born in Turkistan in the late ninth century, is one of the earliest, most influential, and most esteemed figures in the Islamic philosophical tradition.[2] Nietzsche, on the other hand—a nineteenth-century German by nationality, but a so-called "good European" by choice—seems to represent the apex of modern Western secularism, not least because of his thorough going critique of metaphysics and morality. It would appear that these two figures—one a medieval Islamicate thinker, the other a late modern self-described "godless antimetaphysician"—are separated by such a vast historical, cultural, and philosophical chasm that any fruitful conversation would be highly unlikely.[3] However, there is at least one respect in which they have something significant in common, namely, that al-Farabi and Nietzsche both owe a profound debt to classical Greek thought, specifically to Plato. In particular, although each in his own way ignores, or simply rejects, major aspects of Plato's metaphysics and epistemology, al-Farabi and Nietzsche both aim to recover the project of Platonic political philosophy.[4] The purpose of the following discussion is to examine the strikingly different contexts within which these thinkers reappropriate Plato's political thought, the different ways in which it is put to work, and finally, the troublesome commonalities between them.

Plato: The Philosopher as King

The aspect of Plato's political thought with which I am specifically concerned is the idea of the "philosopher-king," or the ideal coincidence of philosophy and political power. By this I mean Plato's belief in the capacity of philosophers, through their understanding of human nature and their comprehension of the Good, to determine the best possible regime for the human being.[5] Such knowledge, if it is indeed possible, would make the philosopher the true *politikos*, the so-called "statesman" or "political scientist" (literally, the person who has knowledge of the political). That is, such knowledge would confer upon him the right—or one might even argue, the obligation—to rule.

The *locus classicus* of this idea is the *Republic*.[6] The prospect of the philosopher-ruler first emerges in Book V, where Socrates is forced to make a series of increasingly radical and provocative claims in order to show that the regime he and his interlocutors have constructed in speech—the *kallipolis*, the fine and noble city—is indeed "possible" and "best." He characterizes these claims as "waves," which threaten to sweep him away. The final and biggest wave that Socrates faces, not without much hemming and hawing, is one which he fears will "drown [him] in laughter and ill-repute" (473c).

> "Unless the philosophers rule as kings or those now called kings and chiefs genuinely and adequately philosophize, and political power and philosophy coincide in the same place while the many natures now making their way to either apart from the other are by necessity excluded, there is no rest from ills for the cities, my dear Glaucon, nor I think for humankind, nor will the regime we have described in speech ever come forth from nature, insofar as possible, and see the light of the sun." (473c-e)

Socrates is right to be so reticent: As his interlocutors will point out, philosophers are typically perceived as "eccentric" or "completely vicious," and the few admittedly decent ones, those who manage to lead virtuous private lives, are generally "useless" to the city (487b-d). Socrates concedes the various possible corruptions of the philosophical type; he even admits that this type, because of its greatness, is particularly susceptible to corruption when not properly cultivated (491d-492a). However, he argues that philosophers are not intrinsically useless or bad: Rather they become that way because of the corrupt, unjust cities in which they live, and the ways in which power is divorced from knowledge (497b-c). In short, Socrates tries to show that "the tension between the city and the philosophers is neither natural nor necessary."[7]

In order to do this, he has to distinguish the imitations and corruptions of the philosopher from what he calls the "true" philosopher.[8] At the heart of these distinctions is the idea that philosophical natures are "always in love with that learning which discloses to them something of the being that *is* always and does not wander about, driven by generation and decay" (485a-b). In the ambitious education that Socrates proposes for the most excellent and philosophically oriented of the guardians, they acquire an increasingly adequate knowledge of the unchanging Forms or Ideas. This culminates in the Idea of the Good, the source of all knowledge, value and being, and the "divine pattern" (500e) upon which the virtuous and happy regime of the city is to be based. It is precisely this knowledge of the Good that makes the philosophers "useful and beneficial" (505a).[9] As Socrates observes in the allegory of the cave in Book VII, "the person who is going to act prudently in private or public must see it" (517c). But this means that the philosophers, who themselves have no inclination to rule, are as knowers of the Good the *most* qualified to rule, and thus must do so for the benefit of the city. Having given us the unhappy image of the escaped prisoner, who makes his way out of the cave, and eventually manages to gaze upon the sun (or Form of the Good) itself, before descending again to meet his death at the hands of the ignorant many, Socrates nevertheless insists that the philosophers not be permitted to remain enraptured in some theoretical contemplation of the Good, but rather be compelled to take up political matters in the city and bring to bear all they have learned (519c-d).

Assuming that the philosopher-rulers have acquired knowledge of the Good, and carry within their souls, as it were, a pattern for the best possible political regime, the question is then how to bring this into being. In other words, how do the philosophers enable the many to acquire virtue and happiness in spite of their ignorance? We are all familiar with the disturbing answer Socrates gives. As he repeatedly acknowledges, the rulers "will have to use a throng of lies and deceptions for the benefit of the ruled" (459c-d), the most fundamental of which is the "noble lie" (the myth of the metals) that underlies the very class system that makes possible the coincidence of philosophy and political power (414c-415c). He also notoriously advocates war,[10] censorship,[11] an ambitious (but apparently doomed) eugenics program,[12] and ultimately, the rustication of everyone over the age of ten (541a). Thus, the just city is necessarily founded upon deception and coercion. Regardless of how we are to interpret these suggestions—and it's far from clear whether they should be taken at face value—it's hard to avoid the conclusion that, as one commentator puts it, "for all his hopes about the perfectibility of human beings, Plato is always prepared to exercise force on those who remain unperfected."[13]

Al-Farabi's Platonism: The Philosopher, Supreme Ruler, Prince, Legislator and Imam as Single Idea

Now, having sketched out the general contours of Plato's political philosophy, let us look at the ways in which this idea of the philosopher-ruler, and the benefits and costs of his rule, are taken up by al-Farabi and Nietzsche. Al-Farabi is one of the preeminent figures in the Islamic philosophical tradition, which—at least in its early stages—can be characterized as a profoundly creative series of negotiations between Islamic theology and Greek philosophy. Al-Farabi is generally considered the father of Islamic political philosophy, not least because of the way in which he recuperates and reinterprets classical political thought, reshaping it to address the concerns of a new world disclosed by the revealed religion of Islam.[14] His task as philosopher, inhabiting a world shaped by the divine law of the Qur'an, is two-fold: (1) to find a place for the insights and resources of classical philosophy within the horizon of Qur'anic revelation,[15] and (2) to make sense of this new phenomenon of revealed religion within the political philosophical framework he has appropriated from the ancients.[16] In other words, he is trying to make space for Greek philosophy within Islam, and make space for Islam within the framework of Greek philosophy, and the only way he can do this is to transform both.

Al-Farabi's specific aim, as a political philosopher, is to explore the characteristics and conditions of the best possible regime, or what he sometimes refers to as the "virtuous city."[17] The virtuous city is one in which the citizens can attain supreme happiness, that is, the final perfection to be achieved by the human being, "in the measure that innate disposition equips each of them for it" (AH 52; cf. AH 20). In one of his key works of political philosophy, appropriately entitled *The Attainment of Happiness*, he observes that there are two methods by which supreme happiness is achieved in nations and cities. The first is instruction, which is concerned with the theoretical virtues, that is, the sciences that make intelligible the principles of being, culminating in the knowledge of God. The second is the formation of character, which is concerned with the moral virtues and practical arts (AH 38). Al-Farabi will argue, as Plato does, that the supreme happiness that is the goal of the virtuous city is possible only if there is expert and virtuous rule by its leaders. This in turn requires that the statesman be a philosopher, and vice versa.

Appropriating Plato's emphasis on the necessary coincidence of philosophy and political power, al-Farabi distinguishes between the "true" philosopher [*al-faylasuf al-haqq*] and various types of "mutilated" philosophy [*al-falsafa al-batra'*].[18] He speaks, for instance, of the "counterfeit" philosopher [*al-faylasuf al-zur*], whose intellect is either inadequately prepared for, or incapable of, acquiring the theoretical virtues; the "vain" philosopher [*al-faylasuf al-bahraj*], who has theoretical knowledge but lacks the moral virtues; the "false" philosopher [*al-faylasuf al-batil*], who is both knowledgeable and virtuous, but who cannot practically bring his wisdom to bear in the city (AH 60-62). These distinctions suggest that the true philosopher must (1) possess theoretical knowledge of first principles, (2) must exemplify the various moral virtues, and (3) must be capable of (a) effectively conveying his theoretical insights to the multitude and (b) forming the character of the citizenry.

> When the theoretical sciences are isolated and their possessor does not have the faculty for exploiting them for the benefit of others, they are defective philosophy [*al-falsafa al-naqisa*]. To be a truly perfect philosopher [*al-faylasuf al-kamil 'ala al-itlaq*] one has to possess both the sciences and the faculty for exploiting them for the benefit of all others according to their capacity. Were one to consider the case of the true philosopher, he would find no difference between him and the supreme ruler . . . the true philosopher is the supreme ruler. (AH 54)

To exploit the theoretical sciences "for the benefit of all others" means for al-Farabi to present complex philosophical truths in the form of simple, powerful, compelling images. It means translating the rigorous, highly technical, and admittedly rather dry and colorless discourse of philosophical demonstration into persuasive rhetorical speeches (AH 44, 55).[19] The former is a privilege accessible only to the "elect" who can attain happiness though a virtue that is rooted in genuine knowledge. The "vulgar" are constitutionally incapable of acquiring such justified true belief, but can nonetheless attain happiness by means of the philosopher's practical dispensation of true belief, through the popularized medium of images and persuasive speech.[20]

One of al-Farabi's great innovations is to assign this popularization as the appropriate function of religion. Religion serves to present the insights of philosophy in a form accessible to the vulgar. On this point he is blunt and unapologetic:

> [T]hese things are *philosophy* when they are in the soul of the legislator. They are *religion* when they are in the souls of the multitude. For when the legislator knows these things, they are evident to him by sure insight, whereas what is established in the

> souls of the multitude is through image and persuasive argument.
> Although it is the legislator who also presents these things through
> images, neither the images nor the persuasive arguments are intended
> for himself. As far as he is concerned, they are certain. He is the one
> who invents the images and the persuasive arguments, but not for the
> sake of establishing these things in his own soul as a religion for
> himself. (AH 59)

Religion and philosophy are not to be understood as at odds with one another (al-Farabi, like his predecessor al-Kindi, goes to great lengths to demonstrate their compatibility), but that is because the former is ultimately an "imitation" or "similitude" of the latter [*al-milla muhakiatun li al-falsafa*] (AH 55).[21] This peculiarly Platonic way of framing the matter—in terms of original and copy—suggests that there can only be *one* true philosophy (which al-Farabi will argue is that of Plato and Aristotle, whose thought he believes is harmonizable), but that there is *not* one true religion, be it Islam or any other.[22] Religion is essentially a tool in the hands of the philosopher, and its specific content must be determined by the particular nature and character of the people to whom philosophical truth is popularly presented (AH 40, 54).[23] The philosopher, as a good rhetorician, needs to know his audience.

Thus, in his attempt to negotiate the apparently competing truth claims of Islam as revealed religion and the philosophy of Plato and Aristotle, al-Farabi will understand prophetic revelation as an imaginative disclosure of the same truths known demonstratively and intellectually in philosophy.[24] And because this is the means by which philosophy is brought to practical fruition, he will conclude that "[T]he idea of the Philosopher, Supreme Ruler, Prince, Legislator and Imam is but a single idea" (AH 58).

Unlike Plato, al-Farabi does not see the need for deception and misdirection on the part of the philosopher-ruler.[25] The religious doctrines by which true belief, virtue and happiness are made possible to the multitude are not simply "a throng of lies and deceptions for the benefit of the ruled," as Socrates suggests in the *Republic* (459c-d), but rather imagistic and persuasive presentations of philosophical truth. However, not all of the vulgar will necessarily be receptive to the philosopher's well-intentioned, edifying efforts. There will always be those who are too obstinate and recalcitrant to participate in the attainment of their own happiness. In such cases, compulsion is required and the philosopher is justified in turning to the "craft of war" in order

> to conquer the nations and cities that do not submit to doing what will
> procure for them that happiness for whose acquisition the human
> being is made. For every being is made to achieve the ultimate
> perfection it is susceptible of achieving according to its specific place
> in the order of being. The human being's specific perfection is called

supreme happiness, and to each human being, according to his rank in the order of humanity, belongs the specific supreme happiness pertaining to this kind of human being. The warrior who pursues this purpose is the just warrior, and the art of war that pursues this purpose is the just and virtuous art of war. (AH 43)[26]

Although al-Farabi is elsewhere rather circumspect about the question of just war,[27] like Plato, he seems convinced that force sometimes must be exercised on those who, through their own intransigent ignorance and viciousness, resist the perfection of their nature and the attainment of happiness.

Nietzsche's Platonism: The Philosopher as Commander and Legislator

Despite the Islamic context in which al-Farabi wrote, it certainly makes sense to speak of him as a kind of Platonist. On the other hand, the phrase "Nietzsche's Platonism" would appear to be something of an oxymoron: At least with respect to questions of knowledge, being and value, Nietzsche's thought offers us the most uncompromising version of *anti*platonism formulated in the history of European thought. However, at the same time, Nietzsche's *grosse Politik* can be understood as an appropriation of Platonic political philosophy.[28] For in spite of his radical questioning of any doctrine of Being or stable eidetic structure, Nietzsche accepts Plato's teaching on the coincidence of philosophy and political power, appropriating the idea of the philosopher-ruler who understands human nature and how it is to be transformed.[29]

Even in his earliest writings, Nietzsche grants a unique and privileged status to the philosopher: "Let us think of the philosopher's eye resting upon existence," he suggests in his third *Untimely Meditation*, "he wants to determine its value anew. For it has been the proper task of all great thinkers to be lawgivers [*Gesetzgeber*] as to the measure, stamp and weight of things." (SE 3, p. 144). The central thesis of this early essay is that the real philosopher has an educative (i.e., life-transforming, invigorating) effect on us. But Nietzsche's more general aim is to clarify what he sees as the true purpose of education and culture, which begins as an attempt to compensate for the aleatory character of nature, and ends in the transfiguration and perfection of the human being. This is effected through the deliberate cultivation of great, exemplary individuals, for whose production great sacrifices are required on the part of the many, but who in turn expand for us the horizon of human perfectibility.[30] This idea lies at the heart of Nietzsche's political philosophy and remains constant in his writings, up through the final works of 1888.

By the time Nietzsche writes *Thus Spoke Zarathustra*, it seems clear that the philosopher is uniquely responsible for engineering this productive transfiguration of human nature.[31] The figure of Zarathustra emerges as a kind of Platonic philosopher, prophet and law-giver, who has achieved insight into the nature of things (human nature in particular) and now claims the right—or again perhaps the obligation—to bring about a revaluation of all values (that is, the creation of new, this-worldly, life-affirming values) and to legislate the future of the human. In *Beyond Good and Evil* it becomes clear that this is the *true* task of the philosopher, and like Plato and al-Farabi, Nietzsche will expend a great deal of energy distinguishing the authentic philosophical type from its various corruptions, e.g., the scholar, the scientific human being, the epistemologist (BGE 204), the "philosophical laborer" or systematizer (BGE 211), and so forth. "*Genuine philosophers* [*eigentlichen Philosophen*]," Nietzsche claims, are "*commanders and legislators* [*Befehlende und Gesetzgeber*]: they say, 'thus it shall be!' they first determine the Wither and For What of humanity . . . With a creative hand they reach for the future, and all that is and has been becomes a means for them, an instrument, a hammer. Their 'knowing' is creating, their creating is a legislation, their will to truth is—will to power" (BGE 211, cf. 203). For Nietzsche, the perfection of the human is no longer teleologically oriented by the Idea of the Good or by God, but rather by the farthest reaches of the philosopher's creative vision.[32]

However, Nietzsche nonetheless shares with al-Farabi the conviction that religion can be a useful tool in the hand of the philosopher-legislator.

> The philosopher as we understand him, we free spirits—as the human being of the most comprehensive responsibility who has the conscience for the over-all development of humankind—this philosopher will make use of religions for his project of cultivation and education, just as he will make use of whatever political and economic states are at hand. The selective and cultivating influence, always destructive as well as creative and form-giving, which can be exerted with the help of religions, is always multiple and different according to the sort of human beings who are placed under its spell and protection. (BGE 61)

What follows this announcement is a remarkable discussion of the ways in which religion might be used to contribute to the flourishing of different types of human beings with different capacities: the strong and independent, the ruled, the ordinary.[33] But this is in turn counter-balanced by an examination of the *dangers* of religion when it breaks free from philosophy and tries to play the legislator on its own: "one always pays dearly," Nietzsche observes, "when religions do *not* want to be a means of education and cultivation in the philosopher's hand, but insist on having their own *sovereign* way, when they themselves want to be ultimate ends and not means among other means" (BGE 61). Wherever religion has arrogated to itself such sovereignty, it has invariably resulted in the diminishment and degeneration of humanity. By the end of the discussion, Nietzsche is so appalled at the damage that he can hardly contain himself: "'O you dolts,'" he bursts out, "'you presumptuous, pitying dolts, what have you done! Was that work for your hands? How have you bungled and botched my beautiful stone! What presumption!'" (BGE 61).

This image of the philosopher-legislator as sculptor recurs in a number of different texts, and it offers us some insight into the opportunity cost of Nietzsche's "great politics." For instance, in the second part of *Thus Spoke Zarathustra*, Nietzsche's prophet speaks of creation as the "great redemption from suffering," and then turns his creative gaze on humanity:

> "[M]y fervent will to create impels me ever again toward the human being; this is the hammer impelled toward the stone. O people, in the stone there sleeps an image, the image of my images. Alas that it must sleep in the hardest, the ugliest stone! Now my hammer rages cruelly against its prison. Pieces of rock rain from the stone: what is that to me? I want to perfect it; for a shadow came to me—the stillest and lightest of all things once came to me. The beauty of the *Übermensch* came to me as a shadow. O my brothers, what are the gods to me now?" (Z II, "On the Blessed Isles")

The hammer rages "cruelly," of course, because the raw material upon which Zarathustra works is the human being, a living, suffering organism, with its own designs and goals (no matter how mediocre or wrong-headed). But as Nietzsche will repeatedly observe, cruelty and suffering are necessary conditions for growth and self-overcoming—they have "created all enhancements of the human being so far" (BGE 225). To do away with suffering, as Nietzsche believes religions and moralities of pity have tried to do, is to make the human being ridiculous and contemptible. In a passage from *Beyond Good and Evil* that picks up on the sculptor metaphor, Nietzsche says that "in the human being creature and creator are united," and adds

> *your* pity is for the "creature in the human being," for what must be formed, broken, forged, torn, burnt, made incandescent and purified—that which *necessarily* must and *should* suffer[.] And *our* pity—do you not comprehend for whom our *converse* pity is when it resists your pity as the worst of all pamperings and weaknesses? Thus it is pity *versus* pity. (BGE 225)

Thus, in spite of his challenging critique of the morality of *Mitleid*, Nietzsche himself admits to a feeling of pity or compassion for the not yet fully formed human animal.[34] Of course, his pity is not for the human being as creature, but rather as *creator,* and it is a pity that nonetheless recognizes the necessity and desirability of imposing violence upon human nature (cf. BGE 188). In short, Nietzsche, like Plato and al-Farabi, acknowledges the right and the obligation of the philosopher-legislator to employ force as well as manipulative rhetoric in the transfiguration and perfection of humanity.[35]

We Good Platonists

Numerous papers in this volume have made a compelling case for philosophy as an antidote to terror; here we see the ways in which it sometimes *requires* and *justifies* terror. Even if we agree with Socrates that "fine things are hard" (497d), we might ultimately want to consign the Platonic lineage of political perfectionism to the trash-heap of history—or perhaps, as Richard Rorty has argued, the private sphere.[36] But let us resist this conclusion, at least for the moment. For despite an almost instinctive modern antipathy towards Plato's political philosophy, we ourselves may very well subscribe to many of its basic tenets.

What thoughtful person doesn't believe in the ideal coincidence of power and knowledge? Perhaps we no longer believe that philosophers—whether they are "the real thing" or some corrupted imitation—possess the privileged insights that would grant them the authority to determine the appropriate conditions of human flourishing. We might still concede a comparable—albeit piecemeal—expertise to other fields or disciplines, or we might simply deny that any such knowledge is possible in the first place. But surely we still believe that some people are more qualified than others to make decisions concerning the appropriate goals of human life.[37] And is it not so much the better if those people can convey their insights through powerful, persuasive speech on behalf of those who either don't have the capacity, or inclination, or time, or energy to arrive at such conclusions themselves? Perhaps we are *all* Platonists in this respect.

Even if we reject the notion of one best regime, or a single univocal conception of the "good life," we presumably still believe that some strategies of living are better than others, that some are simply more conducive to human flourishing. Presumably, we believe in the cultivation of virtue or excellence as a necessary (if not sufficient) condition for a good life, and we believe everyone should lead a good life. Here you may want to hedge a little: yes, we believe in excellence, but not *compulsory* excellence. No insight into the conditions of human flourishing would legitimate *compelling* someone to be virtuous and happy. And yet, I suspect that all of us would concede the unfortunate necessity of coercive intervention at *some* point in the life of the ignorant, the vicious, or the self-destructive. In this respect, too, perhaps we are all Platonists.

The problem, of course, is that the rubric of community that I have been so casually employing here—the royal "we"—often turns out to be a false unity that masks a more fundamental multiplicity. "We" all believe in the happy marriage of wisdom and power, "we" all believe in some rank ordering of regimes for human life, and "we" all, no matter how uncomfortably, concede that coercive force sometimes needs to be exercised on the vicious. We all believe these things, even if we ultimately subscribe, as al-Farabi and Nietzsche do, to different rank-orderings of values, different conceptions of the good life, and perhaps even radically different conceptions of virtue and vice. The question then is, where does that leave us—we good Platonists?[38]

Acknowledgement: I would like to thank Doug Allen, Charles Butterworth, Fred Dallmayr, Anne Eaton, Joseph Prabhu, Joel Smith, Gary Steiner, Karsten Struhl, and Jeff Turner for their many helpful comments and suggestions.

Notes

1. All quotes in the following discussion are from *The Republic of Plato*, trans. Allan Bloom, 2nd ed. (New York: Basic Books, 1968), and will be cited in the text by Stephanus numbers.

2. Particularly among the *mashsha'iyun* (the "walkers," i.e., the Peripatetic or Aristotelian tradition of Islamic philosophy), al-Farabi is often referred to as the "Second Teacher," after Aristotle. For a pithy discussion of this honorific title, see Seyyed Hossein Nasr, "Why Was Al-Farabi called the Second Teacher?" in *The Intellectual Tradition in Persia*, ed. Mehdi Amin Razavi (Surrey: Curzon Press, 1996), 59-65. In my discussion of al-Farabi, I opt for minimal transliteration of Arabic terms, eschewing all diacritics.

3. I use Marshall Hodgson's term "Islamicate" here (rather than "Islamic") to indicate any and all philosophical thought that emerges from within the context of a culture predominantly informed by Islam, whether or not its presuppositions and conclusions are necessarily Muslim. In doing so, I deliberately set aside the question of whether al-Farabi ought to be characterized first and foremost as a Muslim thinker who uses philosophical means to clarify, understand and defend the revelations of his faith, or as a philosopher whose conclusions ultimately go beyond (and even throw into question) the fundamental commitments of his religious and cultural milieu. For a discussion of the usefulness and appropriateness of the term "Islamicate," see Marshall G. S. Hodgson's magisterial *The Venture of Islam*, 3 volumes (Chicago: University of Chicago, 1974), esp. vol. 1, 56-60. For a discussion of problems surrounding the delineation of the rubric "Islamic philosophy," see Oliver Leaman's Introduction in *History of Islamic Philosophy*, ed. Seyyed Hossein Nasr and Oliver Leaman (London: Routledge, 1996), 1-10.

4. Nietzsche's rejection of Plato's metaphysics is self-evident; al-Farabi's is more subtle and indirect. For a discussion, see Leo Strauss, "Farabi's Plato," in *Essays in Medieval Jewish and Islamic Philosophy*, ed. Arthur Hyman (New York: KTAV Publishing House, 1977), 391-427. "[A]ccording to Farabi," he writes, "Plato's philosophy is essentially political" (396). Later, in his examination of al-Farabi's *Philosophy of Plato*, he observes that "Farabi's silence about the ideas and about the immortality of the soul shows certainly that he does not hesitate to deviate from the letter of Plato's teaching if he considers that teaching erroneous. He may have believed that Plato himself considered the doctrines in question merely exoteric. But he may, or he may not have believed that the teaching which he ascribes to Plato by his silence as well as his speech, was the Platonic teaching: he certainly considered it a true teaching. His *Plato* is then not a historical work" (410). Cf. Strauss, "How Farabi Read Plato's *Laws*," in *Islamic Philosophy, Volume 10: Al-Farabi*, ed. Fuat Sezgin, et al (Frankfurt am Main: Institute for the History of Arabic-Islamic Science, 1999), 297-322. Herbert Davidson points out the real orientation of al-Farabi's metaphysics when he writes, "The universe envisioned by Alfarabi is fashioned of Aristotelian bricks and of mortar borrowed from Neoplatonic philosophy." Herbert A. Davidson, *Alfarabi, Avicenna, and Averroes, on Intellect* (Oxford: Oxford University, 1992), 44.

5. Throughout this paper, I shall use the masculine pronoun when referring to Plato's, al-Farabi's, and Nietzsche's respective conceptions of the philosopher-legislator, not because I think this is an unproblematic assumption, but because in the language of all three, that figure is portrayed as male. On this point, Plato is arguably the most prescient of the three, since although he uses the masculine term *archôn*, or "king," for ruler (*Republic* 473d), he later qualifies this by pointing out that what he has said about the philosopher-rulers applies to women just as much as men (540c).

6. Cf. Plato's *Seventh Letter* 326a-b and 328a. Although one finds an increasing emphasis on law rather than the philosopher-ruler in Plato's later political texts (i.e., the *Statesman* and *Laws*), the latter remains as a regulative theoretical ideal, with law-based regimes serving as a practical compromise in the absence of the true *politikos*. See, e.g., *Statesman* 291c-302b and *Laws* 875c-d; cf. *Republic* 540e-541a and 592b. On the fundamental continuity of Plato's political philosophy, see Huntington Cairns, "Plato as Jurist," in Paul Friedlander, *Plato*, Vol.1 (Princeton, N.J.: Princeton University Press, 1958), esp. 286-90, W. K. C. Guthrie, *A History of Greek Philosophy*, Vol. 5 (Cambridge: Cambridge University Press, 1978), 183-88, 332-36 and 381-82, and R. F. Stalley, *An Introduction to Plato's* Laws (Indianapolis, Ind: Hackett, 1983), 13-22.

7. Bloom, n. 5, 468.

8. When making this distinction, Socrates typically employs the language of *alêtheia*, *mimêsis*, and *pthora*. See, e.g., *Republic* 474b, 475d, 480a, 484b, 485d-e, and 487a-497b (esp. 491a and 495c); cf. *Phaedo* 64a-69e, where he speaks of the *alêthôs philosophoi*.

9. For clear discussion of this general idea, see Richard Kraut, "The Defense of Justice in Plato's *Republic*," in *The Cambridge Companion to Plato*, ed. Richard Kraut (Cambridge: Cambridge University Press, 1992), 319.

10. *Republic* 373d-375c, 466c-471c, and 521d.

11. *Republic* 377a-398b, and 595a-608b.

12. *Republic* 458c-461e and 546a-547a.

13. Nickolas Pappas, *Plato and the Republic* (London: Routledge, 1995), 121.

14. The definitive study of al-Farabi's political philosophy is Muhsin Mahdi, *Alfarabi and the Foundation of Islamic Political Philosophy* (Chicago: University of Chicago, 2001), but see also Richard Walzer's commentary on al-Farabi's *Virtuous City* in *On the Perfect State* (Oxford: Oxford University Press, 1985), 331-503, Charles E. Butterworth, "Al-Farabi's Statecraft: War and the Well-Ordered Regime," in *Cross, Crescent and Sword: The Justification and Limitation of War in Western and Islamic Tradition*, ed. James Turner Johnson and John Kelsay (New York: Greenwood Press, 1990), 79-100, Miriam Galston, *Politics and Excellence: The Political Philosophy of Alfarabi* (Princeton, N.J.: Princeton University Press, 1990), and Joshua Parens, *Metaphysics as Rhetoric: Alfarabi's Summary of Plato's "Laws"* (Albany, N.Y.: SUNY Press, 1995).

15. See *The Attainment of Happiness*, section 63, in Alfarabi, *The Philosophy of Plato and Aristotle*, rev. ed., trans. Muhsin Mahdi (Ithaca, N.Y.: Cornell University Press, 2002). All quotes in the following discussion are drawn from this work, henceforth abbreviated as AH and cited in the text by section. For a meticulous explication and analysis of this text, see Mahdi, *Alfarabi and the Foundation of Islamic Political Philosophy*, 173-95.

16. Despite the profound influence of Aristotle's corpus upon al-Farabi's logic, metaphysics, theology, psychology and ethics, his political philosophy shows no significant trace of Aristotle's *Politics*, drawing almost exclusively upon Plato's *Republic* and *Laws*. Although almost all of Aristotle's major writings were translated into Syriac and Arabic, his *Politics* seems not to have been among them. See e.g. Richard Walzer, *Greek into Arabic: Essays on Islamic Philosophy* (Cambridge, Mass.: Harvard University Press, 1962), 243. Shlomo Pines makes the case, however, that Aristotle's *Politics* (or at least relevant portions of it) were in fact available to al-Farabi. See his "Aristotle's Politics in Arabic Philosophy," in *Israel Oriental Studies* 5 (1975), 150-60.

17. *Principles of the Opinions of the Inhabitants of the Virtuous City* (usually just referred to as *The Virtuous City*), along with its companion text, *The Political Regime*, are "popular" works by al-Farabi that offer models of regimes based on his more technical works of political philosophy, e.g., *The Philosophy of Plato and Aristotle*, of which *The Attainment of Happiness* makes up the first part. For an illuminating discussion of the relation between these texts, see Muhsin Mahdi, *Alfarabi and the Foundation of Islamic Political Philosophy*, 1-11.

18. On the "true philosopher," see AH 54, 59 and 62; on the "mutilated philosopher," see AH 60.

19. Al-Farabi is most explicit about this in the second part of *The Philosophy of Plato and Aristotle*: "[Plato] made it known that Thrasymachus was more able than Socrates to form the character of the youth and instruct the multitude; Socrates possessed only the ability to conduct a scientific investigation of justice and the virtues, and a power of love, but did not possess the ability to form the character of the youth and the multitude; and the philosopher, the prince, and the legislator ought to be able to use both methods: that Socratic method with the elect, and Thrasymachus' method with the youth and the multitude." (*Philosophy of Plato*, sec. 36). Much could be said here about (1) the importance of Aristotle's *Rhetoric* in understanding al-Farabi's political philosophy, and (2) al-Farabi's hierarchical understanding of the relation between logic, rhetoric and

poetics. On these topics, see respectively Charles E. Butterworth, "The Rhetorician and His Relation to the Community: Three Accounts of Aristotle's *Rhetoric*," in *Islamic Theology and Philosophy: Studies in Honor of George F. Hourani*, ed. Michael E. Marmura (Albany, N.Y.: SUNY Press, 1984), 111-19, and Deborah L. Black, *Logic and Aristotle's* Rhetoric *and* Poetics in *Medieval Arabic Philosophy* (Leiden: Brill 1990), 1-19, 31-51, 63-71, and 78-94.

20. I leave aside here the vexed question of whether true opinion, received through images and persuasive speech, ultimately has the same transformative and soteriological effect upon the soul as knowledge (i.e., certitude about necessary things), which the philosopher acquires through demonstration. That is to say, is ultimate happiness (predicated as it is upon the immortality of the soul) available to the multitude as well as the elect? This question is a difficult one, at least in part because, as Ibn Tufayl points out, al-Farabi's actual views on the immortality of the soul are far from clear: "In *The Ideal Religion* [i.e., *The Virtuous City*] he affirms that the souls of the wicked live on forever in infinite torments after death. But in his *Civil Politics* [i.e., *The Political Regime*] he says plainly that they dissolve into nothing and that only the perfected souls of the good achieve immortality. Finally, in his commentary on Aristotle's *Ethics*, discussing human happiness, he says that it exists only in this life, and on the heels of that has words to the effect that all other claims are senseless ravings and old wives' tales. This makes mankind at large despair of God's mercy. It puts the wicked on the same level with the good, for it makes nothingness the ultimate destiny of us all." Ibn Tufayl, *Hayy Ibn Yaqzan*, trans. Lenn Evan Goodman, 4th edition (Los Angeles: Gee Tee Bee, 1996), 100.

21. For a comparative examination of al-Kindi and Nietzsche, see Peter S. Groff, "Al-Kindi and Nietzsche on the Stoic Art of Banishing Sorrow," *Journal of Nietzsche Studies*, 28 (Fall, 2004).

22. See in particular *The Harmonization of the Two Opinions of the Two Sages: Plato the Divine and Aristotle*, in Alfarabi, *The Political Writings: Selected Aphorisms and other Texts*, trans. Charles E. Butterworth (Ithaca, N.Y.: Cornell University Press, 2001), 117-67. It may seem strange to attempt to harmonize Plato and Aristotle, who take strikingly divergent stances on so many points. Indeed, as various commentators have pointed out, only a limited number of translated Platonic dialogues were available to al-Farabi, and his accounts of some of these sound at times fanciful. However, it should be noted, first, that al-Farabi does not claim that Plato and Aristotle agree on every point, but rather only the fundamentals, and second, that he does not take all their claims at face value. Al-Farabi sums up his position best in the conclusion to *The Attainment of Happiness*: "So let it be clear to you that their *purpose* is the same in what they presented and that they *intended* to present one and the same philosophy" (AH 64, italics mine).

23. This is in part what Muhsin Mahdi calls the "question of realization." As he formulates it, "To know is one thing; to realize what is known—that is, what is known to be possible or realizable—to bring it about, to have it actually exist among humans and cities and nations, that is something else. . . . How do you bring into being in cities and nations the things you know? Can you bring them into being outside your mind exactly as they are known, or do they have to be modified according to certain conditions? What are

the conditions that make realization possible?" (Mahdi, *Alfarabi and the Foundation of Islamic Political Philosophy*, 56-57, cf. 60-62).

24. On al-Farabi's account of prophecy and its relation to imagination and the Aristotelian notion of the active intellect [Gr: *nous poiêtikos*; Ar: *al-'aql al-fa''al*], see Fazlur Rahman, *Prophecy in Islam: Philosophy and Orthodoxy* (Chicago: University of Chicago, 1958), 11-14, and Herbert A. Davidson, *Alfarabi, Avicenna and Averroes, on Intellect* (Oxford: Oxford University Press, 1992), 58-63. On the importance of the imagination in Islamic philosophy, see Oliver Leaman, "Poetry, Mirrors, and Paintings: Imagination in Islamic Philosophy," in *Essays in Islamicate Philosophy*, ed. Peter S. Groff (Lewisburg, Pa.: Bucknell University Press, forthcoming).

25. I leave aside here any consideration of the role of dissimulation in al-Farabi's own philosophical corpus. For two forceful statements of the esoteric/exoteric distinction in al-Farabi's writings, see Strauss, "Farabi's Plato," and Charles Butterworth and Thomas Pangle's Foreword to Alfarabi, *Philosophy of Plato and Aristotle*, vii-xx. For a critique of this interpretive approach to Islamic philosophy, see Oliver Leaman, *Introduction to Classical Islamic Philosophy*, 2nd edition (Cambridge: Cambridge University Press, 2002), 205-236.

26. In spite of al-Farabi's emphasis on justified war in this passage, he makes no mention of *jihad* ("struggle" in the lesser sense, which involves an active armed conflict with evil), instead settling upon the more neutral term *harb*, which refers to war in general. Cf. al-Farabi's *Selected Aphorisms* 58 and 67, where he does use the language of *jihad*.

27. For a thorough-going discussion of the question of just war in al-Farabi, see Charles Butterworth, "Al-Farabi's Statecraft: War and the Well-Ordered Regime," 79-100.

28. See *Ecce Homo*, "Why I am a Destiny" sec. 1, in *On the Genealogy of Morals and Ecce Homo*, trans. Walter Kaufmann (New York: Vintage, 1967). Henceforth, all references to Nietzsche's works will be cited in the text by abbreviation of the English title and section number. With the exception of occasional emendations, I rely chiefly on "Schopenhauer as Educator" in *Untimely Meditations*, trans. R. J. Hollingdale (Cambridge: Cambridge University Press, 1983), *Thus Spoke Zarathustra*, trans. Walter Kaufmann (New York: Viking Penguin, 1954), and *Beyond Good and Evil*, trans. Walter Kaufmann (New York: Random House, 1966).

29. Stanley Rosen has argued for this point most vociferously in his book *The Mask of the Enlightenment: Nietzsche's Zarathustra* (Cambridge: Cambridge University Press, 1995), ix-x. Cf. Daniel W. Conway, who argues that Nietzsche "retrieves the founding question of politics [i.e., "what ought humankind to become?"] in order to call humankind itself and its future, into question." Conway, *Nietzsche and the Political* (London: Routledge, 1998), 3. Laurence Lampert gives perhaps the richest portrait of Nietzsche as a Platonic political thinker in his *Nietzsche and Modern Times: A Study of Bacon, Descartes, and Nietzsche* (New Haven, Conn.: Yale University Press, 1993), and *Nietzsche's Task: An Interpretation of Beyond Good and Evil* (New Haven, Conn.: Yale University Press, 2001).

30. Nietzsche does not explicitly employ the language of "cultivation" or "breeding" [*Züchtung*] in "Schopenhauer as Educator," but leans heavily upon it in his later writings, from *Beyond Good and Evil* to the final works on 1888.

31. One must, of course, use the term "human nature" cautiously, especially when dealing with Nietzsche. As I have argued elsewhere, "if we can speak of a Nietzschean conception of human nature, it ought not to be understood in terms of some ahistorical, transcultural essence, but rather has to do with the natural *history* of the human, as it emerges and continues to develop from the interplay of fully natural forces and events. The human being, as Nietzsche never tires of reminding us, is no *aeterna veritas*: 'man too has become'. . . . When Nietzsche speaks of recovering the 'terrible' and 'eternal basic text of *homo natura*' . . . it has to do with understanding and affirming the ossified contingencies of our origins and the whole non-teleological course of our developmental history—what Nietzsche calls our 'granite of spiritual *fatum*' . . ." Peter S. Groff, "*Amor Fati* and *Züchtung*: The Paradox of Nietzsche's Nomothetic Naturalism," *International Studies in Philosophy*, vol. 35, no. 3, 31.

32. Note that the philosopher often purports to speak for "nature," a privilege Nietzsche sometimes arrogates to himself, but one that he also unmasks (e.g., see BGE 188 and 9, respectively).

33. For a similar stance towards the role of myth, see Z II, "On the Blessed Isles." Cf. al-Farabi's remark about exploiting the theoretical sciences for the benefit of the multitude, "according to their capacity" (AH 54). Plato, al-Farabi and Nietzsche all subscribe to a hierarchical conception of the human being, although their criteria of rank-ordering differ radically. Nietzsche's insistence upon *Rangordnung* is often minimized or marginalized by Neo-Nietzschean thinkers (e.g., Deleuze, Foucault) who appropriate and develop the anti-universalist, anti-essentialist and anti-foundationalist elements of his thought. However, Nietzsche himself seemed not to recognize any irreconcilable tension between what we might characterize as the premodern and postmodern aspects of his thought. For a discussion of Nietzsche's affirmation and suspicion of hierarchical thinking, see Peter S. Groff, "Who is Zarathustra's Ape?" in *A Nietzschean Bestiary: Becoming Animal Beyond Docile and Brutal*, ed. Christa Davis Acampora and Ralph R. Acampora (Lanham, Md.: Rowman and Littlefield, 2004), 17-31.

34. Cf. Nietzsche's description in BGE 62 of the human being as "the *as yet undetermined animal*" [*das noch nicht festgestellte Tier*].

35. One might argue that Nietzsche stands apart from Plato and al-Farabi, inasmuch as he offers us no actual or ideal regime. Indeed, Nietzsche's philosopher is not a ruler in any strict sense at all: rather, he seems confined to the periphery of his city or state, divorced from all the real institutions of power (Nietzsche's own disenfranchised, nomadic later years are instructive here). Whether we see Nietzsche as a legitimate figure in this Platonic lineage depends on how seriously we take his claims about the true nature of power and legislation: e.g., "Genuine philosophers are commanders and legislators" (BGE 211), "the greatest thoughts are the greatest events" (BGE 285), and so forth. Nietzsche's Platonic stance is perhaps best captured in one of Zarathustra's speeches: "the greatest events—they are not our loudest but our stillest hours. Not around the inventors of new noise, but around the inventors of new values does the world revolve; it revolves inaudibly" (Z II, "On Great Events"). Nietzsche's philosopher-legislators are

such powerful individuals because they impress their will on the millennia, creating the world-views that people will inhabit and the value-systems that will shape their lives. For Nietzsche, then, the coincidence of (genuine) philosophy and political power is not so much an ideal as a fact.

36. Richard Rorty, *Contingency, Irony and Solidarity* (Cambridge: Cambridge University Press, 1989), see esp. Chapter 3.

37. As Lenn E. Goodman puts it, "No one, I trust, will rush from a reading of Farabi to a campaign for philosophical monarchy. But the idea of the philosopher king remains a powerful tool of analysis, because it raises to high relief the core questions of political legitimation. Is it judgment or lineage, faith or philosophy, gender or education, wealth or insight that legitimates authority?" Lenn E. Goodman, *Islamic Humanism* (Oxford: Oxford University Press, 2003), 10.

38. One might object that subscribing in some mitigated way to (1) the ideal coincidence of knowledge and power, (2) the superior aptitude of some to determine the appropriate goals of human life, and (3) necessity of coercive intervention in the lives of the ignorant and vicious does not necessarily qualify one as a Platonist. However, if I am right about these three claims being at the heart of Platonic political philosophy, then even our qualified assent to them suggests that our concerns and ways of thinking are not so distant from figures like Plato, al-Farabi and Nietzsche as we might think.

6

Jihad as Right Effort: A Buddhist Justification of *Jihad* in the Life of Abdul Ghaffar Khan

Jim Highland

Many of the Buddha's teachings encourage us to follow a path meant to guide people away from suffering to a better existence. Too often the goal of this path is misunderstood as one that is far off and only applies to the individual. But the Buddha's teachings encourage a way of life that is helpful to others as well as to ourselves. Furthermore, the steps along this path are not taken for the sake of some final goal, but are themselves the goal: a way of living free from anxiety, fear and suffering. In this chapter, I will discuss several Buddhist practices as the kind of activities we need to promote in the face of intolerance and terrorism, and I will make a similar assertion about *jihad*.

I believe we can find meanings of *jihad* that assert a nonviolent struggle to genuinely help our neighbors and oppose injustice. This will be evident in the example of the Pashtun leader of nonviolent resistance in the Frontier of British India, Abdul Ghaffar Khan, also known as Badshah Khan. I will argue that many aspects of his life exemplify a *jihad* which is both nonviolent and political. Furthermore, while violent and intolerant kinds of *jihad* are certainly discouraged by, if not antithetical to Buddhist practices, the *jihad* that Khan lived and encouraged is, I argue, justified from a Buddhist perspective, in that it encourages efforts to help other people resist injustice and mitigate suffering, and does so in a manner very similar to that of right effort and the *paramita* of exertion. His *jihad* to span religious differences, educate his people, bring self-rule to those suffering under foreign occupation, and transform ancient, but cruel cultural practices are as much an example of Buddhist teachings as they are an aspect of Islam we should encourage to flourish.

Abdul Ghaffar Khan: Service, Islam and other Faiths

Khan[1] worked all of his life to see the true spirit of Islam flourish. As he understood it, that spirit was not confined to one culture or one religion. Nevertheless, he grew up in an area that was, and still is, overwhelmingly Muslim: what is today called the semi-autonomous region of Pakistan. He turned down a position in the British military, arranged through his father's political influence, when he realized it would compromise his devotion to other members of his tribe and ultimately to God. But Khan also resisted the intolerance, and disregard for anything outside Islam, of many in his community. He had no desire to endure the narrow-minded views and habits of others, whether they were Muslim or not. He described his experience learning the Qur'an at a local mosque as an ordeal. The *mullah*, like many people of his country, did not value learning beyond the memorization of the Qur'an. In his autobiography, Khan described the *mullah* who taught him as "devoid of learning and practically illiterate . . . . He knew some *surahs* of the Holy Koran by heart. He was even able to read the Holy Koran. But I very much doubt whether he understood one word of it!"[2]

Khan's parents, like most parents of his region, were very happy that he was learning the Qur'an, but he explained that beneath the approval of this kind of learning, most people regarded any other learning as a distraction from the religious life. The *mullahs*, of course, supported this view: "...for they insisted that all this worldly learning was *kufr*—against religion!"[3] But his parents were different; both valued knowledge more generally and sent Khan and his older brother, who later studied medicine in Britain, to schools after they completed their religious training. Indeed, the *mullahs* tried to stop this by spreading rumors about Khan's parents, but could not challenge them openly because his father was a respected leader in the community.[4]

For Khan, service and care for others were as much a part of religion as knowledge of the Qur'an. Indeed, the name of his nonviolent soldiers (Khudai Khidmatgars, Servants of God) openly declared that the social aims of the movement were motivated by Khan's understanding of religion. Khan did not hide this understanding by any means:

> My religion is truth, love, and service to God and humanity.
> Every religion that has come into the world has brought the
> message of love and brotherhood. And those who are
> indifferent to the welfare of their fellowmen, those whose

hearts are empty of love, . . . they do not know the meaning of Religion.[5]

Indeed, in a speech in 1931, he told people of his region that he and his followers came to awaken them to their ignorance of their own religion, to awaken them to the deplorable conditions in which they were living. Among other things, they would teach them better personal hygiene, and how to spin their own clothing. These and other efforts would not only improve their condition but help them realize their independence from the British. He asserted that the Khudai Khidmatgars had sworn to serve the creatures of God, but he added: "Remember this also that the Musalmans alone are not the creatures of God. The Hindus, Sikhs, Musalmans, Jews, Christians and Parsis, in short, all the creatures that live in the world, are the creatures of God."[6] Their work in helping the needy, in promoting cooperation among people of different faiths, and in opposing the British was all an effort to oppose tyranny. As Khan stated: "Their object is to rescue the oppressed from the tyrant. They would stand against a tyrant whether he is a Hindu, a Muslim or an Englishman."[7]

In fact, Khan had developed a great desire to help the people of his community and country while studying at an English Mission High School in his youth, and credited his interest in service to his teachers there, since his friends, who went to other schools, did not develop such a desire:

> Our headmaster, Mr. Wigram, used to give scholarships to three or four poor or orphaned students from his own salary. These things impressed me very much and I said to myself: "Look at us, Muslim Pathans, we don't have enough sympathy to help or serve our poor needy brothers! And these people are foreigners, they belong to a different nation and a different faith, yet they have come here to serve our people. What sympathy and love for humanity they must have!"[8]

Khan, though inspired by Gandhi's call to service, was a devout Muslim by all accounts, except those of the British, and later Pakistanis, who were trying to discredit him for political reasons. Mahadev Desai explained that while Khan obviously liked Gandhi's actions against the British:

> It is his [Gandhi's] pure and ascetic life and his insistence on self-purification that have had the greatest appeal for him [Khan], and his whole life, since 1919 onwards has been one sustained effort for self-purification. I have the privilege of

having a number of Muslim friends, true as steel and ready to
sacrifice their all for Hindu-Muslim unity, but I do not yet
know one who is greater than or even equal to Khan Abdul
Ghaffar Khan in the transparent purity and the ascetic severity
of his life, combined with extreme tenderness and living faith
in God.[9]

It will be easier to see how Khan's life was a kind of *jihad* after I explain
some of the meanings of the word *jihad*. After that, I will present some of the
traditional teachings about the practice of *jihad* (which are far from Buddhist
practice, generally). Then I will argue that Khan's life is a precedent for *jihad* as
right effort, by explaining the similarity of exemplary actions from Khan's life
with right effort and the *paramita* of exertion. If my explanations of the more
violent kinds of *jihad* seem heavy-handed, it is only to better contrast the more
militant views, held by a minority of Muslims, with the more peaceful views
that I believe the majority of Muslims hold. Furthermore, while much of the
secondary literature on *jihad* discusses the tragic consequences of violent *jihad*,
or debates whether it is a collective or individual duty, I am going to focus on
the nature and goal of *jihad*.

Historical *Jihad*

Jihad literally means "effort," "striving," and "struggle," but also refers to a
kind of effort and struggle that is often misunderstood in the West, and often
debated by Muslims thinkers themselves. The Mass Media focus on *jihad* as a
militant struggle or Holy War. When we teach classes on the world's religions,
the unit on Islam often points out two aspects: a militant, though often
defensive, effort, called the "lesser *jihad*," and an internal effort to follow God's
Will, called the "Greater *jihad*." But this dichotomy is unsatisfactory in that it
suggests that *jihad* can only be public when it is violent, and can only be
nonviolent when it is directed solely to oneself. Furthermore, the more it is
studied, the more meanings we find for the practice of *jihad*. These include
practices aimed at establishing justice, such as a *jihad* against ignorance, a *jihad*
against colonialism, a *jihad* to feed the starving. These are all legitimate aspects
of *jihad*. But before we argue specifically for a Buddhist justification of *jihad*,
we need to recognize that *jihad*, like many human efforts, has often been
directed toward goals which sanction horrible violence. If we are going to
suggest a political but nonviolent kind of *jihad*, we need to contrast it with more
violent kinds of *jihad*.

In the early period of expansion, Muslim thinkers could point to the Medinan suras (chapters) of the Qur'an for direction on when, and how, *jihad* should be part of the extension of Islamic rule. One passage from the 4th sura exhorts Muslims to continue fighting despite recent successes, and suggests rewards in the afterlife for those who practice such a *jihad*.[10] One commentator argues that this suggests that the more peace-loving Muslims, who wanted to stop fighting after success in Medina, had to be persuaded to continue the violent *jihad*.[11]

Furthermore, Muslim jurists in the 'Abbasid period developed an understanding of the world as divided between lands under Islamic rule (the *dar al-Islam*) and lands not yet under Islamic rule (the *dar al-Harb*). The state of war which existed in the latter would only be lifted when Islamic rule was universal. The advance of Islamic rule was not questioned, only the timing and the manner of that advance. Exponents of this understanding of *jihad* often point out that *jihad* mitigates the violence that can accompany such an expansion of rule. Women, children, monks, and others, who pose no threat and do not denounce Islam or fight against it, are protected.[12] But, while these people are not to be harmed, this view of *jihad* asserts that *jihad* as persuasion can and should still be practiced on all. The goal is not so much to help people (though that may be a secondary goal) as to convince them to follow the Islamic way of life. What is implied is that while the order of Islamic rule is being imposed, violence ought to be limited. At the same time *jihad* as the continual effort to bring others to the religion must still continue through less violent means of persuasion. Indeed, the tax (*jizyah*) that non-Muslims must continue to pay, and the manner in which they are to make this payment, are a continual reminder and incentive for non-Muslims to consider a change in their religious commitment.[13]

Those who advocate *jihad* as the expansion of Islam are confronted with verses of the Qur'an which assert that religion must be freely chosen. For example, a verse from the second sura of the Qur'an is often cited: "There is no compulsion in faith!"[14] But such objections can be met with another aspect of *jihad* which requires the effort to uphold justice and strive against injustice. If Muslims who are freely choosing their faith are being mistreated or persecuted in a non-Muslim state, it is the duty of other Muslims to ensure either that the wrongdoers are stopped and the mistreatment is ended or that the local authorities are replaced by ones who will treat Muslims justly. Indeed, this can become an argument for extending the *dar al-Islam*.

Another objection to *jihad* as the forceful expansion of Islamic rule is often raised by reference to the Meccan suras and the hadith[15] regarding the Prophet Muhammad's actions and advice to followers before the *Hijra*, the emigration to

Medina. At this time, Muslims were advised to spread Islam through their words and deeds, but not to enter into open combat against non-Muslims.[16]

This objection is often met with the assertion that the Prophet was, in the pre-Medinan period, simply acknowledging the military weakness of his fellow Muslims. Going to war at such a time, it is argued, was impractical. So, the Prophet advised Muslims to wait until their numbers were sufficient to be successful in battle. When he became better established in Medina, the character of *jihad* changed from peaceful persuasion to military force. From this perspective, the history of Islamic expansion is one of a continual effort, now overt and violent, now peaceful and persuasive.[17] As such, the kind of *jihad* which issues from a position of relative strength is more forceful, while the kind which issues from a position of relative weakness is less forceful and obvious.

So much more can be said about *jihad* throughout Muslim history, but my aim is not just to give background about *jihad*, but to focus on the kind of *jihad* practiced by a devout Muslim leader of the Pashtun people. Unlike the kind of nonviolent *jihad* that is still part of an expansion effort, the efforts I will describe aim to help others act, and interact, with greater intelligence and compassion, regardless of their religious background. This *jihad* can be observed in the life and actions of Abdul Ghaffar Khan.

Khan's *Jihad*

Abdul Ghaffar Khan's efforts to help his people, both during British rule of India and afterwards, exemplify a peaceful kind of striving for justice and goodwill which issues not from a position of relative weakness, but from a condition of moral strength. Yes, he had studied the Meccan suras of the Qur'an, but he had also been inspired by the actions and wisdom of Gandhi. Khan went to great lengths to help his fellow Pashtuns in whatever ways he could. At a time when the British did not allow schools other than their own and were suspicious of anyone traveling around from village to village in what was then known as the North-West Frontier, Khan visited hundreds of villages and set up schools to cultivate social reforms and lift people out of poverty and ignorance.[18]

The Frontier had been the source of some uprisings, and the British, who ran the area like a police state, regarded the people as bloodthirsty savages. After attending several conferences of Muslim thinkers and learning more about Gandhi's activities, Khan also began to work toward a nonviolent way to remove the British from power. His efforts, which he regarded as a divine mission, were a kind of nonviolent *jihad*. He was committed to helping the Pashtun[19] people live more prosperously and more justly. Indeed, removing the

British was only one part of this effort. Along with social improvements in hygiene and self-reliance, Khan wanted to transform some of the customs of his people, especially ancient codes of honor and revenge which often wasted the lives and energies of everyone involved, without benefiting either side.

Though he was Muslim, his *jihad* was not aimed at converting people. Indeed, Islam was already strong with his people. Nor did he aim at extending Islamic rule through the rest of India. When the nonviolent protests that he and Gandhi had helped organize brought about the opportunity for independence from Britain, Khan worked for a united, independent India. He wanted to see Hindus and Muslims living together despite their religious differences. When battles broke out between Muslims and Hindus, Khan, like Gandhi, traveled to hot spots to try to calm people's fears and end the violence. When his homeland became part of Pakistan, Khan's efforts to establish religious harmony were interpreted as pro-Hindu sentiments. For those sentiments, as well as for his efforts to establish a more democratic and just government (he argued for a semi-autonomous province of the Pashtuns within Pakistan), he spent years in Pakistani jails or in exile in Afghanistan. In all of this, his *jihad* was unlike, if not opposed, to the kinds of *jihad* which, either violently or nonviolently, strive to advance one religion over others.

He was striving to lead Pashtun people to a better way of life, but doing so nonviolently. In a way, it could be said that by advancing social justice for his people, Khan was advancing Islam, but not at the expense of other religions. Indeed, his kind of nonviolent *jihad* required strength and bravery, but not for war or missionary work. Regardless of their numbers or military strength, Khan knew that his fellow Pashtuns were a brave and strong people. They survived some of the worst brutality of the British, as well as the even more disruptive violence stemming from their own codes of honor and revenge, and yet they were fearless. He convinced people who were renown for their bravery in battle to fight the British nonviolently. This was not a *jihad* that expressed itself nonviolently in efforts to convert others to Islam because of a Muslim people's relative weakness and inability to conduct a war of conquest. Like Gandhi, Khan regarded nonviolent resistance as an action of the strong, not an accommodation of the weak.

For these reasons, Khan's efforts were truly nonviolent. They were only meant to help people. Khan's *jihad* was a sacred effort to unite and uplift a people who were suffering under brutality from outside and from within. It also sought harmony between people of different religions. It did not imply a temporary truce, nor a peaceful coexistence, but a mutual openness to what is helpful in other religious traditions. How else could he have been so inspired and dedicated to a non-Muslim such as Gandhi?

Since this paper explains Khan's actions as a kind of *jihad*, we need to consider the dearth of that concept in Khan's writings and speeches. Because attempts to drive out the British were often called *jihads*, the term was associated almost exclusively with violent actions in Khan's time. Indeed, in an attempt to thwart Khan's efforts to promote Hindu-Muslim unity and self-rule in India, the British media often used the term *jihad* to describe the actions of Khan and his followers (referred to as Red Shirts):

> Holy war threat in India started by Abdul Ghaffar Khan with the help of the Red Shirts . . . . Khan Abdul Ghaffar Khan turned the Red Shirts into Khudai Khidmatgars to whom he sent call after call to a *jehad*, a holy war: "You shall be the foundation of the work to free the world from all infidels . . . . And there is no better *jehad* than to free your motherland from slavery, from foreign yoke."[20]

It is true that Khan called for overthrowing the British, but he never called for violent means to bring about such an overthrow.

The only instance I can find in printed texts of Khan using the term *jihad* is from a Bombay 1931 speech. He chastised fellow Pathans, and all Muslims, for not standing against the atrocities of British rule more vigorously. After asserting that the Congress was not a Hindu organization, but was working to free all the people of India from British despotism, Khan explained: "I ask you what *jehad* is. According to the teachings of the Prophet, *jehad* is to say the truth before the tyrant kings. If we are Muslims, then we should act on the sayings of our Prophet."[21] He asserted again and again that fighting against other Indians of different cultures and faiths prevented them from fulfilling their duties to God: "The Prophet teaches us to help the oppressed people and destroy the tyrants."[22]

If you believe that the destruction of tyranny is only possible by violent means, then you could take Khan's words as a call for a violent jihad. But later that year, back in his country in the town of Rustam, Khan described how he and his Khudai Khidmatgars would defy a new regulation, called Section 144, which forbade meetings and demonstrations in that part of India. Here, Khan mixed the language of war and nonviolence as he exhorted listeners to take up the service his followers were providing: "Do not fear death. Section 144 is your test. If you cannot oppose this order, how will you come out to the battlefield? Pay no attention to the order. Be ready and come out to the non-violent battlefield."[23] So, though he understood their efforts as a *jihad*, he did not want the violent connotations of the word, as used by many, transferred to his movement. But it is clear that he consciously used other terms associated with war to assert that this nonviolent effort required no less courage, discipline and teamwork, and that it would be more effective in overthrowing the tyranny of the British rule than would a violent war.

Political change, as well as religious change, had come to Khan's part of the world many times in the past, and he did not want his people, so eager for self-rule, to overlook the value of different perspectives. Even when he could not study the teachings of other religions directly, Khan had an understanding of their historical importance, and in his autobiography dated 1969, also expressed a genuine appreciation of the intrinsic value of numerous religions besides Islam. He was aware that before Islam came to his country, the people were Hindu and then Buddhist, and he described studying the Hindu Bhagavad Gita "profoundly and reverently." Furthermore, he stated that despite having a great desire to study Buddhism, he had yet done so. He explained: "I was also very interested in studying Buddhism because our people were Buddhists before they embraced Islam. But, alas, I have never come across any book on Buddhism that I could have studied." He knew some Persian and was interested in studying about Persian religion, especially since Zoroaster came from an area close to his country, but he could not get books about him. He learned about the New Testament in the Christian Mission school he attended, and described reading from the Old Testament in one of his prison stays. He also described listening to Sikh fellow prisoners recite from the Adi Granth.[24]

Indeed, Khan described other religions with connections to his country with great pride, and regarded them as part of his heritage, not merely beliefs to be tolerated. Without understanding this, Khan's significance and authority are difficult to fully understand. Buddhism, Khan explained, had made his country and people strong: "When Buddhism was spreading, our country made great progress, evidence of which can be found in the relics of that age. Even today two magnificent statues of Gautama the Buddha can be seen in Bamian. They are probably the largest statues of Buddha in the world . . . . they present an unparalleled example of the perfection in the art of sculpture."[25] Describing Buddhist monasteries and universities which had existed in this land, he stated: "Our country had progressed to such an extent that we were able to reach out as far as China and the Far East in order to spread our culture and the message of Buddha."[26] Khan argued that the original name of his country was Afghanistan or Pakhtunistan and stressed that it was the birthplace of the Aryan culture that later moved westward into Iran and Europe and southward into India. For him, the religions that developed in these cultures are part of his Pathan heritage.

The genuineness of Khan's regard for numerous religions shines brighter in his description of the way the Arabs brought Islam to his country. Khan explained that the Arabs who came to the Hindukush mountains were not filled with the piety that the Prophet had transmitted to them originally. They were merely conquerors: "The Arabs were intoxicated with the idea of extending their Empire, and blinded by the desire to conquer other countries. The result was that our splendid culture was taken away from us, but they did not give us, in its place, the true spirit if Islam."[27]

It may sound shocking to hear a devout Muslim make such declarations, for how could a people conquered in such a manner have accepted Islam so wholeheartedly? Though Khan does not often discuss the Sufis, Islamic mystics, he gives a nod to their influence in the spread of Islam in his country: "There were, however, some lovers of learning and seekers of God wandering through the Islamic world in search of the real Islam, who acquired scholarship in Islamic philosophy, learning, and mysticism. Of this we can be truly proud."[28] In another part of his autobiography he mentions the high regard of his people for the Sufi saint Khwaja Mu'inuddin Chisti, and for pilgrimages to his shrine at Ajmer in Northwest India.[29] This suggests that Khan was influenced by a branch of Islam which was much more tolerant of religious difference and devoted much more to the spirit of Islam rather than to strict obedience to specific practices and beliefs. Indeed, the family of the Sufi poet, Jalal al-Din Rumi, came from Balkh, an ancient city in what is now Northern Afghanistan, not far from Khan's homeland in the Hindukush mountains.[30]

Buddhist Practices and *Jihad*

I will discuss Khan's *jihad* in relation to Buddhist traditions now, for several reasons. One reason is that both Islam and Buddhism have traditions of missionary activity. But while in Islam, there is more emphasis on encouraging others to take up specific practices in a more rigid manner, in Buddhism the emphasis is more flexible. Though one of the Bodhisattva vows is to "save the many beings," there is great flexibility in how this is done. As Buddhism spread, people were not asked, and certainly not forced, to give up their religious beliefs and customs wholesale. Instead, Buddhists, especially in the Mahayana tradition, found ways to incorporate Buddhist teachings into local traditions, not to advance a new religion, but to help people free themselves from suffering.[31] The kind of *jihad* I am ascribing to Khan also focuses on exercising the kind of effort which helps people to free themselves from suffering.

We can see this in his efforts to reform the tribal code of revenge, *badal*, efforts which resemble the *paramitas* in general. The *paramitas* are activities which can help us out of a life of suffering, but should not be regarded as rules or commandments which you either follow or disobey. As the Tibetan Buddhist teacher Pema Chödrön explains, "They train us in stepping beyond the limitations of dualistic views altogether and developing a flexible mind."[32] She describes them as "journeys of exploration,"[33] rather than commandments, in the sense that they encourage us to look for answers in what is close-at-hand. Our present condition is filled with opportunities that she calls a "fundamental richness."[34] Rigidly following beliefs and practices blinds us to the opportunities for help all around. These opportunities can include people, habits and customs, like *badal*, that at first seem far from helpful.

Badal was prominent in the Pashtun culture. Revenge killings were passed down like family heirlooms. Families had been torn apart by this energy; cycles of revenge killings had persisted so long that no one knew how they started. Fear of death was not so important as maintaining one's honor. But Khan did not ask anyone to give up all aspects of *badal*. Instead, he focused on the great energy and endurance that was so characteristic of the custom, and the sense of honor and commitment which accompanied them. Khan sensed that this kind of energy and endurance would be vital for turning around the British. So he presented nonviolent resistance to his fellow Pastuns as a grander kind of *badal*. If fighting one's enemy with weapons was a respected example of courage, how much more so to fight one's enemy without weapons at all. The effort would still be directed toward struggling against one's enemy; it would still be a *jihad*, but as part of a collective effort to transform that enemy into the kind of friend who would recognize that British rule must end.[35]

Khan's *jihad* also resembled another aspect of the *paramitas*. Robert Aitken, a Zen Buddhist teacher, describes the *paramitas* as encouraging us to see through the unhelpful surface features of various character traits, to the more helpful features within. Laziness, perfectionism, and even anger are not, in themselves, obstacles to a better way of life. They are diamonds-in-the-rough, so to speak. When we work on them properly, he explains, ". . . laziness becomes patience. Anger becomes passion for justice."[36] In his discussion of not indulging in anger, as part of the *paramita* of moral discipline, Aitken points out that once we let fade the violent musings, that often accompany anger, the experience "reveals the power of anger and its possibilities." We can learn about ourselves, the responsibilities that challenge us, and how we can act to fulfill them. He further emphasizes his point, stating "I vow to find the place of equanimity where my anger can come forth to save everybody and everything."[37] In a similar manner, Khan looked to the custom of revenge killings for the energy to help bring his people out of poverty and injustice nonviolently.

Khan's *jihad* was filled with energy. He traveled to hundreds of villages in the North-West Frontier, in his efforts at education and social reform. On one occasion fairly early in his life, he began to wonder why he was doing it all. He was in danger of being captured and jailed by the British. It would have been so much easier to return home. Or, he could have just resolved to carry on grudgingly. But he took his doubts seriously. With no obviously answers, he decided to perform a fast. He found a mosque and fasted for several days. From what we can tell, the skies did not part and he did not hear a voice telling him what to do. But he gained a new strength, and from then on, as one biographer puts it, "his activities and words are stamped with a singleness of purpose—the service of God—that does not alter over the course of eight decades."[38]

His experience is similar to what we find expressed in the *paramita* of exertion (also called the *virya paramita*). Aitken describes this *paramita* as ". . . the advancement of single-minded spiritual vigor."[39] The manner of this vigor is carefree and unflustered, despite difficulties. Chödrön describes this *paramita* as a practice of connecting with "energetic joy" and with "our appetite for enlightenment."[40] In the midst of our daily lives, we have to find our way to this *paramita*. The energy to carry on is not generated in spite of our circumstances, but because of them. As Pema Chödrön remarks: "Exertion is not like pushing ourselves . . . . It's like waking up on a cold, snowy day in a mountain cabin ready to go for a walk but knowing that first you have to get out of bed and make a fire. You'd rather stay in that cozy bed, but you jump out and make the fire because the brightness of the day in front of you is bigger than staying in bed."[41] This cannot be forced, or planned. Somehow, we connect with the richness of our present condition and it pulls us forward. As she explains, the *virya paramita* "allows us to act, to give, to work appreciatively with whatever comes our way."[42]

We can see more of Khan's life exemplifying the *virya paramita* in the following account from one of his many stays in prison. One day, a guard was watching Khan perform his daily chore of grinding corn. The guard knew of Khan and did not think that such good man should have to perform the same duties as common criminals. Here is their conversation, after the guard told Khan to stop grinding the corn, narrated by our principle biographer:

> "You are the only one in this prison who is here on behalf of God. How could I justify myself before Him if I made you grind corn?" Khan stopped grinding, but when the guard left he resumed. The guard was watching him through the slot in the door and came back into his cell. "I allowed you to stop," he said, somewhat indignant. "Why are you still grinding?" Khan pointed to the prisoner in the next cell. "Do you see that man? He is a robber and murderer and you have him grinding

corn. Why should I mind grinding for my cause, which is pure and holy?"[43]

The conversation could have ended there; a holy man defying his guard even when the guard's actions were from good intentions. But Khan had sensed that he could help this guard, not by making promises or threats, but simply by being direct and honest with him about the guard's own situation: "'You are a good man,' Khan said. 'Why have you become part of this evil system?' 'I must feed my children.' Khan went back to grinding the corn. A few days later he found he had a different guard. The first man, he was told, had found another job."[44]

There is so much in this little event, and so much of it was unspoken. By working with his present circumstances, Khan became mindful that the guard was ready to be prodded to become even more caring than he had been when he allowed Khan to stop grinding the corn. He was ready to consider that his occupation, while important for feeding his children, was a source of suffering, for himself and others. Only a few well placed comments and questions were needed to precipitate the change in the guard. Instead of seizing upon an opportunity to relax, Khan mustered the strength to continue his efforts to help others. So even in jail, Khan could direct himself along the lines of the *virya paramita*.

Thich Nhat Hanh describes the *virya paramita* as "the perfection of diligence, energy, or continuous practice." It is a cultivation of the potential in ourselves and others to be helpful, and the desertion of the potential to be unhelpful. Describing these potentials as seeds, Hanh explains: "The Buddha said that in the depth of our store consciousness, *alayavijñana*, there are all kinds of positive and negative seeds—seeds of anger, delusion, and fear, and seeds of understanding, compassion, and forgiveness . . . . We should learn to recognize every one of these seeds in us in order to practice diligence."[45] We can help ourselves and others better when we cease to water the unhelpful seeds and water only the positive ones. Certainly, Khan could have watered seeds of resentment and bitterness when he responded to the guard, but he refrained. Instead, he watered seeds of compassion, helping the guard to recognize that in some ways he was just as much a prisoner as Khan himself.[46]

As such, Khan's efforts were also an example of right effort. Right effort (also known as right diligence) is one of the folds of the eightfold path and is an integral part of Buddhist practice. It is the effort to let go of unhelpful thoughts and feelings whenever they arise. It is also the effort to encourage and cultivate helpful thoughts and feelings whenever they arise. Indeed, Hanh describes right effort and the *virya paramita* in similar terms.[47] It requires being mindful of our thoughts and feelings. This is difficult because violence, hatred, anger and fear often blind us to our feelings and thoughts. Right effort, in conjunction with other aspects the eightfold path, such as right action, right livelihood and right speech, encourages us to act without violence. In doing so, we not only spare others of immediate harm, we also give ourselves a better opportunity to be mindful of the thoughts and feelings that motivate us. As we prune away those that are unhelpful, our actions can grow to better benefit both ourselves and others.

In the account of Khan's talk with the guard, we can also see several practices that support right effort. One is right mindfulness: Khan was not so wrapped up in his own suffering, or his own plans, that he overlooked a compassionate guard. Another practice is right speech: Khan spoke honestly to the guard. He did not threaten him or try to persuade him of anything. He simply explained what the true circumstances were: you are a good man helping to support an evil system. Indeed, this was the case: treatment in the jail was based on a prisoner's ability and willingness to pay bribes to the deputy jailer. After he heard the guard's excuse for working there, he did not lecture him about right livelihood, though something along those lines was what he was hinting at. Instead he practiced that other part of right speech: silence. Telling him to quit his job and find another would have been easy, but perhaps the silence allowed the guard to consider who was living a freer life, Khan in jail or a guard afraid to quit a job he deplored. We are left to wonder, but Khan's authority cannot be disregarded.

Another set of incidents at the same jail illustrates how right livelihood also nourished the right effort that Khan exercised. As mentioned earlier, most prisoners lived in a cycle of bribery and deceit. They paid bribes to the deputy jailer to avoid punishments such as solitary confinement or difficult chores. When they broke rules, they paid more bribes to avoid those punishments. Arguments sprang up between prisoners as their lives became more self-centered and unmindful of those around them. In all, their desire to avoid hard work and unpleasant circumstances, as well as to exercise a pretend freedom by breaking rules, led them into further trouble.

So, Khan would refuse to break rules. He would also refuse to pay bribes to avoid hard work or unpleasant circumstances. He would continue to grind his corn in solitary confinement. In a sense, he was practicing right livelihood. The labors he had been assigned were not, to be sure, jobs he had chosen, or for which he was receiving just compensation. Nevertheless, they were part of what he was called to do. He could have avoided the jail term he was serving, during the time just described, had he paid a bribe of sorts to British officials and promised to stop traveling around to villagers to help educate them. But he had refused both the bribe and promise, declaring that for him, educating others was as sacred a duty as doing one's daily prayers.[48] Grinding corn was just part of that vocation. But Khan understood that the consequences of how we take up that vocation can be momentous. I believe he would agree with Thich Nhat Hanh's explanation of Right Livelihood: "Our vocation can nourish our understanding and compassion, or erode them. We should be awake to the consequences, far and near, of the way we are earning our living."[49] Our present activities will have their consequences, so we must be mindful of them. The other prisoners' activities amplified the already corrupt interactions at the jail. Khan did not want to add to this.

But instead of adding to it, his efforts to go about his work mindfully, exercised authority among his fellow prisoners. People began to be drawn to his example. Many stopped paying the bribes and resigned themselves to carrying out their work like Khan. As the cycle of bribery slowed, so did the cycle of arguments and fights between prisoners.[50] Khan's activities exemplified right effort in that they drew others to better ways of living without verbal or physical force. His efforts were a *jihad* that came from understanding and compassion, rather than from fear.

Conclusion

When we understand Khan's efforts to transform the lives of people for the better, we can truly talk about a nonviolent *jihad*. Such a *jihad* is not conducted in place of a violent *jihad* based on a present state of physical or military weakness. It is a *jihad* that serves others as much as it serves ourselves. Like the Greater *Jihad*, *jihad* as right effort involves an inner striving to overcome the obstacles to a better way of living. But like the lesser *Jihad*, it draws us into the public world of service to others. It may be called serving God, or serving others as we follow God's Will. It may also be called being drawn into service by the fundamental richness of our present circumstances. In the end, the names are not as important as the effort itself which, I have argued, is justified in light of similar Buddhist practices. I have offered the example of Abdul Ghaffar Khan to illustrate this kind of effort in the context of Islam, but there are others. We can find examples of this *jihad* in any religious tradition, so long as we look past the other examples of effort that the media find easier to present.

Notes

1.Technically, the term "khan" simply means a tribal chief. Abdul Ghaffar Khan was also called Badshah Khan, which means "king of the khan." It was not a political title, but one given to him by fellow Pashtuns out of love and respect. I will often just refer to him as "Khan" in this paper for the sake of brevity.

2. Abdul Ghaffar Khan, *My Life and Struggle: Autobiography of Badshah Khan*, as narrated to K. B. Narang, trans. Helen H. Bouman (Delhi: Hind Pocket Books, Shiksha Bharati Press, 1969), 12. (This text transliterates Qur'an as "Koran.")

3. Abdul Ghaffar Khan, *My Life and Struggle*, 13.

4. Khan, *My Life and Struggle*, 14.

5. Khan, *My Life and Struggle*, 195.

6. D. G. Tendulkar, *Abdul Ghaffar Khan: Faith is a Battle* (Bombay: Gandhi Peace Foundation, Popular Prakashan, 1967), 128.

7. Tendulkar, *Abdul Ghaffar Khan*, 128.

8. Khan, *My Life and Struggle*, 28.

9. Tendulkar, *Abdul Ghaffar Khan*, 175.

10. Suhas Majumdar, *Jihad: The Islamic Doctrine of Permanent War*, (New Delhi: Voice of India, 1994, 2001), 12. Citing Q.4:77, the passage suggests that these people were afraid to lose their lives. A previous passage from this sura suggests a context of fighting for a just cause, not necessarily the expansion of Islam.

11. Majumdar, *Jihad*, 13.

12. Louay M. Safi, *Peace and the Limits of War: Transcending Classical Conception of Jihad*, (Herndon, Virginia: International Institute of Islamic Thought, 2001), 38-39. He cites Ibn Taymiyah.

13. Majumdar, *Jihad*, 6.

14. Abdul Aziz Said, Nathem C. Funk, Ayse S. Kadayifci, eds., *Peace and Conflict Resolution in Islam*, (Lanham, Md.: University Press of America, 2001), 8 (citing Q.2:256).

15. Hadith are writings about the life of the Prophet Muhammad, which include descriptions of his actions and habits, as well as sayings attributed to him. Information in the hadith is very influential, but not as influential, or revered, as that of the Qur'an.

16. Safi, *Peace and the Limits of War*, 6 (citing Q.29:69, 29:6, and 25:52), 42-43.

17. Majid Khadduri, *War and Peace in the Law of Islam* (Baltimore: The Johns Hopkins Press, 1955), 56.

18. One of my main sources for the biographical information about Abdul Ghaffar Khan is Eknath Easwaran, *Nonviolent Soldier of Islam: Badshah Khan, A Man to Match His Mountains* (Tomales, Calif.: Nilgiri Press, 1984, 1999).

19. Khan and his biographers often use the terms "Pathan" and "Pakhtun" to refer to Khan's culture, which is often referred to as "Pashtun" today.

20. *The Daily Express*, quoted in Tendulkar, *Abdul Ghaffar Khan*, 130.

21. Tendulkar, *Abdul Ghaffar Khan*, 85.

22. Tendulkar, *Abdul Ghaffar Khan*, 86.

23. Tendulkar, *Abdul Ghaffar Khan*, 85.

24. Khan, *My Life and Struggle*, 194.

25. Khan, *My Life and Struggle*, 15.

26. Khan, *My Life and Struggle*, 16.

27. Khan, *My Life and Struggle*, 17-18.

28. Khan, *My Life and Struggle*, 18.

29. Khan, *My Life and Struggle*, 36-7. The intense intolerance of the Taliban, from the suppression of Sufism to the destruction of the Buddha statues at Bamian are all the more painful and ironic, given the fact that the Taliban's power base was, and continues to be, the Pashtun tribes in Afghanistan and Pakistan, the very tribes of Khan and his nonviolent soldiers. It is not that people turned away from Khan's nonviolent message, but that the rulers of Pakistan, especially after 1948, acted to imprison, mistreat and/or murder Khan and his followers, since Khan openly likened them to the British for not making more strides toward democracy and for oppressing the Pashtuns.

30. Balkh had also been a center of Buddhism before the advent of Islam.

31. This is not to say that Islam did not also undergo changes as it spread. But in the teachings about *jihad*, there is very little of this flexibility for the purpose of truly helping others while, at the same time, respecting their religious traditions.

32. Pema Chödrön, *When Things Fall Apart: Heart Advice for Difficult Times* (Boston: Shambhala Publications, 1997), 99.

33. Pema Chödrön, *When Things Fall Apart*, 100.

34. Pema Chödrön, *When Things Fall Apart*, 101.

35. See Easwaran, *Nonviolent Soldier of Islam*, 41.

36. Robert Aitken, *The Practice of Perfection: The Paramitas from a Zen Buddhist Perspective* (New York: Pantheon Books, 1994), 17.

37. Aitken, *The Practice of Perfection*, 32.

38. Easwaran, *Nonviolent Soldier of Islam*, 71.

39. Aitken, *The Practice of Perfection*, 67.

40. Pema Chödrön, *When Things Fall Apart*, 106.

41. Pema Chödrön, *When Things Fall Apart*, 105.

42. Pema Chödrön, *When Things Fall Apart*, 106.

43. Easwaran, *Nonviolent Soldier of Islam*, 89.

44. Easwaran, *Nonviolent Soldier of Islam*, 89.

45. Thich Nhat Hanh, *The Heart of the Buddha's Teachings: Transforming Suffering into Peace, Joy, and Liberation* (New York: Broadway Books, 1998), 206.

46. Hanh, *Buddha's Teaching*, 206-209.

47. Hanh, *Buddha's Teaching*, 99-104.

48. Easwaran, *Nonviolent Soldier of Islam*, 83-84.

49. Hanh, *Buddha's Teaching*, 113.

50. Easwaran, *Nonviolent Soldier of Islam*, 89.

7

Standing Up to Terrorists: Buddhism, Human Rights, and Self-Respect

Christopher W. Gowans

In recent years, there has been considerable debate about whether or not Buddhism can provide support for, or is even consistent with, the contemporary idea of human rights. The predominant view is that there is considerable affinity between Buddhism and human rights. But some have dissented from this position. In my judgment, though there are grounds supporting a Buddhist embrace of human rights, this embrace has more difficulties and complications than are commonly recognized. In this essay, I draw attention to one difficulty that has received little attention, and I explore to what extent it may be overcome.

Many philosophers maintain that there are important connections between human rights and self-respect, connections that are reflected in many struggles for human rights. It is thought that the idea of human rights entails that we are morally permitted, and perhaps obliged, to have self-respect—where this means sometimes assertively demanding that other persons respect our rights. In this, there is an obvious implication for responding to terrorists. As commonly defined, terrorism involves outrageous violations of human rights, and our possession of human rights is thought to warrant actively opposing those who terrorize us.

In view of the Buddha's no-self teaching—and its associated values of non-attachment, compassion, forgiveness, etc.—it is natural to wonder whether followers of the Buddha could properly value human rights understood to imply the importance of self-respect. Could a sincere adherent of the Buddha's teaching stand up to terrorists who violate his or her human rights?

There has been a tendency to dismiss such concerns. Part of my argument is that there is a real issue here that those interested in Buddhism and human rights should not ignore. However, the balance of my argument is that a partial resolution of this issue is possible based on a distinction between the ideal of the fully enlightened person and the path required to attain this ideal. At the end, I propose that in this regard the Buddha's outlook implies a different approach to violations of our rights and to the threat of terrorism than is common in the West.

My concern is philosophical, not historical. I explore whether the teaching of the Buddha, as represented in the *Sutta Pitaka* of the Pali canon, is compatible with a particular feature of the contemporary idea of human rights, as expressed in interpretations of documents such as the *Universal Declaration of Human Rights* (affirmed by the United Nations in 1948).

A Problem for a Buddhist Embrace of Human Rights

To begin, recall the debate between Damien Keown and Craig K. Ihara. Keown claimed that, despite the fact that neither Pali nor Sanskrit has a word for 'rights', "the concept of rights is implicit in classical Buddhism."[1] His argument was simple. The Buddha explicitly endorsed many duties, and duties entail rights. Therefore, the Buddha implicitly endorsed many rights and hence employed the concept of rights. Keown went on to argue that "there is every reason why it would be proper for Buddhism" to affirm the *Universal Declaration*.[2]

The first premise of Keown's argument appears to have merit: In the "Sigalaka Sutta," the Buddha outlined numerous reciprocal obligations between parents and children, pupils and teachers, etc.[3] It is plausible to think of these obligations as duties. However, as Ihara pointed out, we should question the general thesis that duties entail rights (namely, that a person A has a duty to do X entails that another person B has a right to A's doing X).[4] This thesis has been widely discussed, and there are numerous apparent counter-examples. For instance, consider a citizen's duty to vote, a judge's duty to punish a criminal, a person's duty to give to charity, and a person's duty not to take his or her own life. In each case, it is hard to identify a specific person to whom the duty is owed and thus who may be said to have a right to performance of the duty.

In Keown's defense, it might be said that *some* duties entail rights. For example, many find it natural to suppose that a professor's duty to grade fairly entails a student's right to be graded fairly, and that a parent's duty to support his or her children entails a child's right to be supported by his or her parents. Moreover, these are just the sort of duties the Buddha appeared to endorse.

It would be a mistake, however, to rely on such intuitions to resolve the dispute. Persons in the modern Western world find it natural to think these duties entail rights because they already find it natural to think in terms of rights.

The conceptual framework of rights dominates their thinking. It does not follow that the Buddha also would have found this natural—or even intelligible. We should not suppose there are Platonic concepts of duties and rights to which we and the Buddha have equal access: Moral concepts are thoroughly embedded in historical and cultural contexts. In view of this, we need first to think carefully about what contemporary discourses and practices imply about the concept of human rights, and then to reflect on how well this concept might comport with the Buddha's teaching. When we do this, we will discover important affinities, but also deep divergences. Both need to be kept in mind.

In the human rights movement, the understanding of human rights has several multifaceted and complexly related dimensions. These include beliefs about the meaning of human rights, their justification, and the nature and relative importance of specific rights. The "Preamble" to the *Declaration* affirms its faith "in the dignity and worth of the human person and in the equal rights of men and women."[5] The delineation of rights in the articles that follow suggests that human rights are individual moral entitlements possessed equally by all human beings simply in virtue of being human. Human rights proponents generally agree that there are human rights so-defined. But what does it mean for a human being to possess an individual moral entitlement?

A prominent theme in philosophical accounts that resonates with much of the practice of human rights advocacy is that human rights and self-respect are closely connected. For example, Joel Feinberg says that "to think of oneself as the holder of rights is . . . . to have that minimal self-respect that is necessary to be worthy of the love and esteem of others."[6] Again, Robin S. Dillon holds that an important form of self-respect includes "understanding and properly valuing one's equal basic rights."[7] In a different connection, Jeffrie G. Murphy maintains that resentment responds "to wrongs against one's self" that include "direct violations of one's rights," and he believes that self-respect is the main value resentment defends. Someone who does not resent such wrongs, he says, "is almost necessarily a person lacking in self-respect."[8] The absence of self-respect is often called servility. According to Thomas E. Hill, Jr., we have a duty to avoid servility and to maintain self-respect. Servility, he says, results "from misunderstanding of one's rights" or "from placing a comparatively low value on them."[9] The importance of self-respect has also been ascribed to social movements supporting human rights. For example, Laurence Thomas argues that the 1960s civil rights movement "enhanced [the] self-respect" of blacks, and that "*the* goal" of the movement was to achieve precisely this.[10]

In these discussions, it is not always clear exactly what the connection between human rights and self-respect is thought to be—for example, whether it is conceptual or empirical, and whether human rights entail the importance of self-respect or the reverse (or both). For our purpose, what is important is the contention that to say persons have human rights implies that self-respect is a good, something that is morally permitted and perhaps morally obligatory. Let us call this the *self-respect conception of human rights*. That self-respect is a good, and that the idea of human rights implies that it is a good, is widely affirmed in contemporary Western accounts.

In these accounts, to have self-respect implies having a proper appreciation of one's value or worth, and living one's life in a manner that is consonant with this appreciation. Two forms of self-respect are commonly distinguished.[11] The first must be earned through the development one's moral character. Since persons differ in their moral character, self-respect in this sense is warranted in varying degrees: Those with a better character should have greater self-respect than those with a worse character. This is not what is primarily relevant here. The second form of self-respect implies a proper appreciation of one self's intrinsic value as a human being, where it is understood that each human being has the same intrinsic value (irrespective of what he or she does). This is what those who accept the self-respect conception of human rights typically have in mind. The *Declaration* affirms the equal worth and dignity of each person. In view of this, it seems reasonable to consider recognition of this fact about persons as a good: The person with self-respect, in this sense, has this recognition about him- or herself, and lives in accordance with it.

Often interpretations of human rights and self-respect develop an account of that in virtue of which human beings have equal worth and dignity. For example, Immanuel Kant believed rationality (understood in terms of autonomy) renders a person an end in himself in virtue of which "he possesses a *dignity* (an absolute inner worth)" that is "on a footing of equality" with all other rational beings. This, he says, "instills in him respect for himself."[12] In any case, the self-respect that the idea of human rights is thought to render important centrally involves the belief that one has an intrinsic worth that is equal to the worth of every other human being.

This understanding of self-respect is consistent with some variations in what specifically constitutes having self-respect. Though there is a core notion of affirming one's intrinsic worth as a human being, which feelings, attitudes and actions are involved in valuing one's intrinsic worth, which aspects of these are most important, and which modes of expressing this appreciation are proper—all these may differ to an extent through history and across cultures. In some cases—such as those concerning modes of dress, physical comportment, and manners of speech—these differences may be regarded as acceptable subjective variations. In other cases—such as how much importance should be assigned to attending to one's material well-being or to the development of one's talents—these differences may involve more significant issues about which it is important to try to resolve the disagreement.

Let us now consider a practical implication of self-respect that is often stressed in the West. In philosophical accounts of rights, a common theme is that living in accord with an appreciation of one's equal worth and dignity implies, in some circumstances, assertively demanding that other persons respect one's rights. "For a person to have human rights," Alan Gewirth says, "is for him to be in a position to make morally justified stringent, effective demands on other persons."[13] Jack Donnelly agrees: "A [first-person] rights claim...involves a powerful *demand* for action."[14] The best-known representative of this view is Feinberg. He argues:

> A world without claim-rights, no matter how full of benevolence and devotion to duty, would suffer an immense moral impoverishment. Persons would no longer hope for decent treatment from others on the ground of desert or rightful claim....The harm to individual self-esteem and character development would be incalculable. A claim-right, on the other hand, can be urged, pressed or rightly demanded against other persons. In appropriate circumstances the right-holder can "urgently, peremptorily, or insistently" call for his rights, or assert them authoritatively, confidently, unabashedly . . . . A right is something a man can *stand* on, something that can be demanded or insisted upon without embarrassment or shame.[15]

Elsewhere Feinberg writes that "not to claim in the appropriate circumstances that one has a right is to be spiritless or foolish."[16] Likewise, Hill says that a servile person, someone lacking self-respect, maintains a deferential attitude toward others "by acting as if his rights were nonexistent or insignificant."[17] Again, Bernard R. Boxill says: "The powerless but self-respecting person will declare his self-respect. He will protest. His protest affirms that he has rights."[18] Echoing this theme, Martin Luther King, Jr. writes: "freedom is never voluntarily given by the oppressor; it must be demanded by the oppressed."[19]

For our purpose, the key suggestion in these remarks is that having human rights implies not only that self-respect is a good, but that self-respect sometimes morally permits and may require assertively demanding that other persons respect one's rights. Let us call this the *self-assertive demand conception of human rights*. Though perhaps somewhat more controversial than the self-respect conception, the self-assertive demand conception resonates strongly with a good deal of discourse and practice in the human rights movement. Arguably, the extent to which this movement has been successful in bringing about respect for human rights is due in large part to the fact that people have assertively demanded that their rights be respected.

We can now see why it appears problematic for Buddhism to embrace human rights as understood in these two conceptions. The heart of the problem is the Buddha's no-self teaching. Let us first note some representative expressions of this teaching in the *Middle Length Discourses*. The Buddha says he teaches a path to overcoming suffering (*dukkha*) and does "not see any doctrine of self that would not arouse sorrow, lamentation, pain, grief and despair in one who clings to it." To overcome suffering we must cling to no doctrine of self. Moreover, a person who does not cling is someone who "personally attains *Nibbana*." An essential part of the path to this attainment is meditation. The Buddha tells his son to meditate so that "the conceit 'I am' will be abandoned." A person who has attained *Nibbana* does not even have the thought, "*I* have attained *Nibbana*." In short, "it cannot happen that a person possessing right view could treat anything as self."[20]

For the Buddha, our ultimate reality is a selfless reality, and the key to overcoming suffering and attaining *Nibbana* is the existential realization of our selflessness. It is obvious why this creates a problem for the self-respect and self-assertive demand conceptions of human rights. As Dillon says, "self-respect is respect for one's self,"[21] and this can hardly be considered a good if there is no self. Hence, it would seem that a Buddhist has reason to reject a conception of human rights that implies that self-respect is a good. If a fully enlightened person abandons the conceit 'I am', it is difficult to see how such a person could be morally permitted or required to assertively demand that other persons respect his or her rights. If a conception of human rights implies this, it would seem that a Buddhist has grounds for questioning that conception. Moreover, if the ideal is to live literally selflessly, then persons seeking to achieve this ideal might be expected to have reservations about the value of assertively demanding that other persons respect their rights.

Those who think Buddhism can and should embrace human rights may object that there is no real problem here because either the Buddha's teaching or the idea of human rights has been misunderstood. First, it might be argued that Buddhism does not preclude all senses of self. For example, a distinction was drawn early on in Buddhism between ultimate truth and conventional truth. It is said that though there are no selves in ultimate truth, there are selves in conventional truth (what we ordinarily think of as selves). However, though this distinction might be relevant to a solution, it does not show that there is no problem to be resolved: If in ultimate truth there are no selves, then the value of self-respect and related notions looks precarious. Those who affirm that self-respect is a good typically would deny that the self one is to respect ultimately is an illusion.

Second, it might be claimed that the basic idea of human rights does not require the self-respect or the self-assertive demand conceptions. However, much reflection and practice in the human rights movement suggests that this would significantly diminish, if not eviscerate, the idea. That each person has an inherent worth or dignity appears fundamental to human rights, and it seems a short step from this to a positive assessment of respect for this worth in oneself. Moreover, the value of individuals asserting their rights appears just as important. Not only would the human rights movement have a very different cast without this, many would agree with Feinberg that giving this up would be "an immense moral impoverishment."

Other preemptive dismissals of the problem may be proposed. But I urge that we pause long enough to recognize that there is an important issue here. We should not hastily endorse the compatibility between Buddhism and human rights. Doing so may prevent us from appreciating real obstacles within Buddhism to embracing human rights, obstacles that must be overcome if this embrace is to be genuine and enduring. Or it may preclude us from realizing that Buddhism suggests an understanding of human rights that is significantly different from Western accounts, an understanding that might teach valuable lessons to persons in the West. Buddhism and the human rights movement are deeply different normative outlooks, rooted in widely divergent historical and cultural contexts, philosophical orientations, and practical concerns. Reconciliation and accommodation should be understood more as a project to develop over time than something to accomplish promptly on the basis of brief reflection. In the remainder of this paper, I hope to move this project forward.

Towards a Resolution of the Problem

Let us begin by making some assumptions favorable to a Buddhist embrace of human rights. First, let us suppose there is a response to the objection that Buddhists need not worry about social justice because the doctrines of *kamma* and rebirth imply that the most important concern of justice—happiness in proportion to morality—is assured no matter what we do. Second, let us allow that there is an answer to the contention that seeking to attain the transcendent state of *Nibbāna* suggests that Buddhists should be rather indifferent to the ordinary affairs of this world. Third, let us agree that the central presupposition of human rights, that each person has inherent and equal dignity, may be justified from a Buddhist perspective—presumably because each person has the capacity for enlightenment. Fourth, let us grant that the Buddha's teaching would give followers of this teaching little or no reason to violate the rights specified in the *Declaration*. Finally, let us admit that many of the duties implied by the rights in the *Declaration*, such as the duty to respect human life and property, could be warranted from a Buddhist standpoint—for example, by reference to the basic ethical precepts. A positive Buddhist appraisal of human rights would have to defend each of these assumptions. For the sake of argument, let us suppose this could be done.

We also need an interpretation of the Buddha's no-self doctrine. It is widely recognized that his position implies a distinction between a primary sense in which there are no selves and a secondary sense in which there are selves (the distinction between ultimate and conventional truth suggests one form of this). There are many reasons such a distinction is required: The most obvious is that the doctrines of *kamma* and rebirth seem to presuppose a self. Here I can only summarize what I believe is the best understanding of this distinction.[22] Let us say that a substance-self is an entity that is distinct from other entities and has strict identity through time, while a process-self is a unified nexus of processes that are interdependent on other processes and in constant change. A process-self lacks distinctness and identity, and is consonant with the Buddha's teaching concerning dependent origination and impermanence. On my interpretation, the Buddha believed that substance-selves have no reality, but process-selves have a form of contingent reality. A person's process-self exists only insofar as the person mistakenly believes he or she is a substance-self, as manifested in craving, clinging, attachment, etc. As long as this mistaken outlook persists, the process-self will suffer and be reborn and suffer again, and so on. But it is possible to abandon the mistaken outlook and thereby overcome suffering. This is what happens when a person attains *Nibbana*, provisionally in this life and ultimately after death. With final *Nibbana*, the process-self ceases: All that remains is pure selfless existence beyond conditioning and change.

On the basis of this interpretation, it might be thought that there is something in the Buddha's teaching that could possess human rights and be objects of self-respect—namely, process-selves. However, in typical Western approaches, it is persons understood as substance-selves, as distinct entities with identity, that are thought to have the inherent dignity that makes them worthy of human rights and self-respect. For the Buddha, since process-selves depend on a mistaken outlook, and since full enlightenment ultimately brings about their elimination, it does not seem they could have the value Western approaches assign to substance-selves. I will argue that the idea of process-selves does have a role to play in a more positive Buddhist assessment of the self-respect and self-assertive demand conceptions of human rights. But the more fundamental consideration is our ultimate selflessness.

Such an assessment needs to consider both the ideal Buddhists aspire to achieve and the path to this ideal. In the *Sutta Pitaka*, the ideal is to be an *ara-*

hant—a "fully accomplished" person. The *arahant* has followed the Eightfold Path and grasped the transcendent reality of *Nibbana* in an enlightenment experience. The *arahant* is said to have "reached the true goal" and to be "completely liberated through final knowledge."[23] After death, he or she will permanently escape the cycle of rebirth and attain final *Nibbana*. But our concern is with the life of the *arahant* during the interval between the enlightenment experience and death. In this transitional stage, the *arahant's* process-self persists in many respects, but she has fully understood the Buddha's no-self teaching. Having attained "the perception of non-self in all things without exception," we are informed, the notions of 'I' and 'mine' vanish in the *arahant*.[24] She "has abandoned the conceit 'I am', has cut it off at the root."[25] True, "knowing the world's parlance," she employs 'I' and other personal pronouns in her speech. But she "uses such terms as mere expressions."[26] In all important respects, she does not *think* in these terms. For example, the *arahant* "has no such thought, 'There is one better than I; there is one who is equal; there is one who is worse'."[27] She does not even have the thought "*I* have attained *Nibbana*."[28]

How, then, does the *arahant* live? We are told that he "has abandoned craving" and "does not cling to anything in the world."[29] He has destroyed lust, hatred, and delusion,[30] and "evil unwholesome states…are far away from him."[31] In the *arahant*, "pride and contempt have fallen off like a mustard seed from the point of a needle."[32] He "resents nothing."[33] When he is struck, he does not "give way to anger."[34] On the contrary, he "is friendly amidst the hostile, peaceful amidst the violent."[35] The *arahant* is "kindly and dwell[s] compassionate towards all living beings."[36] He is calm in thought, speech and deed,[37] and he "utters gentle, instructive, and truthful words."[38]

In view of this description, how might the *arahant* be depicted with regard to human rights? On the one hand, it is evident that, as friendly, kind, and compassionate, the *arahant* would be very unlikely to violate anyone's human rights. In this respect, she has considerable affinity with this contemporary moral outlook. On the other hand, a different perspective emerges when we consider the self-respect and self-assertive demand conceptions of human rights. The first of these takes the idea of human rights to imply that self-respect is a good, that the belief that one's self has an intrinsic worth equal to all other persons is morally permitted and perhaps obligatory. Since the *arahant* is regarded as wholly good, but as having no thoughts pertaining to herself, self-respect would not be a good for her. Of course, the *arahant* does think there is a sense in which all human beings have an equal inherent worth insofar as they all have the capacity for enlightenment. It is just that, having no thoughts concerning herself, she does not apply this general truth to herself. She does not have self-respect, nor does she think she should or even may have it. Hence, a conception of human rights that says self-respect is always a good is incompatible with the Buddhist ideal of the *arahant*.

The self-assertive demand conception says that the idea of human rights implies that on some occasions people may or should assertively demand that other persons respect their rights. It is evident that the *arahant* would not do this on any occasion, and would not think he may or should make these demands. This is clearly implied by the passages quoted above. Moreover, we are told that the *arahant* is one "who without resentment endures abuse, beating, and punishment, whose power, real might, is patience."[39] This is obviously not a person who values assertively demanding that his rights be respected. Therefore, a human rights conception that says such demands are sometimes good conflicts with the Buddhist assertion that *arahant* is the ideal. It should not be supposed that the *arahant* has nothing to say to terrorists and others who violate people's rights. However, this will take the form, not of standing up for himself, but of speaking honestly, kindly, and gently so as to guide the perpetrators of these violations to a better way. The *arahant* has compassion for oppressors and oppressed alike, for both terrorists and their victims.[40]

Does this mean the *arahant* is servile? It might seem that it does: She lacks self-respect and acts as if her own rights are insignificant. But this is misleading. As ordinarily understood, the idea that self-respect is good and servility bad presupposes that each of us is a distinct self with identity. The servile person is thought of as a substance-self who mistakenly believes (or acts as if) she has less inherent worth than other substance-selves. Since the *arahant* rejects the presupposition that we are substance-selves, the issue of the value of self-respect and servility (as ordinarily understood) does not arise for her. She does not think she is a self who has less inherent worth than other selves. She does not make any comparisons between herself and others. Hence, though the *arahant* does not have or value self-respect, the same can be said of servility as well.

Since the Buddha taught that the *arahant* is the ideal, and the *arahant* neither has self-respect nor demands that his rights be respected, there are Buddhist grounds for having reservations about the self-respect and self-assertive demand conceptions of human rights. However, this is only part of the story. The *arahant* is an exceptional person, to say the least. Though the Buddha thought each of us could become an *arahant* eventually (meaning in this or some future life), he also thought this goal was very difficult to achieve. Much of his teaching pertains to the path we need to follow to reach this goal. The Buddha believed we ordinarily live as if we are substance-selves and suffer on account of this mistaken perspective. The path he taught is a complex set of intellectual, moral, and meditative disciplines that are meant to effect a radical transformation of a person from this state to the state of an *arahant*, from giving primacy to (what we take to be) ourselves to living selflessly. He thought this transformation typically involved stages of progress. For example, in a standard description, he said a person could become a stream-enterer, then a once-returner, then a non-returner, and finally an *arahant*.[41] Each of the three preliminary stages denotes both a level of accomplishment and a set of goals made possible by that accomplishment. At least for most of us, we cannot become *arahants* all at once.

The Buddha suggested that in some respects our moral orientation should change as we progress through the stages to full enlightenment: the greater our progress, the higher our immediate moral aspirations. We might think of this as similar to a person who undertakes a long program of training to reach a physically high level of achievement—for example, a weight-lifter or a ballet dancer. Suppose the ultimate goal is to lift 350 pounds or to perform a difficult sequence of leaps. Most persons starting out the program should not try to do this right away: Doing so is likely to result in injury and to impede progress toward the goal. If a weight-lifter has been successful in lifting 150 pounds, then it would be reasonable to try to lift a bit more, say 175 pounds (but not, in the immediate future, 200 pounds); and similarly for the ballet dancer. Through a process of increasingly demanding training, the ultimate goal might be reached. But at a given stage, what these persons ought to do is determined by both the ultimate goal and the current level of achievement: They ought to move toward the goal in a manner that is feasible given what they have done so far. This may be seen as an 'ought-implies-can' principle. Similarly, what a person on the Buddhist path to enlightenment ought to do is determined by both the goal of *arahantship* and the current level of progress on the path. The goal is to live selflessly, but what ought to be done at a given time will depend on the extent to which a person's initial orientation to think in terms of self has been transformed by the existential realization of selflessness.

This means that in some respects different people will have different moral standards depending on their progress on the path (though the Buddha thinks there are some minimal standards that apply to all persons). This recognition of different moral standards may appear to entail a denial of the principle of universalizability, but it is consistent with one version of this principle: It might still be said that everyone *at a given stage of progress* ought to act in the same way.

Once we see this developmental framework, it becomes possible to suppose that it is good for some persons on the path to have self-respect, and to demand that their rights be respected, even though these things are not good for the *arahant*—the ideal that constitutes the goal of the path. The Buddha does not directly say this: He is not concerned to address the positive evaluation of these self-orientations that is so common in our culture. But a Buddhist position on this issue may be constructed based on what he does say.

In order to understand the idea of moral development, let us consider one important factor in the Buddha's depiction of progress on the path—overcoming what he calls the fetter of ill-will. He says that the non-returner destroys ill-will, while the once-returner attenuates it.[42] The context implies that the stream-enterer has not even attenuated it (or perhaps has done so only to a very limited degree). Moreover, the Buddha says that "the underlying tendency to ill-will lies within" infants and later becomes "habitual" as they grow older.[43] The overall picture is that we are born with a tendency to ill-will that becomes ingrained in our character, but this tendency can gradually be overcome and finally eliminated. The Buddha believes ill-will is rooted in the belief that one is a self distinct from other selves. Hence, as the realization of selflessness grows, the tendency to ill-will diminishes. Someone at the stream-enterer stage has some ill-will and should strive to attenuate it, but it may be too soon to try to destroy it completely. At this stage, a measure of ill-will is accepted, so long as efforts are made to diminish it. By contrast, someone at the once-returner stage should try to destroy it altogether. What a person ought to do with respect to ill-will is determined by his or her progress on the path.

This only takes us so far. There is no suggestion that ill-will is considered good for a person at any stage on the path. Ill-will is provisionally allowed in the stream-enterer: It is not favorably evaluated. However, there is a collection of self-oriented values that are frequently assessed positively for persons on the path. For example, the Buddha says, "you should live as islands unto yourselves, being your own refuge, with no one else as your refuge."[44] Moreover, he emphasizes the character traits of "self-restraint," "self-control," and "self-examination."[45] Much of his teaching stresses the importance of self-discipline. Thus, one step on the Eightfold Path—right effort—states that an adherent "awakens zeal...makes effort, arouses energy, exerts his mind, and strives" to have wholesome states and be free of unwholesome ones.[46]

The repeated affirmations of the great value of various forms of self-reliance and self-discipline show that the Buddha believes many persons on the path should be encouraged to have self-oriented values in some sense. There is much emphasis in his teaching on what we might call individual responsibility. Though presumably persons following this teaching have some grasp of the no-self doctrine, the Buddha implicitly recognizes that many of them nonetheless continue to have a powerful propensity to think and act as if they were substance-selves. As a result, their process-selves persist in significant ways. The values of self-reliance and the like are meaningful and necessary for persons in this condition. For example, in order to overcome hatred, persons need to examine and regulate an ensemble of feelings and beliefs that are part of their process-selves. However, as these persons gain a deeper realization of their selflessness, these self-oriented endeavors may be expected to become less important. With the full enlightenment of the *arahant*, they will have no significance at all.

This feature of the Buddha's teaching provides us with a model for a Buddhist understanding of the value of self-respect in the modern world. Self-respect typically means having an appropriate appreciation of one's intrinsic and equal value as a human being. On the Buddhist approach, we may suppose, human beings have intrinsic and equal worth on account of their capacity for enlightenment. Strictly speaking this capacity is not a feature of one's self since ultimately there is no self. Rather, pure selfless existence is a hidden dimension of each person that enlightenment reveals. The worth of human beings is rooted in this dimension and our capacity to discover it. However, given the strong tendency to think and act as if we were selves, even among persons on the path, we find it natural to think of the capacity for enlightenment as a feature of ourselves. In recognition of this, it may be said that *Buddhist self-respect* is having a proper appreciation of "one self's" capacity for enlightenment, a capacity shared equally with all other human beings. Though the term 'self-respect' is literally a misnomer in this context, and the Buddha does not employ it, Buddhist self-respect nonetheless may have an important role to play for contemporary followers of the Buddha still in the grip of self-oriented ways of thinking and being—for reasons similar to those supporting the value of self-reliance and the like. For example, each of us needs to have confidence that he or she can attain enlightenment, and it is natural to base this on the belief that "one's self" has this capacity. But as our realization of selflessness deepens, such "self-respect" will become less important (though presumably not the confidence), and it will disappear altogether in the *arahant*. Hence, it can be said that self-respect so-understood is sometimes a good for persons on the path even though it is not a good in any sense for an *arahant*.

It might also be said that assertively demanding that one's rights be respected is a good for some persons on the path. In direct ways, violation of a person's rights can significantly impede pursuit of the path to enlightenment. Such oppression often damages a person psychologically by communicating the message that the person has little or no worth, and this might undermine Buddhist self-respect. Given our habitual understanding of commitment, as involving something "one's self" is determined to do, a person committed to the Buddhist path may have reason to express resistance to oppression and to demand that his or her rights be respected (recall the Buddha's own determination to seek enlightenment in the face of parental opposition). As with self-reliance and self-discipline, this may have important instrumental value in pursuing enlightenment. It might even be said that, at early stages, failure to make such demands is a sign that a person is not really committed to the Buddhist path. However, once again, this is only because the person is still in the grip of living as if he or she was a substance-self. As the person is liberated from this grip, different moral perspectives open, and eventually that of the *arahant* may be attained.

Since a person on the path may have reason to endorse the value of having Buddhist self-respect and of sometimes demanding respect for his or her rights, Buddhism is compatible with qualified forms of the self-respect and the self-assertive demand conceptions of human rights: It can allow that for persons not yet fully enlightened self-respect and assertively demanding that one's rights be respected are sometimes good. To this extent, the apparent incompatibility between Buddhism and these conceptions may be overcome. This is a significant conclusion, but it must be qualified in three respects.

First, Western accounts typically presuppose that distinct selves with identity possess human rights and to deserve self-respect. The Buddha's no-self teaching is a metaphysically incompatible understanding of human nature. It maintains that the only sense in which we are selves is as interdependent and ever-changing process-selves. Moreover, these selves are maintained by a delusion: Our ultimate reality is pure selfless existence. It is this reality and our capacity to realize it that is the source of our worth, not the fact that we are substance-selves or process-selves.

Second, Western defenses of the value of self-respect and demanding that one's rights be respected usually take this value to have deep and far-reaching moral significance. For example, Dillon cites a long list of Western moral philosophers who have recognized that self-respect has "profound moral importance."[47] Self-respect and standing up for one's rights cannot be said to have this significance in an account based on the Buddha's teaching. They have only provisional worth as "skillful means" to enlightenment.

Finally, it makes a difference that the ideal of the *arahant* is the focal point of the Buddhist picture. Buddhist self-respect may be an instrumental good for a person on the path, but the ultimate goal of the path is a selfless state in which self-respect has no place. The follower of the path is committed to transcending self-respect. Likewise, demanding that one's rights be respected may also be an instrumental good, but the aim is a transformation that makes possible a higher moral perspective. Near the beginning of *The Dhammapada*, we hear these words: "'He abused me, he struck me, he overpowered me, he robbed me'— those who harbour such thoughts do not still their hatred."[48] Since the aim is to overcome hatred, followers of the Buddha eventually need to strive to move beyond thoughts of resentment towards those who have violated their rights. This ideal takes us considerable distance away from Murphy's defense of resentment and Feinberg's praise for the man who stands up for his rights.

Two Approaches to Human Rights

My argument has been that a partial reconciliation is possible between the Buddha's teaching and the self-respect and self-assertive demand conceptions of human rights. Though they share much common ground, they also imply rather different approaches to our encounter with terrorists and others who violate our rights. Proponents of the human rights conceptions typically portray human beings as distinct selves who should be confident about their own inherent and equal worth, and who may and sometimes should stand up and aggressively challenge those who fail to respect this worth by violating their rights. This suggests, and is frequently associated with, a *politics of confrontation* that is a familiar feature of the modern world. In this politics, self-respect is sometimes thought to appropriately issue in anger and resentment towards oppressors, along with emphatic demands that they immediately change their ways.

By contrast, the Buddha's teaching allows that the politics of confrontation has a place for many persons, but falls short of an ideal to which we all ought to aspire. Its place is secured by the value persons on the path to enlightenment may give to Buddhist self-respect and demanding respect for their own rights. However, the ideal we ought to strive for is rather different—a *politics of reconciliation* rooted in the belief, not that human beings are distinct selves, but that we are all interconnected and have the capacity for liberation from suffering through the realization of our ultimate selflessness. From this perspective, we should have compassion and loving-kindness for both oppressors and the oppressed, for terrorists as well as their victims; and we should try to end violations of human rights, not through angry and resentful demands, but through moral example along with gentle, peaceful, and truthful persuasion and encouragement. This is not indifference or passivity, but it is not confrontation either. The aim is not merely to modify behavior, but to move hearts and minds. The underlying value is more compassion than respect.

Arahantship is an extraordinary ideal by any measure, and no doubt most followers of the Buddha are far from attaining it. For them, the politics of confrontation may have a natural and proper role to play in their lives. But it matters that the *arahant* is the ideal, that there is a fundamental commitment to work to transcend the politics of confrontation and move towards the politics of reconciliation. This commitment is a distinctive contribution Buddhism brings to contemporary human rights concerns, and it marks a difference from many Western approaches to human rights violations. By way of conclusion, I want to suggest that the debate about Buddhism and human rights, as well as discussions of Buddhist responses to terrorism, would benefit from further dialogue about the respective merits of these two approaches. To get a sense of relevant issues, let us consider some criticisms that may be advanced by advocates of the politics of confrontation against the politics of reconciliation, and briefly discuss how Buddhists might respond to these criticisms.

An initial objection is that an *arahant* would allow him or herself to be used by terrorists and others intent upon oppression, and so could be an unwitting tool of evil. Hence, *arahantship* is not a legitimate ideal. A Buddhist response would point out that an *arahant* is not passive. Though there is no standing up for oneself, the life of an *arahant* is animated by loving-kindness for all beings. An alternative to evil is manifestly present, though not in the mode of confrontation. The extraordinary life of an *arahant* is thought to have tremendous transforming power. An *arahant* radiates compassion, generosity, and forgiveness, and thereby demonstrates what these values really mean and why they have such importance—as well as the fact that human beings are capable of living in accordance with them. Hence, an *arahant* can have great, practical effect in the world, and those on the path to *arahantship* can have a similar but lesser effect in proportion to the progress they have made. There is no suggestion of silently or indifferently allowing oppression to march forward, much less tacitly advancing its aims. Passivity is not the only alternative to confrontation.

A related objection is that it is doubtful that the politics of reconciliation could be as effective as the politics of confrontation in ending terrorism and bringing about respect for human rights. A Buddhist approach, it may be said, is unrealistic and utopian. There is no question that the politics of confrontation has often achieved good results. However, a Buddhist perspective would invite us to look more closely at these results. Confrontation might modify behavior in the short-term, but deep and long-lasting change requires inner transformation. This is a central theme in the Buddha's teaching. For this purpose, reconciliation may be more effective than confrontation. From a Buddhist standpoint, it might also be questioned how much significance should be assigned to these consequentialist considerations. For a person who has realized selflessness, compassion and loving-kindness are self-evidently good ways of relating to human beings. They are not justified simply on the ground that they produce the best results as commonly understood.

In this connection, it may be objected, more pointedly, that an adequate response to terrorism sometimes requires a strong form of the politics of confrontation that employs violence to prevent terrorist attacks. Respect for human rights, it may be said, implies a willingness to use force to prevent violations of those rights, whether the violations are of one's own rights or the rights of other persons. The objection is that Buddhism, with its emphasis on nonviolence, could never permit the use of violence for this reason.

There certainly is an emphasis on nonviolence in the Buddha's teaching. One of the ethical parts of the Eightfold Path, right action, includes "abstaining from killing living beings." "With rod and weapon laid aside, gently and kindly," we are told, a follower of the Buddha "abides compassionate to all living beings."[49] The use of violence to compel others to respect one's rights appears deeply contrary to the teaching of the Buddha.

Some contemporary socially engaged Buddhists interpret this teaching as implying strict pacifism, the view that violence is never justified no matter what the circumstances or consequences. However, the Pali canon does not directly support this position. Pacifism is not explicitly affirmed, and some texts suggest that violence may sometimes be permitted and that there may be room for flexibility in applying moral rules. In general, the Buddha's teaching contains a variety of ethical elements, duties as well as virtues, and the commitment to nonviolence is one of its central elements. But his teaching does not directly address theoretical issues such as the justification, scope, and qualifications of moral rules, and it does not confront the complex questions contemporary pacifism needs to face about the relationship between absolute prohibitions and consequentialist considerations.

It could plausibly be argued that progress toward enlightenment involves a gradual reduction of the occasions when violence would be warranted or permitted. However, it does not follow that the *arahant* is completely nonviolent. Indeed, though an *arahant* is said to be "peaceful amidst the violent,"[50] it might be argued that true Buddhist compassion requires using minimal force to protect innocent persons from terrorist attacks when nothing else will do so. Moreover, even if an *arahant* were completely nonviolent, it would not follow that those on the path to enlightenment should be. Indeed, the model of progress suggests the contrary. Asoka, the famous 3rd century BCE Indian political leader, explicitly advocated Buddhism in his edicts, yet still maintained his army.

What the Buddhist emphasis on nonviolence clearly insists on is that we never simply assume a violent response is justified, even when—perhaps especially when—it seems most natural and necessary. Rather, we are to interrogate relentlessly the motivations underlying such a response with an array of inquiries rooted in the Buddha's teaching. In the case at hand, we should ask questions such as: Would violence directed at actual or potential terrorists truly be rooted in compassion and loving-kindness rather than the self-centered reactions of fear, anger, and hatred? Would a violent response actually reduce the likelihood of terrorist attacks or would it be more likely to deter some terrorists only by creating many more? Is there a nonviolent alternative that more fully expresses our commitment to compassion for all persons, and that is more likely to bring about a reduction in terrorism in the long run? Have we carefully considered the possibility that our own actions—perhaps rooted in greed, indifference, or hostility—have given terrorists reason to oppose us? Could it be that terrorist actions, though clearly unjustified, are nonetheless inspired by injustice for which we ourselves have some responsibility?

As followers of the Buddha advance on the path to full enlightenment, increasingly they should and are able to pursue such questions with the utmost seriousness. This suggests that a Buddhist response to the objection that terrorism must be opposed with violence would be complex. There certainly is a deep skepticism about all forms of violence in our lives, and an imperative constantly to seek alternatives even when the end is obviously good and violent means appear to be just and effective. This implies a critique of the common view in the United States that violence is obviously the main way to confront terrorism. On the other hand, Buddhism is not unconcerned about consequences. It does not suppose that consequences are the only thing that matters, that we ought to do whatever would have the best overall consequences. Basic moral precepts, such as those classified under right action and right speech, as well as fundamental virtuous dispositions such as compassion, loving-kindness and generosity are the central sources of guidance. These permit and indeed sometimes require consideration of consequences, but they also enjoin us to act appropriately towards each living being. It is up to each practitioner to apply these values in particular circumstances, consistent with his or her progress on the path. There is no Buddhist algorithm for doing this.

Proponents of the politics of confrontation may say that there is danger of naiveté in this stance. But the Buddha's teaching tells us that there is a much greater danger in uncritically following our natural instincts towards violence and acquiescing to the ease with which we find "good reasons" to resort to it. From the standpoint of consequences, there is greater courage in seeking to break the cycle of violence than in perpetuating yet another round of it.

Another criticism from the politics of confrontation is that self-respect and assertively demanding that one's rights be respected need not issue in hate, nor even anger or resentment. It may be said that appropriate expressions of self-respect are compatible with, and in fact should be shaped partly by, compassion and love for others. This touches on a fundamental feature of the Buddha's *Dhamma*. It may be allowed that this is true up to a point. But the Buddhist position is that attachment to self is always problematic in the end: It inevitably pulls us toward anger, resentment, hatred, etc. Hence, any belief in one's self and its importance tends to work against compassion and loving-kindness in the long run.

Finally, it might be argued that the ideal of the *arahant* is so extraordinarily difficult to attain that most followers of the Buddha could embrace the politics of confrontation virtually without qualification. The aforementioned issues arise only for the handful of persons at or near the goal of *arahantship*. For all other Buddhists, there is no real obstacle to embracing the self-respect and self-assertive demand conceptions of human rights. Here a Buddhist might respond by saying that, as long as ideals are taken seriously, they do make a practical difference. Hence, even for a person who has made little progress on the path, the ideal of the *arahant* guides life in significant ways, ways that may not be evident to persons who reject the ideal and advocate a contrary approach.

These are some of the issues that should be pursued in a debate about whether a Buddhist politics of reconciliation ought to be an ideal. In this short synopsis, I have not tried to resolve these issues. My point is that, however much common ground they share, most Western approaches to human rights differ in important respects from what the Buddha's teaching implies, and from a Buddhist perspective, these approaches would benefit from reflection on this teaching.

Let me bring this discussion to a close by relating it to His Holiness the Dalai Lama, a prominent Buddhist proponent of human rights who has had much tragic personal experience with those who have violated these rights in Tibet. He says, "it is natural and just for nations, peoples and individuals to demand respect for their rights." I have tried to show how it could make sense for a Buddhist to think this. But he offers this remark in the context of a broader argument that stresses the overriding importance of compassion and universal responsibility as the central values that are important in bringing about respect for human rights. For example, he says that "in relation to the question of human rights violations and concern for human rights, the key point is the practice of compassion, love, and forgiveness."[51] I have also tried to show why this argument expresses the deeper moral truth from a Buddhist standpoint.[52]

Notes

1. Damien Keown, "Are There Human Rights in Buddhism?" in *Buddhism and Human Rights*, eds. Damien Keown, Charles S. Prebish, and Wayne R. Husted (Richmond Surrey: Curzon, 1998)., 22.

2. Keown, "Human Rights," 31.

3. Maurice Walshe, trans., *The Long Discourses of the Buddha* (Boston: Wisdom Publications, 1987), 467-68.

4. See Craig K. Ihara, "Why There are No Rights in Buddhism: A Reply to Damien Keown," in *Buddhism and Human Rights*, 44.

5. "Universal Declaration of Human Rights," in *The United Nations and Human Rights 1945-1995*, ed. United Nations Department of Public Information (New York: United Nations Reproduction Section, 1995), 153.

6. Joel Feinberg, "The Nature and Value of Rights," in *Rights, Justice, and the Bounds of Liberty: Essays in Social Philosophy* (Princeton, N.J.: Princeton University Press, 1980), 151. Cf. 155.

7. Robin S. Dillon, "How to Lose Your Self-Respect," *American Philosophical Quarterly* 29 (1992): 133.

8. Jeffrie G. Murphy, "Forgiveness and Resentment," in Jeffrie G. Murphy and Jean Hampton, *Forgiveness and Mercy* (Cambridge: Cambridge University Press, 1988), 16.

9. Thomas E. Hill Jr., "Servility and Self-Respect," *The Monist* 57 (1973): 97.

10. Laurence Thomas, "Self-Respect: Theory and Practice," in *Philosophy Born of Struggle: Anthology of Afro-American Philosophy from 1917*, ed. Leonard Harris (Dubuque, Iowa: Kendall/Hunt Publishing Company, 1983), 181.

11. For example, see Dillon, "Self-Respect," 133-34.

12. Immanuel Kant, *The Metaphysics of Morals*, trans. Mary Gregor (Cambridge: Cambridge University Press, 1991), 435-36 (Prussian Academy pagination).

13. Alan Gewirth, *Human Rights: Essays on Justification and Applications* (Chicago: The University of Chicago Press, 1982), 11.

14. Jack Donnelly, *Universal Human Rights in Theory and Practice* (Ithaca, N.Y.: Cornell University Press, 1989), 10.

15. Joel Feinberg, *Social Philosophy* (Englewood Cliffs, N.J.: Prentice-Hall, 1973), 58. Feinberg is speaking of legal claim-rights here, but later he relates these to human rights, understood as existing independently of legal institutions (see 84 ff.).

16. Feinberg, "Nature and Value of Rights," 151.

17. Hill, "Servility and Self-Respect," 97.

18. Bernard R. Boxill, "Self-Respect and Protest," *Philosophy & Public Affairs* 6 (1976): 69.

19. Martin Luther King, Jr., "Letter from Birmingham Jail," in *Why We Can't Wait* (New York: New American Library, 1964), 80.

20. Bhikkhu Nanamoli and Bhikkhu Bodhi, trans., *The Middle Length Discourses of the Buddha* (Boston: Wisdom Publications, 1995), 231, 163, 531, 846, and 928.

21. Dillon, "Self-Respect," 133.

22. For more details, see Christopher W. Gowans, *Philosophy of the Buddha* (London: Routledge, 2003), pt. 2.

23. *Middle Length Discourses*, 87.

24. Nyanaponika Thera and Bhikkhu Bodhi, trans., *Numerical Discourses of the Buddha: An Anthology of Suttas from the Anguttara Nikaya* (Walnut Creek Calif.: AltaMira Press, 1999), 177.

25. *Middle Length Discourses*, 233.

26. Bhikkhu Bodhi, trans., *The Connected Discourses of the Buddha*, vol. 1 (Boston: Wisdom Publications, 2000), 102.

27. *Numerical Discourses*, 165.

28. *Middle Length Discourses*, 846.

29. *Middle Length Discourses*, 233 and 344.

30. See *Connected Discourses*, vol. 2, 1295.

31. *Middle Length Discourses*, 370.

32. Acharya Buddharakkhita, trans., *The Dhammapada: The Buddha's Path of Wisdom* (Kandy, Sri Lanka: Buddhist Publication Society, 1985), sec. 407.

33. *Dhammapada*, sec. 95.

34. *Dhammapada*, sec. 389 (taking the holy man to be an arahant).

35. *Dhammapada*, sec. 406.

36. *Numerical Discourses*, 217.

37. See *Dhammapada*, sec. 96.

38. *Dhammapada*, sec. 408.

39. *Dhammapada*, sec. 399.

40. It should also not be supposed that the *arahant* is completely unconcerned with his well-being. See F.L. Woodward, trans., *The Book of the Gradual Sayings*, vol. 2

(1933; reprint, Oxford: Pali Text Society, 1962), 186. This follows from the fact that he is a person and is concerned with the well-being of all persons. But he is not concerned, we might say, with his well-being *as his own.*

41. For example, see *Middle Length Discourses*, 235-36.

42. For example, see *Middle Length Discourses*, 116 and 235-36.

43. *Middle Length Discourses*, 538.

44. *Long Discourses*, 245.

45. Respectively: F.L. Woodward, trans., *The Book of the Gradual Sayings*, vol. 1 (1932; reprint, Oxford: Pali Text Society, 1960), 139; *Dhammapada*, sec. 159; and *Numerical Discourses*, 250. The use of 'self' in such expressions is not merely the result of translation.

46. *Middle Length Discourses*, 1100.

47. Robin S. Dillon, "Introduction," in *Dignity, Character, and Self-Respect*, ed. Robin S. Dillon (New York: Routledge, 1995), 2.

48. *Dhammapada*, sec. 3.

49. *Middle Length Discourses*, 1100 and 914.

50. *Dhammapada*, sec. 406.

51. Dalai Lama, "Humanity's Concern for Human Rights," in *Reflections on the Universal Declaration of Human Rights: A Fiftieth Anniversary Anthology*, eds. Barend van der Heijden and Bahia Tahzib-Lie (The Hague: Martinus Nijhoff Publishers, 1998), 105 and 102.

52. I have benefited from valuable comments on this paper from Coleen Gowans, Doug Allen, and several participants at the Society for Asian and Comparative Philosophy Asilomar conference held in May 2003.

8

The Bodhisattva Code and Compassion: A Mahayana Buddhist Perspective on Violence and Nonviolence

Wendy Donner

The foundation of Buddhist ethics features the first precept of non-harm that rules out violent intentional killing. Mahayana Buddhism, with its central emphasis on the bodhisattva and compassion, qualifies the foundational teaching in several respects. In Mahayana ethics, the bodhisattva acting from compassion, not anger, may justifiably use force and even kill in extreme situations to prevent greater suffering. In this paper I explore this Mahayana perspective using the writings of the Dalai Lama, Robert Thurman and other Buddhist thinkers.[1]

Mahayana Buddhism and the Bodhisattva

According to Paul Williams, a bodhisattva in the Mahayana Great Vehicle tradition is a "being who has taken the vow to be reborn, no matter how many times this may be necessary, in order to attain the highest possible goal, that of Complete and Perfect Buddhahood for the benefit of all sentient beings."[2] The bodhisattva is a generator of great compassion, and his or her actions are directed at helping other beings. The sutra says: "Great compassion . . . takes hold of him. He surveys countless beings with his heavenly eye, and what he sees fills him with great agitation . . . . And he attends to them with the thought that: 'I shall become a saviour to all those beings, I shall release them from all their sufferings!'"[3]

The Prajnaparamita sutras differentiate this goal or aspiration from that of non-Mahayana traditions, in which the aspiration is personal liberation. The

123

bodhisattva does not aspire to the enlightenment of the non-Mahayana schools, the goal of which is to become an arhat, who seeks individual liberation and a form of nirvana that is the cessation of mind and body. On the contrary, "the Bodhisattva regards the pursuit of liberation as something to be achieved by oneself and for oneself in isolation from others as a misguided aspiration. Bodhisattvas are unwilling to be satisfied merely by securing their own liberation and, deeply moved by the sight of the sufferings of other sentient beings, feel compassion for them and determine to become Buddhas so as to be able to provide the maximum benefit to others."[4] In other words, the goal is the welfare and liberation of all beings and the means to that goal is the bodhisattva's attainment of Buddhahood. Indeed, Taigen Dan Leighton argues that it is viewed as "the fundamental violation of the spirit of bodhisattva ethics" to attempt to attain individual awakening and so abandon the realm of suffering.[5]

The path to Buddhahood takes eons. The practices are many forms of the ten perfections: generosity, ethics, patience, effort, meditation, wisdom, skillful means, powers, vow (aspiration), and pristine awareness (innate wakefulness).[6] The wisdom of emptiness is the object. It is wisdom that "destroys the ignorance that mistakenly believes that persons and phenomena exist in and of themselves, as solid, autonomous, intrinsic entities."[7] As progress on the path increases, the wisdom of emptiness deepens, and abilities to help others correspondingly increase. Buddhist teaching and history are a treasure-trove of myths and stories of the panorama of enlightened activity of bodhisattvas acting to help sentient beings. They act in their various guises—from the extraordinary to the ordinary, from the awesome and radiant to the mundane, and from the visionary and transcendent to the immanent.[8] The nirvana of the bodhisattva is non-abiding nirvana, "a nirvana which embodies two dimensions—the upward movement away from samsara, away from greed, hatred, and delusion, and a downward movement returning to the maelstrom of samsaric institutions and persons out of compassion."[9]

Mahayana Buddhism changes the qualifications for becoming a bodhisattva, so that the path to Buddhahood opens to those who are able to feel the compassion and the intention to take on the sufferings of the world. At one and the same time, aspiring bodhisattvas can view themselves as receiving the compassion of advanced or celestial bodhisattvas as well as making them the objects of their devotion. The bodhisattva is an object of veneration and a compassionate savior as well as a paradigm of the dedication to which all ought to aspire. As such they function as archetypes of enlightened activity for human practitioners. There are innumerable bodhisattvas, peaceful or wrathful, and their many aspects represent their infinite capacity to help. According to Robert Thurman, the bodhisattva's mission is to turn the entire universe into a Buddha-land, a domain in which the force of karma is overcome by the power of compassion.

Santideva's Guide to the Bodhisattva Way of Life is the classic study for those determined to take on this responsibility for others.[10] "Santideva states that as soon as a being conceives the spirit of enlightenment, he or she becomes at once a 'Son or Daughter of the Sugatas,' a Buddha-child."[11] A being becomes a bodhisattva at this very moment of the will to enlightenment.[12]

Luis Gomez argues that the bodhisattva mind manifests itself in multifarious forms, from the miraculous celestial bodhisattva to the ordinary human bodhisattva. This covers a broad spectrum of human possibility. Gomez articulates four distinct types of religious ideals represented in the bodhisattva figure. These four kinds of bodhisattva are the celestial or mythical bodhisattva, the ethical bodhisattva, the mystical bodhisattva, and the immanent or ordinary human bodhisattva. The celestial bodhisattvas use miraculous powers to instruct and assist human beings, and they "teach and embody in their behaviour an ethical ideal that makes demands on ordinary humans."[13] Bodhisattvas describe their spiritual state in terms of emptiness and embody a mystical, transcendent ideal. Gomez emphasizes that human aspirants become bodhisattvas at the moment of adopting the precepts. "Ordinary human beings who . . . attempt to follow their ethical and mystical teachings may also be called 'Bodhisattvas' even before they have approached the perfect condition of ideal Bodhisattvas."[14] These four ideals are related and overlap. Gomez considers the celestial bodhisattva as idealized human being and as ethical model for ordinary bodhisattvas. Most importantly, the concept of bodhisattva as ethical ideal bridges and connects the celestial and the earthly dimensions.

The bodhisattva serves as friend to the poor and the helpless. Bodhisattva morality is egalitarian and expresses an ideal of equality. "As a rule...the lower the social status, the greater the possibility that a human being will meet face to face with a Bodhisattva, or manifest him—or herself as a Bodhisattva."[15] This model expresses the continuity extending from advanced holiness down to the initial aspiration to the good. "Thus, common acts of virtue can be seen as the acts of a bodhisattva, and the first aspiration to enlightenment as a manifestation of enlightenment itself."[16] In Mahayana the transcendent spiritual ideal of "emptiness" or "nirvana" is the same as "form" or "samsara," the world as it is.

Mahayana theory holds that bodhisattvas often appear in the guise of ordinary human beings. But the holiness manifesting in the mundane and ordinary "is so conspicuous that it is usually overlooked."[17] All of these archetypal figures represent the ethical and spiritual ideals of the actual human Buddhist practitioners of wisdom and compassion. But the miraculous bodhisattvas set out the standards of behaviour to which those on this path must aspire. "The presence of the sacred in all things points to wisdom (the sameness of all things) and to compassion (regarding all sentient beings as oneself)."[18]

The Bodhisattva as Ethical Model

What does it mean to say that ordinary human beings should use the bodhisattva as an ethical model? The structure of Buddhist ethics is complex, incorporating elements of what in Western philosophical theories are familiar as consequentialism, especially utilitarianism, deontological ethics, and virtue ethics. However, most Western ethical theories do incorporate the three elements of the good, the right, and the noble or virtuous, and what distinguishes these theories as belonging to different classifications gets down to which element is foundational in the theory. Viewed in this light, Buddhist ethical theories are most accurately classified as a form of virtue ethics.

James Whitehill also proposes that Buddhist ethics be classified as a form of ethics of virtue, which he defines as "an ethics that is character-based (rather than principle-driven or act-focused), praxis-oriented, teleological, and community-specific."[19] Whitehill uses the phrase "awakened virtue" as shorthand for "awakened, compassionate virtue-cultivation," which calls attention to the interconnections of the moral and the spiritual. Buddhism "dialectically affirms both the deterministic weight of karma or character dispositions and our freedom from them in the concomitant 'emptiness' of sunyata."[20] In keeping with other theories of virtue ethics, the aim is to develop a virtuous character by emulation and practice of the virtues, so that one acts from the "ground of a well-tempered character, supported by a . . . reasonable knowledge of what one is doing." This is brought about by the meditative practices such as tonglen (exchanging self and others) as well as the repeated and habitual practices of the perfections and compassionate activities.[21] The Sanskrit word "paramita" refers to the practices in which aspiring bodhisattvas train; "paramita" is translated as "perfection" and is understood as a transcendental virtue.[22]

Compassionate Force

The foundational Buddhist precept of non-harm means at least that we should avoid intentional harm to living beings. The law of karma applies only to volitions, so if one intentionally harms, then this will bring harm in return to the person who intentionally caused harm. However, Buddhist ethics is extremely complex, and particularly in the later Mahayana and Tibetan Vajrayana, a balancing of different elements is necessary for ethical deliberation.

Robert Thurman explains the basis for the justifiable use of compassionate force by a bodhisattva. Asanga's Bodhisattva Stages lists the bodhisattva vows, some of which call for breaking the moral precepts in exceptional circumstances in order to bring about a higher good. In Bodhisattva Stages, Asanga states that "a Bodhisattva should kill a killer if that is the only way to prevent him from killing many other people; should rob a tyrant of his country if that is the only way to deliver the people from oppression."[23] Bodhisattva compassion can be fierce, tough love. The Vajrayana bodhisattva path makes much use of wrathfulness and fierceness. Thurman expresses the perspective of many teachers of this tradition when he notes the at-times ferocity of non-violence and compassion. He explains an often-discussed example.

> Asanga argues that a bodhisattva is compelled to kill someone if that is the only way he can save the life of many people, though killing violates a fundamental monastic and ethical precept. Yet even if he has to take life in order to save life, he does not do so aggressively. He acts with regret and love toward the person he must kill. If we define violence as force used in connection with hatred, anger, or aggression, then the taking of life by the bodhisattva is not violence. However, if we do not include this motivational factor in the definition of violence and only consider the effect on others, then this act of the bodhisattva is indeed violence.[24]

Intentions are thus central to the assessment of the moral qualities of action. Donald Lopez echoes this, and also highlights some of the tensions between the basic ethics of the monastic code, the vinaya, and bodhisattva ethics. Lopez says "it is an infraction for a bodhisattva not to be willing to commit one of the nonvirtuous deeds of body and speech (killing, stealing, sexual misconduct, lying, divisive speech, harsh speech, senseless speech) out of compassion for others."[25]

Many people consider His Holiness the Dalai Lama to be the strongest possible advocate of nonviolence, and so it is illuminating to consider some of his philosophical writings on this topic. He says that virtues are the cause of happiness whiles vices are the cause of unhappiness. Attachment and hatred are chief vices or mental afflictions, but "the primary mental affliction is the ignorance that grasps onto the inherent existence of phenomena."[26] His understanding of what are mental afflictions is complicated. He says that afflictions are mental events that disturb the tranquillity of the mind and that also produce an overall balance of long-term mental disruptions and unwholesome behavior. The parallels with Western consequentialism and utilitarianism are palpable. That a mental event disturbs the mind is not sufficient to classify it as an affliction, since there are many wholesome mental events that have this character.

> Compassion is an example of this. In The Guide to the Bodhisattva Way of Life, Shantideva points out that when you cultivate compassion, it may be disturbing. It may give rise to anxiety for other sentient beings. He ponders to himself: Isn't it the case that if you cultivate compassion you will feel suf-

fering? And his response is: Yes, but there is a great purpose for cultivating this temporary uneasiness or unhappiness, because of the great benefit that will follow. If we come back then to the definition of mental affliction—a mental factor that disturbs the equilibrium of the mind—we see this is not simply something that temporarily brings about a disturbance, anxiety, or unhappiness. A mental affliction is a mental distortion that not only creates such a disturbance, but in the long run it produces yet further problems. With compassion, there is a temporary disturbance and a long-term benefit.[27]

This background is used to explore the role of compassionate anger. If the incitement for the anger is compassion, this is not ordinary anger, for while the mind may be disturbed, "it has no malice, no intent to give harm. In other words, there is no element of hatred."[28] Such anger can lead to forceful or violent action. The wrathful deities or principles of Tibetan Vajrayana Buddhism are an expression of this. Ordinary anger, in contrast, is aroused by attachment.

There are occasions when an enlightened being seeks to help another sentient being and finds that circumstances do not allow a peaceful approach or engagement. A violent engagement is required in order to serve the sentient being on that occasion, and circumstances induce a wrathful expression....You recognize this evil propensity, or vice; you know it must be dispelled because of the ensuing harm it would bring about; and...out of great compassion arising from the wish to avert the great harm, you see that you must dispel the vice. Recognizing that there is no way to dispel that vice other than through an act of violence, you may take the life of the person who bears that vice, without ever losing compassion for that person, and while being willing to take on that act yourself.[29]

In this context, being willing to take on that act yourself means being willing to take on the karma of that act, or, in other words, being willing to take on the suffering of others, in this case, the suffering of the person who is about to act harmfully. This willingness to take on the suffering of others is the heart of the bodhisattva attitude. In Western moral philosophy, examples are often posed for reflection which revolve around the dilemmas presented when an agent must decide whether it would be justified to use force, or even to kill someone who was about to cause great destruction or kill many innocent people. Usually reflection on such examples includes a calculation of the consequences for all those involved in the situation and who will be affected by the outcomes being considered. This reflection includes, as one factor, calculating the long-term effects on the person who decides reluctantly to use force or even to kill to avert catastrophe. The person reflects on the long-term consequences of the anguish that would be caused to the agent who chooses to avert catastrophe. What can they live with? This reflection on the effects on the agent is one of the factors that must be taken into account when looking at the fruits of action for those involved in the situation.

The Dalai Lama considers further how his philosophy would approach such moral situations.

> Two things need to be taken into the balance. On the one hand, something is proscribed, such as killing; on the other hand, it's always a contextual event. That is, one needs to ask: What is the greater need given this circumstance? Something may be proscribed, yet in certain circumstances, the benefit of engaging in it may be greater than the harm created by avoiding it. We find this principle of balance...even in the Vinaya, the most fundamental Buddhist ethics, and it carries through in the Bodhisattva ethics. One's wisdom is continually called forth to judge the specific circumstances in terms of general principles and context.[30]

A general injunction against violence is therefore difficult to implement, for the motivation is the most significant factor, and consequences must also be taken into account. "Violence is just the method, and the method is less important. But the pity is, you don't know the results of your actions until they happen...On a practical level, it's very complicated, so it's much safer to avoid acts of violence."[31]

In these formulations, the main emphasis is on intention and motivation. This is clear in the Dalai Lama's explanation of the kind of anger that is morally wholesome or acceptable. When forceful, even violent action is motivated by compassion, when there is no malice, hatred, or intent to harm, then the action is wholesome and the anger is justified. Although Thurman maintains that whether or not an act is properly classified as violent depends upon the presence or absence of this motivation, whereas the Dalai Lama maintains that action motivated by compassion is indeed violent, yet is a case of justified anger, they appear to agree on the underlying point. Wholesome or justified or right action is rooted in compassion and lacks malice or hatred.

However, the concentration on intention and motivation as key criteria, while it sheds light upon the moral framework, is open to some lines of objection and criticism.[32] Compassion begins with the idea that all sentient beings wish to avoid suffering. The bodhisattva vows to alleviate the suffering of all sentient beings. There are some obvious parallels with utilitarianism on this issue. But mental-state accounts of utilitarianism face the problem of the difficulty of measuring internal mental states of suffering and happiness. The Buddhist framework also is faced with objections based on the difficulty of assessing the subjective motivations of others. While in many cases, others can be confident in judging that actions are motivated by hatred or malice, this cannot always be relied upon, and the moral worth of the actions may depend, in large measure, on the assessment by agents of their own motivation. In addition, although mindfulness and compassion meditative awareness practices are designed to increase practitioners' knowledge and understanding of their habitual motivations and emotional patterns, there is still plenty of room for self-deception to operate even in seasoned practitioners. The Dalai Lama recognizes this limitation when he acknowledges that, despite the discipline and training in self-honesty of these meditative practices, "the human mind is so devious that it would be able to find loopholes."[33]

The Dalai Lama's reflections upon these problems reveal that his system of ethics is actually quite intricate and relies a great deal upon the traditional combination of compassion and wisdom. His framework does not rely upon motivations in isolation from other factors. He notes that we must judge whether mental events and actions in the long run produce problems or benefits, thus adding in significant consequentialist elements. He says that "one's wisdom is continually called forth to judge the specific circumstances in terms of general principles and context," thus adding in a method of balance of different factors. This also can be viewed as strengthening the theoretical approach by making it less rigid and rule-governed than the early Buddhist ethics' reliance upon specific and detailed rules governing aspects of conduct.

In a recent article, Robert Thurman makes crystal clear what is at stake in these deliberations. He notes that

> If there were a really bad person who was about to launch nuclear weapons or engage in germ warfare, the most compassionate thing would be to have somebody take him out without hurting innocent people. In the Theravada ethic, you say, 'We don't know the real story here. I don't know whose karma is what, so I can't get involved'. But in the bodhisattva ethic, if you see someone about to kill a bunch of people, you have to stop him or you're an accomplice. If you don't stop him, not only are you letting others lose their lives, but you're also harming the killer because he's going to have very bad karmic effects. You try to stop him without killing, but if you have to kill, you do. You get bad karma, too, but because you're acting out of compassion, not hatred, the good karma will outweigh the bad.[34]

This contemporary example also resonates with an often-discussed classical example of a story about the Buddha in an earlier lifetime. Donald Lopez tells the story to illustrate this principle. In this earlier lifetime, the future Buddha, as leader of 500 sea traders, learned that a thief on the ship planned to murder the 500 to steal the ship's goods. The future Buddha decided that the only way to stop this mass killing was to kill the thief himself. In so doing, the future Buddha, it is explained, not only saved 500 lives, but also protected the thief from the negative karma of 500 murders. The killer of the thief, the future Buddha, "rather than amassing the negative karma of murder himself, was able to reduce his own path to enlightenment by one hundred thousand aeons by means of his compassionate act."[35]

Kenneth Kraft also asks whether resort to force or violence can be justified in extreme circumstances. He says that many Buddhists maintain that some form of violence may be justified if this prevents greater violence. He also highlights the differences between Western engaged Buddhists and Buddhist activists in Third World and Asian countries. For Buddhists facing brutal and tyrannical regimes, "'engagement' takes the form of a life-and-death struggle for political and cultural survival. Those involved in such conflicts typically have little interest in the theoretical implications of nonviolence...some reluctantly conclude, 'We see no way to defend ourselves but to fight back'."[36] At a gathering of the International Network of Engaged Buddhists, cherished views on nonviolence can be confronted. "For example, an American whose advocacy of nonviolence remains untested may be drawn into conversation with a Burmese student who associates nonviolence with impotence, having seen his companions gunned down in the city and ambushed in the jungle."[37] Joanna Macy says that she cannot pass judgment on those who take up arms: "For us as members of this Empire to sit by and say, 'Oh, but the response should be nonviolent, and it is wrong to take up arms...' Well, I simply cannot bring myself to do that."[38]

The Dalai Lama also specifically addresses this in the context of peace and nonviolence. He says that peace is not simply the absence of violence, but it is an expression of compassion and caring. "And if you see there is violence, some problem existing somewhere, and you remain disconnected from that prob-

lem, then that is not nonviolence....If you are seeing that there
is a problem, but you fail to get involved, you are just watching the suffering of others...Nonviolence requires that you are
fully engaged in the problem, fully involved, trying to solve
the problem."[39] He says that in order to distinguish violence
and nonviolence, we must look beyond the surface appearance. We must look to the motivation as the basis of the
distinction. "Now, if you undertake a harsh action, some
wrathful action, with genuine motivation to save or protect, or
in order to achieve some great benefit for a great number of
people, that action is essentially nonviolent. It is violent in
appearance, but not in essence."[40]

When asked how one can judge one's own motivation, the Dalai Lama
replies that, without wisdom, it can be difficult to judge this. "Generally, every
event is a mixture of positive and negative. So, then, which percent is higher, the
positive or the negative? A hundred percent right is almost impossible."[41] The
circumstances must be brought in to the decision-making procedure. But then if
there are no alternatives and "your failure to do something violent will create a
disaster to many people, you must do something forcefully to stop it."[42] He also
reiterates that the long-term consequences will affect the quality of the action
chosen now. "It may be that you stopped this wrongdoing and your motivation is
sincere, but due to this event, unexpected consequences may arise which are not
good. In the long run you may perhaps make the situation worse. It is very difficult to predict."[43] The Dalai Lama appears to conclude that in situations of uncertainty about these long-term consequences, not acting is safer than acting.
However, I will argue shortly that this claim is open to objection.

Justification of Compassionate Force

Now I turn to an exploration of the arguments given to support the use of compassionate force in extraordinary circumstances where the use of such force results in a great benefit or in a reduction in suffering. The Dalai Lama says,"In
the ethics of the Hearers, the main point is to refrain from harming others. In the
Bodhisattva ethics, you are concerned not only with not harming others, but also
with restraining your own reluctance to help others."[44] I will explore some
points raised by the examples of the Dalai Lama and Robert Thurman.

Firstly, the examples illustrate that in bodhisattva ethics, in assessing the
justification for proposed courses of action, the distinction between action and
non-action is blurred if not entirely extinguished. As Thurman says, according to
this framework if you do not take action to stop a killer, then you become an
accomplice. The bodhisattva practices are designed with the goal of "restraining

your own reluctance to help others," that is, restraining your inclination to stand back, not get involved, or not act when compassionate action is required. The wholesomeness or justification of the action depends primarily upon the intention, goal or motivation, but also upon the effects or consequences of acting or not acting. Secondly, and correspondingly, the negative karma produced by not acting to stop someone from killing many often is greater than the negative karma created by killing one "bad person" who is about to kill many others. Similarly, the story of the historical Buddha illustrates that compassionate force in many cases can strongly accumulate positive karma.

Thirdly, a reluctance to get involved based upon concern that one will create negative karma for oneself through killing is misplaced or inappropriate in the bodhisattva ethics. Practitioners vow to take responsibility for others, to take on their suffering, even, if advanced enough, to descend into hell to help those beings there. The merit that is accumulated is given away to all sentient beings, not grasped at or hoarded for oneself. In the meditative practice of tonglen, or exchange of self and others, and in the practice of "give-and-take," "one works to share with . . . [others] every iota of happiness one may be fortunate to possess, and to relieve them of every suffering they may have."[45] So a willingness to take upon oneself any negative karma created by compassionate force is part and parcel of the bodhisattva path.

Fourthly, if we dig a little deeper into the reluctance of an ordinary bodhisattva to act because of concern that one's motives and intentions are mixed, we find that non-action is not necessarily the safer course. An ordinary bodhisattva faced with this extraordinary circumstance may initially be inclined to caution and the safety of not acting. The reasoning may be: "Since I am not very advanced on the bodhisattva path, my wisdom and compassion are also not the deep wisdom and compassion of the celestial bodhisattvas. How can I emulate them and model my behaviour on theirs in this situation? My motives inevitably will be mixed, and though my intention may be to act from compassion, there will be some anger present and thus some unwholesome feelings. If I act even partially from anger, my action is unjustified and negative karma is created. So I must reluctantly not act until I have reached a level of awakening that I can act purely from compassion without any taint of unwholesome anger."

However, this form of reasoning is also misplaced. For in this circumstance, ordinary bodhisattvas will be subject to mixed motives, and some unwholesome emotions or mental afflictions, whether they act or they refrain from action. (In this line of thought, decisions to urge others to act or not act, or to advocate or be an activist in support of action or non-action are correspondingly justified or unjustified.) If one is faced with a conflict and the suffering of others, and one chooses not to get involved, not to act, the mixed motives are likely to involve fear of taking on a powerful opponent, as well as indifference or aversion to the suffering of others, perhaps masquerading as equanimity or detachment. Jack Kornfield says that "The near-enemy of equanimity is indifference. It feels very equanimous to say, '. . . I'm not really attached to it'…and in a way it is . . . a great relief. Why is that? Because it is a withdrawal. It is a removal from world and life." It is a way "of backing away or removing ourselves from the things which cause fear."[46]

While it may at first sight appear that not acting rather than acting is the safer course if one is not entirely confident that one's compassionate stance is not tinged with anger, I claim that there is no inherent advantage in not acting in these circumstances. It is equally likely that one's motivations for holding back in these circumstances are also tinged with fear, indifference, or aversion. This is just the nature of being at an earlier stage of the path than the celestial bodhisattva models. At this stage, practitioners are still prone to the mental afflictions and undeveloped compassion. So the apparent safety of the decision to avoid acting on anger dissipates with the realization of our equal capacity to hold back because of fear, indifference or aversion. The conclusion is that non-action holds no inherent advantage over action when it comes to relaxing the grip of the afflictive emotions on behavior. Further progress on the path will lessen the afflictive emotions of all types, but acceptance that motives will be mixed both in action and inaction undermines the illusion that action is more subject to risky emotions. And as we must take responsibility to reduce the suffering of others, we must forge ahead in our action or our inaction.

In addition to intentions, the specific circumstances and the consequences must also be taken into account. As the Dalai Lama says, "It may be that you stopped this wrongdoing and your motivation is sincere, but due to this event, unexpected consequences may arise which are not good. In the long run you may perhaps make the situation worse. It is very difficult to predict." But again, the uncertainty of the long-term consequences, and the prospect of unexpected consequences apply equally both to action and inaction. Uncertainty about the long-term and unexpected consequences haunts us whether we act or do not act. Even a cursory exploration of different possible scenarios and unfoldings in complex circumstances should give us pause, if we are tempted to assume that inaction is inherently the safer course to reduce the harm.

A similar point applies to those who object that much of the violence and destruction in the world's political arenas does not come about because of intentional malice or hatred. Yet still, this objection claims, the consequences of horrifying suffering and death serve as a rejoinder to those who invoke the principle of justified compassionate force. This objection also uses clear examples of the systemic violence that is the result of political and economic structures that promote oppression. Yet a similar reply awaits this objection. These points apply equally to the suffering caused by the inaction of allowing those who need help to remain unassisted. Systemic exploitative and oppressive patterns and structures often rely for their power and continuation upon the reluctance of those who are called upon to help to avert their eyes from the suffering. Systemic and structural violence are on a par with systemic oppressive and exploitative structures that continue unchallenged and unabated as a result of the indifference and fear of those who are called upon to help, in the form of compassionate force if necessary.

When faced with the prospect of using compassionate force in extremely complex and subtle circumstances of mass suffering, it is difficult to sustain the claim that it is inherently safer and less risky not to act to use compassionate force. Nor is it simple to argue that the mere absence of war is the peaceful course. A strong case can be made that great suffering can and often does come about as much from a failure to act as from decisions to pursue violent and destructive courses of action like war.

The acceptance and justification of the use of compassionate force to avoid or reduce great suffering has an incontrovertible place within bodhisattva ethics. Formulations of the principle of compassionate force often contain a caveat in the form of a warning that such force should only be turned to as a last resort or in exceptional circumstances. Given the dangerous level of destruction and harm arising from ongoing cycles of violence in many parts of the world, it is not hard to see why these caveats are taken so seriously. Often related objections are raised, in the form of slippery slope concerns. The objections rightly point out that too-easy recourse to the use of force can and often does lead to a slippery slope of justifying violence, and so the objections exhort us to explore other options first before using this last resort.

However, while it is important to appreciate and give due regard to the merits of these objections in serving as a cautionary brake on too-easy justifications of force, my analysis raises questions and challenges about these caveats. One aim of my argument is to challenge us to see the symmetry of what I claim are the twin dangers of producing violence and of standing back from acting because of indifference to suffering. His Holiness the Dalai Lama reminds us that contexts and circumstances must always be assessed and evaluated before embarking on a course of action. In many circumstances, these twin dangers are two sides of the same coin, because often the only way to alleviate the great suffering of horrific circumstances of brutal tyranny, massive human rights abuses, and extreme but all too common cases of genocide, is indeed to use force to stop the suffering. We cannot have our cake and eat it too. In extreme but all too common circumstances, the choice not to use apparently violent force and the choice not to act to stop horrific suffering are one and the same in effect, for in refusing to use force, we allow the consequences of suffering to unfold. So we need to face squarely the reality that the caveat that compassionate force is to be used only as a last resort means that many people will be tortured, imprisoned and murdered before this last resort arrives. And it will be too late for them, at least in this lifetime.

My argument also aims to open up the debate to consider whether exactly the same caveats and warnings then do not also apply to holding back from using compassionate force when circumstances call for it. It is quite easy to see the effects of careless, violent force fueled by anger in current political arenas like the Middle East. The challenge that is here posed, however, is whether we can see as clearly the slippery slope and escalating effects of enduring cycles of suffering that result from inaction fueled by indifference, callousness and aversion in political arenas like Rwanda and Sudan. News stories about horrific suffering caused by violence share space with reports of horrors allowed to happen because of indifference, fear and aversion that lead to just watching, or more often averting our eyes from suffering, because we have not sufficiently trained ourselves to overcome our reluctance to help suffering beings.

The principles and framework of bodhisattva ethics lead to the conclusion that we need to consider with equal care and wisdom these twin barriers to the alleviation of suffering. So we need to consider with equal care and wisdom whether (1) a proposed course of action may in fact be fueling violence rather than using compassionate force to good effect, and whether (2) we may be standing by and allowing suffering to occur out of indifference and fear masquerading as an aspiration to avoid violence.

The bodhisattva ethics is a form of virtue ethics, one that uses the exemplary models of wise and compassionate advanced bodhisattvas, and the myths and stories of their enlightened activities, as examples to be followed. However, the development of these capacities of wisdom and compassion also requires ongoing training and discipline in the paramitas, to awaken unconditional and relative bodhichitta, or the awakened heart/mind.[47] The fearlessness of the compassionate bodhisattva includes a well-trained and disciplined ability to rest in groundlessness and accept ambiguity and uncertainty without moving too quickly into a solidified and too-rigid position on complex questions. And once we reach a perspective, the training in the virtues or paramitas aids in holding the position with lightness and flexibility and undermines rigidity and self-righteousness.[48] Pema Chödron eloquently explains the dangers of holding to perspectives with rigidity and bias. "The far enemy of equanimity is prejudice. We get self-righteous about our beliefs and set ourselves solidly for or against others. We take sides. We become closed-minded. We have enemies. This polarization is an obstacle to the genuine equanimity that informs compassionate action. If we wish to alleviate injustice and suffering, we have to do it with an unprejudiced mind."[49]

In bodhisattva ethics, there is the responsibility to use discriminative wisdom, compassion and habits of virtue and reason to attempt to determine the best course of action or inaction in complex uncertain circumstances. Buddhism holds to the Middle Way, which tries to avoid extremes. Buddhism also holds that we should not cling to or grasp at teachings or positions. This means that although we do have a responsibility, when circumstances warrant, to come to a perspective and to do our best to act from wisdom and compassion, for the benefit of others, we should also be mindful that we do not cling to our position dogmatically. Since the situations are complex, with humility we should realize that others, making an equal effort to act from wisdom and compassion, may reach very different conclusions from our own.

Notes

1. I would like to thank Angela Sumegi and Noel Salmond for many helpful and insightful conversations on the topics in this paper. I would also like to thank Robert Thurman for email correspondence about his position. I would like to express my gratitude to Lama Surya Das, Khenpo Tsewang Gyatso Rinpoche and Ajahn Viradhammo for their teachings. Thanks also to Doug Allen for comments on an earlier draft.

2. Paul Williams, *Mahayana Buddhism: The Doctrinal Foundations*, (London and New York: Routledge, 2002), 49.

3. Quoted in Williams, 50. From E. Conze, *The Perfection of Wisdom in Eight Thousand Lines and its Verse Summary* (Bolinas: Four Seasons Foundation, 1973).

4. Williams, 25.

5. Taigen Dan Leighton, *Faces of Compassion: Classic Bodhisattva Archetypes and Their Modern Expression*, (Somerville, Mass.: Wisdom Publications, 2003), 67.

6. See Leighton, especially pp. 63-82 for a detailed discussion of these practices. I thank Lama Surya Das for clarification of this list. This list is the most complete, but some lists contain only the first six of these perfections.

7. Williams, 25-26.

8. Luis O. Gomez, "From the Extraordinary to the Ordinary: Images of the Bodhisattva in East Asia," in *The Christ and the Bodhisattva* ed. Donald S. Lopez, Jr. and Stephen C. Rockefeller (Albany: State University of New York Press, 1987), 141-91.

9. Williams, 182.

10. Santideva, *A Guide to the Bodhisattva Way of Life*, translated from the Sanskrit and Tibetan by Vesna A. Wallace and B. Alan Wallace (Ithaca: Snow Lion Publications, 1997).

11. Robert A. F. Thurman, "The Buddhist Messiahs: The Magnificent Deeds of the Bodhisattvas" in *The Christ and the Bodhisattva*, ed. Donald S. Lopez, Jr. and Stephen C. Rockefeller (Albany: State University of New York Press, 1987), 76.

12. See also Lama Surya Das, *Awakening the Buddha Within: Tibetan Wisdom for the Western World* (New York: Broadway Books, 1997), especially 142-46.

13. Gomez, 144.

14. Gomez, 144.

15. Gomez, 150.

16. Gomez, 151.

17. Gomez, 164.

18. Gomez, 178.

19. James Whitehill, "Buddhism and the Virtues," in *Contemporary Buddhist Ethics*, ed. Damien Keown, (Richmond, Surrey: Curzon Press, 2000), 19.

20. Whitehill, 22.

21. See also Lama Surya Das, *Awakening the Buddhist Heart* (New York: Broadway Books, 2000), especially "The Bodhicitta Practices of an Awakened Heart," 221-43.

22. Lama Surya Das, 236.

23.Thurman, "The Buddhist Messiahs," 84.

24. Robert Thurman, "Tibet and the Monastic Army of Peace," *Inner Peace, World Peace: Essays on Buddhism and Nonviolence*, ed. Kenneth Kraft (Albany: State University of New York Press, 1992), 78. Reference is to Mark Tatz, trans., *Asanga's Chapter on Ethics with the Commentary of Tsong-Kha-Pa, The Basic Path to Awakening, the Complete Bodhisattva,* by Bodhisattva Yogarcarabhumi (Lewiston/Queenston: Edwin Mellen Press, 1986), 70-72.

25. Donald S. Lopez, *The Story of Buddhism: A Concise Guide to its History and Teachings* (New York: HarperCollins, 2001), 149.

26. HH the Dalai Lama, "The Virtues in Christian and Buddhist Traditions," in *Healing Emotions, Conversations with the Dalai Lama on Mindfulness, Emotions, and Health,* ed. Daniel Goleman (Boston: Shambhala, 1997), 170-175.

27. HH the Dalai Lama, 171-2.

28. HH the Dalai Lama, 173.

29. HH the Dalai Lama, 174-75.

30. HH the Dalai Lama, 176.

31. HH the Dalai Lama, 177.

32. See, for example, Barbara Clayton, "Ahimsa, Karuna and Maitri: Implications for Environmental Buddhism," *Ecumenism*, No. 134, June 1999, 27-31.

33. HH the Dalai Lama, 176.

34. Robert Thurman, "Cool Heroism," *Tricycle: The Buddhist Review*, Spring, 2003, 45.

35. Lopez, 149-50.

36. Kenneth Kraft, "Prospects of a Socially Engaged Buddhism," in *Inner Peace, World Peace: Essays on Buddhism and Nonviolence* (Albany: State University of New York Press, 1992), 24. Quote from All Burma Students' Democratic Front, *Dawn*, 1:9 (May 1989): 1.

37. Kraft, 28.

38. Joanna Macy, quoted in Kraft, 28 Quoted from Catherine Ingram, *In the Footsteps of Gandhi: Conversations with Spiritual Social Activists* (Berkeley: Parallax Press, 1990), 155.

39. HH the Dalai Lama, quoted in Scott A. Hunt, *The Future of Peace: On the Front Lines With the World's Great Peacemakers,* (New York: HarperSan Francisco, 2002, 70-71.

40. HH the Dalai Lama, in Hunt, 87-88.

41. HH the Dalai Lama, in Hunt, 88.

42. HH the Dalai Lama, in Hunt, 89.

43. HH the Dalai Lama, in Hunt, 89.

44. HH the Dalai Lama, in Lopez and Rockefeller, 225.

45. Thurman, "The Buddhist Messiahs," 82.

46. Jack Kornfield, "The Path of Compassion: Spiritual Practice and Social Action," in Kraft, 24-25.

47. Pema, Chodron, *The Places That Scare You: A Guide to Fearlessness in Difficult Times* (Boston: Shambhala, 2002), especially 93-98.

48. Pema Chodron, 96.

49. Pema Chodron., 80.

9

Rootlessness and Terror: Violence and Morality from a Zen Perspective

Michael G. Barnhart

> ". . . the question is not to know whether one accepts or rejects vio-
> lence, but whether the violence with which one is allied is 'progres-
> sive' and tends toward its own suspension or toward self-perpetuation
> . . . the crime has to be set in the logic of a situation . . . instead of
> judging it by itself according to that morality mistakenly called 'pure'
> morality."[1]

In the current political climate, where issues of religiously motivated terrorism
have become the paramount concern, it is particularly risky for a religion to project an appearance of lacking ethical concern for the effects of its actions on
others, especially non-believers. The condemnation of fundamentalist Islam and
its concept of "jihad" is a good example, but suspicion of other religiously ob-
sessed and violent groups and individuals—fundamentalist Christian antiabor-
tion bombers in the U.S., murderous settlers in Israeli-occupied territories, separatist Tamils in Sri Lanka, and so on—also suggests the same concern. Indeed,
many have put the case that any fundamentalism, whether Islamic, Christian,
Hindu, or other, lacks sufficient moral depth to be considered a viable and humane religious option.

Interestingly, the popular image of Buddhism, perhaps because of its association with non-violence, seems to have escaped the scrutiny reserved for others of the world's religious traditions. And while it is hard to come up with a
Buddhist analogue of fundamentalist Islam or Christianity, particularly in their
messianic and crusading forms, nonetheless, I'm not sure that all forms of Buddhism deserve such a free pass. It has long been assumed that Buddhism is nonviolent in its very nature, and indeed though many of its stated precepts enshrine

a doctrinal rejection of killing, injury to any sentient being and so on, Buddhism is not without a history of violence itself. Of course, an obvious case is the repression of Tamils in Sri Lanka. However, it is not clear to what extent this is more an example of human hypocrisy than a deep-seated doctrinal ambivalence. There is another and from the standpoint of Buddhist principles even more troubling case.

Zen Buddhism has had a troubled relationship with ethics and morality for a long time. These troubles have been both external and internal. Outside critics have long complained that either Zen had no conception of morality or was frankly unethical in itself. Internally, some Zen practitioners, for example Masao Abe, have echoed the same concern, though more gently and presumably with reformist intentions.[2] Also, Zen has had a troubled relationship with the Japanese military, the most recent example being the revelation of close and supportive connections between Zen temples and Japan's wartime military leaders. Even philosophers and Zen exponents revered in the West, for example D. T. Suzuki, apparently celebrated the martial ferocity of the Japanese soldier, seeing in it a distinctively Zen value. In view of such revelations and not uncoincidentally after the September 11th terrorist attacks, at least one Japanese Zen temple, Myoshin-ji, has seen fit to offer an apology for its past militaristic associations.[3] All of which raises profound questions regarding Zen Buddhism's moral viability in a world recoiling from terrorist violence and the inevitable overreaction of those who feel threatened, particularly the U.S.

To put the question more explicitly: [1] Is Zen Buddhism ethically challenged? [2] If so, what are the implications for Buddhism generally especially given its extensive list of ethical precepts? [3] What are the possible implications generally for understanding issues of moral responsibility, violence, and terrorism? Does Buddhism offer a comprehensive view as to what violence is, particularly politically motivated violence aimed at noncombatants? And does it sort out issues of moral responsibility in regard either to the perpetration or the response to such acts?

Does Zen Buddhism Have an Ethics?

There is simply no easy way to answer this question. On the one hand, because Zen is a part of the Buddhist tradition generally, it has a very robust and explicit ethic, the First Precept of which forbids any sort of violent act, including the political. Christopher Ives, in his book *Zen Awakening and Society*,[4] provides a specifically Zen version of these precepts, the first of which is simply "Not killing."[37] Furthermore, almost every text from the Mahayana tradition, of which Zen is an offshoot, reaffirms a commitment to nonviolence. Of course, it is true that plenty of Zen Buddhist monks and practitioners have committed violent acts over the course of Zen's history. The Japanese samurai tradition made liberal use of Zen practice and often identified with its emphasis on selflessness and sacrifice. It is also true, as many of the war-related apologies attest to, that Zen temples supported Japanese militarism and imperialism in World War II. However, such practices might be dismissed as lapses or a corruption of the Zen tradition were it not for the fact that it is difficult to see what the connection is exactly between Zen's traditional, Buddhist subscription to nonviolence and the claims it seems to support regarding the relativity of good and evil.

In other words, Zen seems to have a philosophical problem in regard to its approach to issues of metaphysics on the one hand and its ethical precepts on the other. Tom Kasulis brings this conflict out with particular clarity when he comments regarding the Soto-Zen philosopher Dogen.

> Dogen tries to resolve a conflict within the Zen tradition. On the one hand, Zen wishes to be traditionally Buddhist; this entails recognition of various moral edicts passed down through the centuries. On the other hand, as an offshoot of the Mahayana wing of Buddhism and, in particular, of Nagarjuna's viewpoint, Zen considers distinctions such as that between good and evil to be relative rather than absolute. Therefore, Dogen wants to show how it is possible to affirm traditional moral exhortations while simultaneously denying the absoluteness of the distinction between good and evil.[5]

That is, if nonviolence is a good thing, a thing to be done, but nothing is absolutely good (or absolutely bad), then why should I be nonviolent? If doing a good thing isn't *really* good, then why do it? So what if I act violently, if I kill or injure? What exactly is the connection between my seeing that "No *dharma* whatever exists which is not empty"[6] and my performing this or that action, my perpetrating this or that *dharma*?

The same kind of issue emerges when one considers the traditional Buddhist insistence on *anatta* or non-ego as the foundation of the human person. As is well known and in contrast to the traditional Hindu conception of *atman* as our ultimate substance, Buddhism denies this calling the self a mere "counting term" or convenient designator. The self is a relational term and therefore non-substantial. Yet if such is the case, why should we care what we do to the various elements that fall under such a designator? What matter if we injure the body or pollute the mind if these are merely drifting *dharmas*, unanchored in the integrity of a person, a self? That is, if there is no self, how can I hurt anyone? On what can I practice violence? Maybe I can injure the body, but what makes that any worse than breaking a branch on a tree or treading on a stalk of grass?[7] There seems to be a logical gap between a "doctrine" of egolessness or selflessness and positive ethical precepts. Even the general esteem with which compassion (*karuna*) is held in Buddhism generally and Zen especially seems to lack any logical connection with the emptiness of the self or all *dharmas* collectively. Just because there are no selves why should I show compassion? In fact, how do I show compassion to what doesn't exist?

Finally, the same sort of challenge is raised regarding the traditional association of wisdom (*prajna*) and compassion. How does knowing the truth of things make me a compassionate or caring person? Especially, because ultimate wisdom involves seeing the emptiness of things, how can I be caring for that which is fleeting, impermanent, and empty? It is true that wisdom does not involve subscribing to the non-existence of things, and much of what can be said in defense of Zen hinges on this point. As Nagarjuna claims over and over again in the *Mulamadhyamakakarikas*, "The 'originating dependently' we call 'emptiness'."[8] But why does accepting the dependent origination of things require compassion of us? Compassion without wisdom is most certainly blind and wisdom without compassion possibly dangerous, but why would one lead to the other? Again, would knowing of the unlimited interconnections constitutive of my sense of the world make me less likely to kill or injure? Could not knowing such interconnections make me a more effective, perhaps more selfless killer?[9]

One would expect that much would have been said in defense of Zen on these points, but even its most eloquent and sophisticated spokespersons have been at best ambivalent on these questions. Take, for example, Masao Abe's tally of Zen's strengths and weaknesses as a worldview. "In fact, *ri* as an universal principle in the Western sense—i.e., human reason, intellectual reality, the laws of the universe, and particularly moral principles in terms of Ought—was never taken as an ultimate principle. It was always apprehended as something secondary."[10] Hence,

> precisely because of its standpoint of Non-thinking, Zen has in fact not fully realized the positive and creative aspects of thinking and their significance . . . and moral principles and ethical realization based on Subjective practical thinking, have been very conspicuous in the West. In contrast to this, some of these things have been vague or lacking in the world of   Zen . . . That Zen lacks the clue to cope with the problems of modern science, as well as individual, social and international ethical questions, etc., may be thought partly to be based on this.[11]

So, does Zen have an ethic and is that ethic specifically nonviolent? Given the above I don't believe there is any ready or glib answer to the question. However, the argument assailing the logical connection between wisdom and compassion or egolessness and nonviolence or between emptiness and commitment is flawed. The assumption seems to be that on the one hand stands metaphysics with a positive account of ultimate reality and on the other a set of ethical precepts and somehow the one should deductively follow from the other. I don't see that as a reasonable demand. The most one can expect is that the two don't contradict each other, and selflessness and compassion as well as relativity and commitment are certainly logically consistent.

Turning again to Nagarjuna,[12] he observes that were it not the case that phenomena coarise dependently we could never tread the path of wisdom or achieve enlightenment. "You deny all mundane and customary activities when you deny emptiness [in the sense of] dependent co-origination." [36] "For you [one who denies emptiness], some one who is a non-*buddha* by his own nature (*svabhava*) but strives for enlightenment will not attain the enlightenment through the 'way of life of becoming fully enlightened.'" [32] In short, without the co-arising of things, enlightenment itself cannot co-arise through the process of seeking it. Furthermore, if to deny emptiness is to deny the path of enlightenment, then to confirm enlightenment is to confirm emptiness. Thus, as he observes, the higher truth of Buddhist teaching is "not taught apart from practical behavior." [10] Of course, this is not to deny the dependent co-arising of acts of cruelty and so on as well. It is not as though existence logically leads to goodness. But it is true that a certain sort of path, as laid out by the Buddha, is a worldly path of "practical behavior" and is a reliable path to truth. Existence, in the Buddhist sense, does not force you to take the path of enlightenment, but it does open it to you; and pursuing it will get you to the truth of existence.

Of course, one can ask if an understanding or perception of existence as co-arising leads to an ethical kind of path. But I think this is to put the question the wrong way. What is clear is that to pursue a form of life that begins with accepting Buddhist ethical precepts, such as the prohibition on killing, is to pursue a course of practical behavior that makes enlightenment possible. One way of interpreting Buddhist ethics is to see the ethical kind of path as leading to an understanding of existence, to enlightenment, while insisting that it would be unfair to ask more of Buddhism generally.

However, there may be more to it than that. The connection that is usually emphasized between selflessness and enlightenment is that selflessness in the form of ego deconstruction is the key to seeing the interdependence of all things. It is the way we make the truth of existence personal, and a key component to the personalizing of emptiness is the avoidance of greed, ambition, and so on—that is, a kind of selflessness. Avoiding evil and immoral acts is therefore a necessary, although hardly sufficient, condition for treading the Buddhist path. Avoiding evil becomes the basis for a transformation of one's insight so that one goes from simply following a commandment such as "Do not kill" to, as Kasulis

puts it, "authenticating" it in "his or her own spiritual situation."[13] We lose ourselves in the process of acting out the imperative and achieve the state of "without-thinking" that Kasulis and others offer as Zen insight.

Indeed, not just Zen, but much of the Mahayana Buddhist tradition, though
it avoids detailed lists of precepts and virtues, invariably urges its practitioners
to avoid evil and do good. Shinran is a good example of this. Taking the "Primal
Vow," people "seek to stop doing wrong as their hearts move them, although
previously they gave thought to such things and committed them as their minds
dictated." This "is surely a sign of their having rejected this world."[14] To enter
onto the Buddhist way is to follow the path of right, to be right-minded. Why?
Because self-centered action is the root of all evil; one commits evil in the name
of advancing one's self-interest. Avoiding evil follows from the renunciation of
what Shinran calls "self-power," *jiriki*, and the acceptance of the "other-power"
of Amida Buddha.

However, there is a wrinkle here in regard to what was said above regarding
the efficacy of the Buddhist path and its precepts for gaining enlightenment.
Shinran believes that the renunciation through uttering the Vow and committing
oneself sincerely to Buddha comes first. Before that point we are enmeshed in
karmic evil. But to the degree that we suddenly become sincerely aware of that
evil that is ever present in our hearts and minds and always will be as a residue
of the self and our reliance on self-power, we transcend ourselves and "the Buddha receives us without judging whether our hearts are good or bad." So, the
justification for Buddhist precepts is not that they represent a path to enlightenment but that enlightenment removes the temptation of evil acts as a motivating
force within our personality, replacing it with our sincere trust in Buddha. To do
evil is thus to fall from grace. In other words, Buddhist precepts are a litmus test
of our sincerity.

Of course, the Shin approach assumes that all evil is selfishly motivated
which, to return to the moral critics of Zen, is a rather hefty assumption. In fact,
many of the most heinous cruelties of this century, from the Nazi death camps to
contemporary ethnic cleansing, have been carried out in a spirit of selfless service to a greater cause. Clearly, not every practitioner of such atrocities is motivated by personal hatred although I am sure that most are.[15] Moreover, is it
really obvious that selflessness alone is normatively significant? Would a selfless violation of the First Precept against killing be superior to a self-serving
one? Could one commit an evil act with what Shinran calls *shinjin*, a kind of
perfect sincerity? If not, why not?

In addition, in response to Nagarjuna's point regarding the interdependence
of the various elements of the path to Buddhist enlightenment, one can ask if
these various elements are essential? Could there be a path to such enlightenment lying outside of the practice of Buddhist precepts altogether? Shinran's

claim that one authentic expression of the *nembutsu* is enough to secure true enlightenment no matter how much evil is in one's life or heart might suggest the answer is, in fact, yes. As Kasulis concludes, "Zen has thrown us into the midst of relativism. Unlike Joseph Fletcher's situation ethics, though, there is apparently no overriding criterion such as *agape* to guide the individual in a moral dilemma. In the Zen view there is literally nothing to hold onto; to be responsible is simply to be responsive."[16]

The one thing that saves the account according to Kasulis is that Zen, like Mencius, believes that in our fundamental nature, that is, at a pre-reflective level of authentic experience, we are good. "For Zen, compassion and intuitive wisdom are the same because both radiate from the pre-ego mode of without-thinking. Only if the ego has been extirpated can there be compassion without distinctions and wisdom without presuppositions." [98] But again, as we face the moral critics from the standpoint of Zen, one has to ask whether such a fundamental assumption is justifiable. Isn't accepting this assumption itself to beg the question?

Moreover, we can accept the claim that true compassion can only be achieved through overcoming egocentrism, but it doesn't follow that overcoming egocentrism necessarily leads to compassion. If you are trying to be compassionate, you will indeed have to deal with the problem of your own ego. However, if you overcome the ego, how can you be sure compassion will result? Furthermore, if there is no intrinsic connection between the relativity of all things and the value of compassion, what constitutes Zen's fundamental commitment: the belief in the fundamental relativity of all things without moral valuations or the value of compassion whether or not it expresses our fundamental and relativistic nature?

There is another ethical challenge that faces Zen, one that receives less discussion. Even if we accept that Zen and other forms of Mahayana Buddhism do have a basis for insisting on doing good and avoiding evil, do they furnish any moral guidance regarding what counts as good or evil? Texts such as Shinran's seem to presume that the distinction is clear. But clearly reasonable people disagree as to exactly what is good, just, or virtuous. Is abortion a moral evil? Is religious tolerance a political virtue? How do we determine the goods of a good life? Should people be allowed to make what appear to be unreasonable choices for themselves in determining their fate, as in rejecting life-saving medical treatment? What can Buddhism teach us regarding the content of morality? Can it provide guidance in the discussion of such dilemmas?

Some commentators have tried to develop Buddhism's implications along these lines, but almost all such attempts that are at all convincing start with specific precepts and examples from the early and monastic literature. This is no help to Zen, and its almost complete focus on cultivating meditative awareness

seems very far afield from the specific concerns that generate debate over morality's content. One direction that might be open, explored by William R. LaFleur
in terms of Japanese attitudes regarding abortion, is the concept of moral *bricolage* as found in Jeffrey Stout's *Ethics After Babel*.[17] The idea is essentially that,
in this case, Japanese moral attitudes must be seen as a kind of improvised as-
sembling of a variety of ethical sources, a *bricolage* of different materials, that
responds to the specifics of a particular dilemma in a particular place and time.
Again, if this isn't to be a kind of meaningless relativism, being simply "responsive" as Kasulis says, such a process would have to have some point or purpose,
in this case Buddhist compassion. So, content-wise, a Zen ethics would represent not a single rule or set of principles but a general balancing of competing
concerns and points of view in a way that maximized compassion and minimized suffering.

This kind of account is certainly no worse off than a utilitarian ethics that
seeks to maximize happiness or preferences. In fact, it might be in a somewhat
better position to fend off criticisms regarding what the nature happiness is or
how we are to rank competing preferences fairly. A Buddhist *bricoleur* could
not say that compassion was a single uniform measure covering human actions,
as is utilitarian happiness, nor claim that compassion requires a supplemental
account of what is fair. The whole concept of fairness, a Buddhist might argue,
is built into the complexities of interdependent phenomena. Seeing things as
they really are is in essence being fair to all. Such an account still faces criticisms but at least genuflects in the direction of fairness and perhaps a conception
of justice.

So, in what sense does Zen have an ethic? It has an ethics in the sense of an
account of a form of life, as laid out by the Buddha, which provides one with an
opportunity to spiritualize one's inner cultivation. This is the suggestion that
Nagarjuna and Dogen contribute: Nagarjuna through arguing that what we con-
ventionally call enlightenment requires a set of co-arising conventions, the deep
understanding of which leads to higher truth or deep enlightenment, and Dogen
through arguing that pursuing the avoidance of evil can lead to the full accomplishment of doing without-thinking, that is to say, becoming fully cultivated in
Zen-approved sense. The weak point is that each fails to exclude the possibility
that there are perhaps morally unseemly ways of achieving these same results,
although in response it is hard to see how one detaches the results of cultivating
oneself in the Buddhistically approved fashion from the resulting enlightenment
itself. One might get somewhere by pursuing evil and avoiding good, by killing
selflessly perhaps, but how could one claim that one had achieved specifically
Buddhist enlightenment?

Finally, we can say that Zen has an ethic in so far as it expresses the
sensibility of the moral *bricoleur*, cadging bits of this and that to work the most

compassionate response one can. Peter Hershock has described something similar with his term "virtuosic sociality."[18] The challenge is to provide some sort of basis for distinguishing the virtuoso from the amateur. How do we know when we are performing well? Are the indications all internal and subjective? What makes one *bricoleur* more skillful than another? And if compassion isn't measurable, then while we avoid collapsing Zen into a kind of utilitarianism, we forego the objectivity of at least some kind of moral calculus.

What Are Implications for Buddhism Generally?

I want to raise this question because some might say, well so much the worse for Zen. That is why we need to fall back on a more ethically specific form of Buddhism. However, while Zen may be challenged in terms of specifying what is to count as a morally or ethically approved action and why, other forms are challenged by having little to say regarding the value of their precepts. As I have characterized it so far, a Zen ethic essentially comes down to insisting on compassionate involvement in existence as an acknowledgement of the interdependent nature of things, the emptiness of things in Nagarjuna's sense. While compassionate involvement is such an acknowledgement, however, it's not clear that violent and destructive involvement isn't as well. But we need not conclude that a true account of existence must leave us with only one path or form of life from which to choose; that our ethics are on shaky ground if our view of human nature cannot exclude all possible ways of acting. Certainly, if we assume along with Mencius that human beings are essentially compassionate (the child in the well example), then the specifically human acknowledgement of interdependence is through compassionate engagement with others. The difficulty with this solution is, of course, that Zen itself seems to undermine essentialistic assumptions regarding our true nature and therefore whether we are truly compassionate underneath.

Be that as it may, to turn to other forms of Buddhism such as Theravada, that base ethics on the specific precepts of the Buddha, does not remove the problem for Buddhism generally. Though a tradition-minded Buddhism can point to the canonical literature to support its claim that certain ways of conduct are what it is to be a Buddhist, that being a Buddhist is espousing a particular path to universal enlightenment, one can still ask why one must be a "Buddhist," at least in that sense? Though non-injury, refraining from killing, and so on may be traditional Buddhist precepts, what makes Buddhists so confident that exactly these practices are what generate enlightenment? This is not exactly the challenge raised before, whether one has an argument that these are the ultimately "right" principles, but the humbler question as to why one is certain that such conduct is central rather than incidental to achieving an enlightened status. One may accept that traditional precepts are as 'right' as any others; one may also accept that in the chain of interdependency such actions may have had a connection to others achieving their own enlightenment. The question is whether this is always the case? Will such conduct do so for me? Is there an invariable causal connection? After all, Buddhist literature is full of examples of people who live by Buddhist precepts and yet fail to achieve enlightenment. In short, it is far from obvious exactly what the connection is between refraining from certain acts and achieving enlightenment.

Zen Buddhism is all about this connection. Kasulis describes how a Zen practitioner, such as Dogen, takes the non-doing of evil—*shoakumakusa*—first in the usual sense of not producing evil.[19] Then as the one practicing non-doing of evil becomes adept at the producing of non-production, the experience of without-doing and without-thinking that is Buddhist enlightenment of emptiness ensues. Thus, the practitioner moves from rote doing to enlightened doing all through the agency of a form of denial. Thus does ethical action lead to enlightenment. Whatever one makes of such a set of associated claims, the point certainly is to trace out the phenomenological passage from the ordinary to the enlightened state. In which case, the value placed on a certain kind of precept is clear. Not only does avoiding evil express a certain kind of interrelatedness with all things, it also has a direct and internal connection with the very process of gaining enlightenment itself.

So, Zen Buddhism not only can support a traditional Buddhist ethic, or any traditional ethic of avoiding evil and doing good, but it can supply an internal connection between such acting and the very nature of Buddhist enlightenment itself, at least in the sense of experiencing *sunyata*. However, what Zen Buddhism cannot do is supply such precepts *de novo*. To do this would require the kind of deductive link between first principles and ethics that the very relativity of emptiness and dependent co-arising forecloses. But if Zen, which explores the internal and phenomenological link between action and enlightenment, cannot supply such a connection, neither can Buddhism in general. As argued above, it may be unfair to characterize a religious tradition as unethical or unprincipled in the absence of such an explanation. A consistent set of metaphysical and ethical precepts I believe to be enough. So, both Buddhism in general and Zen in particular may be said to have an ethics or to be ethical, and a rejection of violence, at least intentional violence, harm, or injury are component aspects of Buddhist ethics. What they don't obviously have is a foundation.

Of course, it is possible to argue that our analysis points not to a problem for Buddhism in general but Zen in particular. From this perspective, Buddhism is defined by its ethical commitment to the relief of suffering in general, particularly the suffering of others. Buddhism does not promise that compassion will generate enlightenment or wisdom so much as it takes its stand on the independent value of compassion. Compassion, an awareness of *dukkha*, the Bodhisattva-like resolve to save all sentient beings, are the starting points of all Buddhism, the experiential or existential lineaments of Buddhism's *dasein*. Zen or *dhyana* is situated in a Buddhist context. The Buddhist part, the ethical commitment, comes first; the meditative part exists within the broader framework. Therefore, we should take care to avoid tarring Buddhism in general with the specific problems of Zen or even Mahayana itself.

This sort of situational analysis of Buddhism, that Buddhism is centered in a compassionate recognition of the suffering of others and the need to respond, clearly has plenty of textual support and makes good sense philosophically. Furthermore, it represents a fairly widely held view that is not inconsistent with what I've argued so far. Clearly, if Buddhist ethics do not necessarily follow from Buddhist "metaphysics," then perhaps we should treat the ethics separately from the metaphysics. However, insisting on the independent value of compassion relative to wisdom and making compassion the necessary and indispensable condition of Buddhist commitment and hence wisdom and enlightenment entails its own difficulties.

The first of these difficulties is textual. Though early Buddhist documents, such as the "First Sermon" conveying the Four Noble Truths, suggest that the "first truth" of Buddhism is the recognition of universal *dukkha*, this first truth is always articulated in the context of an understanding of dependent co-arising. It is first only in the numerical sense, not in the logically prior sense. There is no document that I am aware of in which any claims are made regarding the priority of any one principle or principles, whether these be ethical or metaphysical sorts of principles. If anything, Buddhist sutras tend to portray these principles as themselves co-dependent or equivalent.[20]

The second difficulty is more philosophical. To elevate compassion or related virtues over wisdom as the central and defining feature of Buddhist faith could amount to claiming either that (1) wisdom is entailed by compassion or (2) compassion is the central influence on or condition for wisdom. The problem is that both of these positions give up too easily on the idea that wisdom can influence or inspire compassion.

The first claim, that compassion entails wisdom, suggests among other things a Buddhist monopoly on compassion, a distinctly uncharitable interpretation of the worth of other religious faiths. If (1) was strictly true, it would itself entail the contrapositive suggestion that if one is not wise in the Buddhist sense, then one is not compassionate. Hence, every Christian, Jew, Muslim, Hindu, Animist, or whatever would be precluded from true compassion unless it could be shown that unbeknownst to them, their beliefs were closet forms of Buddhism all along. Furthermore, to say that one is compassionate is not to say in what way one understands the world. Caring can be for all sorts of different reasons linked to all sorts of different kinds of beliefs about the nature and needs of those towards whom one's compassion is directed. There seems to be little logical entailment between a compassionate disposition and a particular metaphysics or even lack of metaphysics.

The second version of the claim, that compassion influences or conditions wisdom, is attractively modest and faithful to Buddhist texts. However, in that case wisdom ought to have some intrinsic connection with compassion; we cannot treat the two aspects as logically independent. Otherwise, it is hard to see why Buddhists can plausibly maintain that following the precepts has any role in sparking enlightenment. And if wisdom and compassion are intrinsically connected, one would expect that such influence runs both ways.

Now one might counter by claiming that compassion (and related precepts) do influence or inspire wisdom in the sense that one cannot be truly compassionate without achieving a level of selflessness and recognition of interdependence with others. Thus, if Buddhist precepts such as non-injury and selfless giving represent one's path, then Buddhist metaphysics becomes one's philosophical orientation. However, besides the fact that influence or inspiration still does not constitute logical entailment, and it is not clear that it must, there is another issue at stake. To say that compassion requires selflessness and recognition of interdependence seems to suggest that somehow these create compassion. Yes, they create it in one perhaps already compassionate or predisposed to compassion, but that they make such a contribution involves some intrinsic connection between wisdom and the results of a compassionate nature. Of course, one could argue to the contrary and say that no, wisdom does not create compassion but does enlarge it in the sense that one no longer distinguishes between compassion towards oneself or one's friends and compassion towards one's enemies for example. Wisdom and compassion are wholly different but have complementary roles in the development of one's moral outlook. But this is to conceive of wisdom itself in terms that are wholly separate from compassion itself and provides no basis for claims to the effect that wisdom itself influences or inspires compassion.

Therefore, we should avoid all claims that seek to clarify or characterize what it is to be compassionate or see things from a compassionate angle. All such claims inevitably require typifying the world or some slice of the world in a particular fashion, and if one is a Buddhist, in terms of co-arising and dependence. And this again is to see some relationship between compassion and our sense of the world—wisdom in other words.

Personally, I rather think that Buddhists, and particularly Zen Buddhists, do entertain a fairly strong and mutually entailing or dependent relationship between wisdom and compassion. The idea seems to be that wisdom is not really wise unless it is compassionate and compassion is not truly compassionate unless it is truly wise. That is, when wisdom in the form of Buddhist doctrines such as *anatta, anicca, sunyata, pratitya samutpada,* and the like is fully comprehended, it is not a merely intellectual grasping but an affective and experiential transformation into a life of compassion, giving, and so on. Equally when *karuna* and other such virtues are truly internalized they constitutively reshape our comprehension of the world in its entirety. The world of the truly compassionate is impermanent and they themselves egoless. To see it that way, as the whole of one's perspective, is exactly the true mark of compassion. It wouldn't occur to you to represent things as any other way. Yet to allow such thorough mutual influence or identification between wisdom and compassion is to have to take seriously the question of how each follows from the other or is intrinsically related to the other. What is a problem for Zen is also a problem for Buddhism, at least if we choose to understand Buddhism in the manner just outlined.

What Are Possible Implications for Understanding Issues of Moral Responsibility, Violence, and Terrorism?

If the above is where we end up on the question of Zen and ethics, and thus perhaps for Buddhism in general, then the answers we get to questions of violence and moral responsibility are complicated and perhaps somewhat disquieting. The upshot of our discussion suggests Buddhists saying, "Well, we don't condone violence, but we can't give any general answer as to why others shouldn't. If they wish to end their suffering and achieve what we take to be enlightenment, then we can offer a path that starts with following certain ethical precepts and ends in Zen enlightenment. But short of such a quest there is little to say regarding a general moral responsibility to avoid violence." Terrorism, in the sense of politically motivated violence aimed at terrorizing noncombatants, is not a Buddhist option in its rejection of even the most elemental type of compassion. Yet, it remains a human option that Buddhism cannot foreclose. Buddhism cannot even foreclose the possibility of violence hastening enlightenment: traditional Buddhism because it cannot rigorously ground its precepts in the first place and Zen because it cannot foreclose any avenue as a path to enlightenment.

In other words, because of the lack of a deductive connection between the relativity of all things as Buddhism sees the world and the specific acts that Buddhism condones as appropriately articulating our place in the sea of becoming, there seems to be little of a general and moral character that Buddhism can say regarding violent acts. In which case, Buddhism in general can say little to one who, in the name of a new non-traditional Buddhism, might claim the necessity of violence and injury in dealing with a specific situation or the revaluation of moral goods and evils as happened in World War II Japan. Does Zen provide the moral resources to balance off the call to avoid the evil of sedition against the demand for compassionate refusal of wars of imperial conquest? Thus, while it might be clear that Buddhists generally have a responsibility to avoid violence, it isn't clear that they always do. It is also unclear that non-Buddhists have such obligations either.

But while a deductive connection between emptiness and action might furnish a kind of answer, because it would explain why any being would have such obligations as Buddhists recognize, could a less comprehensive connection do the job? Are there ways of rethinking the connection between emptiness and action that might strengthen the evident value placed on non-violence and heighten our general moral obligation to be compassionate? Could it be that Buddhist precepts represent not exactly morally unconditional constraints on our actions, but approximations to an enlightened state?

Let me first of all characterize these precepts as various admonitions to refrain from violence, from inflicting injury in various fashions whether through killing or simply exploiting the vulnerabilities of another. In other words, Buddhist ethics are about avoiding violence in this sense. Let me further postulate without argument that such violence requires a state of mental dissociation between the perpetrator and the victim. Since such dissociation represents a denial of mutual dependence, violence, in the sense of an intention to inflict injury on another, requires a form of blindness or ignorance in the Buddhist sense. To avoid intentional, injury-inflicting action is consistent with placing oneself on the path to enlightenment, and its importance in Buddhist literature makes good sense. Buddhist precepts thus represent an approximation of the path of enlightenment.

This leaves open a significant possibility, however, that action involving non-intended injury is not precluded from the enlightened state or the path to the enlightened state. In which case, the Merleau-Ponty quote with which the essay begins is within the purview of Buddhist principles in the sense that the demands of a certain situation might involve violent action though not "self-perpetuating" violence. That is, violence would have to involve its own "suspension" as he says. Why might such violence pass Buddhist muster?

"Non-intended" could mean at least a couple of things. On the one hand, it could mean completely unforeseen and accidental. I might have no idea, and excusably so, that something I am doing is dangerous. The other possibility is that I may foresee that a certain act will result in injury though I do not intend to bring the injury about; injury is not my aim, so to speak. A surgeon may operate on a patient knowing that the procedure will hurt without intending to bring about pain. The purpose in this case is to help; the pain involved is incidental, even if considerable. However, any invocation of the principle of "double effect" is constrained by the requirement that what is foreseen but unintended *not* be the means whereby that which is intended is brought about. If an action is a means of accomplishing an end, it is as intended as the end. Consequently, I cannot claim that killing one person to save another represents an incidental and unintended side effect. My killing one to save another is instrumental to accomplishing my purpose.

This places a considerable limitation on the sense in which unintended injury might escape Buddhist prohibitions. The most likely scenario whereby I might have a causal role in unintended violence that was not accidental would be a situation such as Gandhi's non-violent resistance acts of civil disobedience. I may know that my non-violent acts may provoke violence on the part of others, but I do them anyhow because they are instrumental to social change. Violence is not my means, though it is inevitable and foreseeable. It is hard to imagine any sort of scenario where violence on my own part would escape the constraint. However, that is hardly an argument that such could never be the case. In other words, a non-violent path in the sense laid down by Buddhism's precepts provides the best objective approximation of the path of full enlightenment.

Notes

1. Maurice Merleau-Ponty, *Humanism and Terror: An Essay on the Communist Problem*, trans. John O'Neill (Boston, Beacon Press, 1969), 1-2

2. See Masao Abe, "Zen and Western Thought" in *Zen and Western Thought* (Honolulu: University of Hawaii Press, 1985), 83-120.

3. Allan M. Jalon, "Meditating on War and Guilt, Zen says It's Sorry," *New York Times*, 11 January 2003, 9(B).

4. Christopher Ives, *Zen Awakening and Society*, Foreword by Masao Abe and John Hick (Honolulu: University of Hawaii Press, 1992).

5. T.P. Kasulis, *Zen Action/Zen Person* (Honolulu: University of Hawaii Press, 1985), 93-94.

6. Frederick J. Streng, *Emptiness: A Study in Religious Meaning* (Nashville, Tenn.: Abingdon Press, 1967), 213, *Karika 19*.

7. As is well known, Krishna makes a very similar claim in the *Bhagavad Gita* when he challenges Arjuna's reticence to kill in battle by arguing that whatever is born and dies (in this case the empirical self) is fundamentally unreal and hence unworthy of concern.

8. Streng, *Emptiness*, 213.

9. David Burton argues a similar point in "Knowledge and Liberation: Philosophical Ruminations on a Buddhist Conundrum," *Philosophy East and West*

52, no. 3 (July 2002): 326-45. His point is that knowledge of impermanence does not necessarily lead to a cessation of craving.

10. Abe, "Zen and Western Thought," 104.

11. Abe, "Zen and Western Thought," 119-20.

12.   The reference is to Chapter 24 in Streng's "Translation of *Mulamadhyamakakarikas*: Fundamentals of the Middle Way" in *Emptiness*, 212-15. Numbers in brackets refer to numbered verses in the text.

13. Kasulis, *Zen Action/Zen Person*, 96.

14. Yoshifumi Ueda and Dennis Hirota, *Shinran: An Introduction to His Thought* (Kyoto: Hongwanji International Center, 1989), 256.

15. Hannah Arendt's "banality of evil" might describe this class of motivations.

16. Kasulis, *Zen Action/Zen Person*, 97.

17. Jeffrey Stout, *Ethics After Babel* (Princeton: Princeton University Press, 1988).

18. See Peter Hershock's *Reinventing the Wheel: A Buddhist Response to the Information Age* (Albany: State University of New York Press, 1999), 287.

19. Kasulis, *Zen Action/Zen Person*, 93-97.

20. An example may be found in *The Vimalakirti Sutra*, translated by Burton Watson (New York: Columbia University Press, 1997) in the chapter translated as "Regarding Living Beings" where Vimalakirti claims that the bodhisattva treats living beings "with a compassion that never despairs, seeing that all is empty and without ego . . . treats them with the compassion of wisdom, which always knows the right time . . . " (84-85) or, "One embraces the view of emptiness and nothingness, yet does not discard one's great pity" (129). Compassion coarises with wisdom in one who is accomplished, in other words.

10

Eliminating the Root of All Evil: Interdependence and the De-Reification of the Self

Jeffery D. Long

As the title of this volume suggests, we are living today in times of terror. How can comparative philosophy help us to cope with and ideally overcome terror? How can it help us envision a world without terror and the steps toward making such a world a reality?

My approach in this paper is to situate the question of terror in the larger context of the question of violence more generally (of which terror is of course a subvariety) and ultimately in the even larger context of suffering (of which violence is a subvariety). My approach, shaped by the Buddhist tradition, is to isolate the basic conditions that make violence possible, the idea being that the elimination of these conditions, should it occur, would necessarily lead to the elimination of violence.

There are many reasons to believe the complete elimination of violence is highly unlikely, if not impossible. Reasons for this which I allude to here include the degree to which practically all human beings are implicated in the phenomenon of structural violence and the arguably superhuman capacity for empathy that a a life of complete nonviolence, on my analysis, would require. But is the pursuit of a world without violence therefore a waste of time? I would like to suggest that it is not, but rather that the attempt to pursue a world free from violence and the employment of a world free from violence as an absolute ideal or limit concept may very well decrease the overall amount of violence in the world and dramatically improve the quality of human existence.

This is the larger context in which the argument of this paper, which is presented as a case for absolute nonviolence, should be understood. The author is no utopian starry-eyed idealist when it comes to assessing the actual likelihood of a nonviolent world ever becoming a reality (although he has been accused of it in the past). In fact, there are good reasons for believing that, short of all beings attaining *nirvana*, such a goal will never be achieved in the realm of time and space. But the potential benefits of the attempt, though short of the ultimate goal, seem well worth the effort.

My Assumptions

What is violence? How does it arise? And how might a cessation of violence be brought about? What is the path to the elimination of violence? The not-so-modest goal of this essay is to at least begin the process of sketching an account of violence and its emergence for the purpose of determining how an end to violence might be effected.

A basic assumption of the approach I am taking is the Buddhist "principle of the conditionality of existence." This is the principle, as given in *Samyutta Nikaya* 2.28, that "(1) When this is, that is; (2) this arising, that arises; (3) when this is not, that is not; (4) this ceasing, that ceases."[1] The assumption is that there are certain basic conditions the presence of which coincides with the arising of violence and the absence of which coincides with the cessation of violence. Therefore, if one can determine what these basic conditions are, one can conceivably develop a path to the elimination of violence through the elimination of the conditions that invariably coincide with its arising, assuming these conditions can be eliminated.

Another assumption I am making here is that violence as such is something that needs to be eliminated. This assumption is again Buddhist. It takes for granted that violence is a form of *dukkha* or suffering which, on a Buddhist understanding, is that which is to be eliminated.

This understanding of suffering is probably the most basic of the assumptions I am employing in this essay. While suffering may indeed have a variety of redemptive or character building features, on a Buddhist understanding these are not features of suffering as such. They are effects of the creative uses that, if we are properly discerning, we may put to our experiences of suffering. For example, through our own experiences of suffering we may learn to develop empathy. We come to understand that we should not inflict upon others the kinds of unpleasant experiences that we, ourselves, wish to avoid. But positive effects of suffering such as these are not intrinsic to the experience of suffering. They are a result of what we do with our suffering. The ultimate goal of the Buddhist path is a state in which there is no suffering at all. Suffering, therefore, in and of itself, is not seen as having an intrinsic positive value in the Buddhist tradition.

While suffering is involved in the path to *nirvana* (for on a Buddhist understanding suffering characterizes all states short of *nirvana*) it is not something that the Buddhist tradition sees as in any sense intrinsically positive. So for all

intents and purposes we may conceive of suffering as that which is to be eliminated.

Although the most fundamental assumptions and the approach to violence
that I am taking in this essay are Buddhist, I shall also draw upon a variety of
non-Buddhist sources in order to make my argument. It will hopefully become
clear by the end of this essay that its very eclecticism is part of the claim that it
advances–that at the root of violence is a false sense of self as an independent
entity. This sense can be dispelled, at least in part, by a recognition of the interdependence and hybridity of all of our "selves": cultural, religious, ethnic, national, or personal. Though I do not make a case for it here, it is my view that a
plurality of paths are possible by which the elimination of a false sense of self
and its replacement by an authentic self-awareness can be attained. My approach
here is primarily Buddhist, but not exclusively so.

What I mean by "a false sense of self as an independent entity" is a reified
sense of the self. Reification "involves a process of abstraction, as with constructions of the imagination, in which we convert the abstraction into a real
thing. We take a mental abstraction...and reify it by giving it substantial reality
and existence independent of its status as a mental abstraction existing in our
minds/imagination."[2] In keeping with the Buddhist No Self doctrine, I take the
self to be the result of just such a process.

My claim is not that simply by de-reifying the self, by undoing this process
of abstraction and giving substantial reality to the self, we can necessarily arrive
at the kind of right understanding that would be required to eliminate violence:
an understanding of ourselves as interdependent entities, an interdependence the
proper response to which is compassion for and solidarity with our fellow beings. On a Buddhist understanding, it is the desire for a separate self-existence
that fuels the process of self-reification. It is this desire that must ultimately be
eliminated if the de-reification of the self is to have any lasting effect–if it is to
lead to *nirvana*. The de-reification of the self, in other words, in a Buddhist context, is a process undertaken not as an end in itself, but as both a step toward and
a product of a right understanding of reality. It is therefore not the same as, for
example, a materialist de-reification of the self.

But if the reified self is a necessary condition for violence and intrinsically
an obstruction to a right understanding of reality, then its elimination (what I call
the de-reification of the self) would be a necessary step in the direction of a
world without violence. In the context of this essay I conceive of the de-
reification of the self not so much in its Buddhist soteriological sense, though
my analysis does draw and depend upon such an understanding. I am conceiving
of it here more as an antidote to prejudice and an alternative to the self-other
dichotomies with which we are being constantly bombarded and which are in-

voked as justifications for acts of violence: nationalisms, ethnicities, and religious identities. I am proposing, in place of these "selves," a not-self. My strategy is to undermine the "selves" that violence is often intended to defend and thereby to undermine violence itself.

What Is Violence? A Working Definition

We should be clear, first of all, what we mean when we speak of violence. What is it that we are saying should be eliminated? The Sanskrit word that is most typically translated with the English word "violence" is *himsa*, a noun derived from the *sannanta*, or desiderative form of the verbal root *han*, meaning kill, strike, or injure. *Himsa*, therefore, refers to a desire to kill, strike, or injure. Let us begin by defining violence, then, in terms of intention, as the desire to bring about injury and any thought, word, or action that arises from this desire. By "injury" we mean *dukkha* or suffering.

Violence, on this definition, is basically a perverse desire, a desire to bring about that which, by definition, is to be eliminated, as well as any thought, word, or deed which flows therefrom. Such a desire is a reversal of *karuna*, or compassion, which is the desire for the elimination of the suffering of all beings. The desire to bring about the end of all suffering is the desire at the root of the bodhisattva path, the path to *nirvana*, which, according to the *tathagatagarbha* doctrine, the doctrine of Buddha Nature, is our true natural state. On this analysis, therefore, violence is a perversion of our most basic nature as interdependently arising beings. When we injure others we injure ourselves. A similar understanding is present in a variety of religious and philosophical traditions, notably Hinduism and Jainism, but others as well. It is the essence, one could say, of the Golden Rule.

How adequate is this definition of violence as the desire to bring about injury and any thought, word, or action that arises from this desire? One possible objection to this definition is that it excludes a number of phenomena that are normally characterized by the word "violent," like a violent storm, or a violent earthquake. A tornado is not, by this definition, violent (unless tornadoes are sentient!) although it is certainly productive of *dukkha*. So unintentional violence, on this understanding, does not occur.

But this only seems problematic if we are talking about the actions of sentient beings. If a comparison can be made with the word "evil," much unnecessary confusion has arisen over the characterization of destructive natural phenomena as cases of "natural evil," rather than simple tragedies. Violence, like evil, has a *moral* character. It involves intention and choice. Insentient phenomena are "violent" only by way of analogy.

But with regard to the actions of sentient beings, it seems that my proposed definition of violence has more serious problems. One could argue, for example, that the thief who robs a wealthy man, perhaps even killing him in the process, in order to provide for his starving children, is acting not out of an intention to do harm, but out of compassion for his children. Similarly, one could argue that someone who kills in self defense, or a soldier acting in the defense of her nation, or even a terrorist seeking to overturn the present, unjust world order for the purpose of bringing about a new order that he takes to be more just, is not engaging in violence, so long as the intention motivating the action is not to bring about injury, but a higher purpose, such as the defense of the innocent. The injury brought about in such cases, one could argue, is merely an unfortunate side effect of actions carried out with intentions that are ultimately pure and benevolent, a double effect argument.

One could respond to this objection that a distinction needs to be made between the ultimate intention that might motivate the actors in these cases, their long term goals, and their immediate intentions. The thief may intend, in the long run, to feed his children; but when he bashes the rich man over the head with a baseball bat, his immediate intention is to render his victim unconscious, and maybe even dead, so he can go about robbing him. The soldier may intend ultimately to defend innocents from harm; but when she has an enemy in the sights of her gun, her intent is to injure that enemy. The terrorist may be trying to create a just world order; but his immediate goal is terror and mayhem.

But the argument would still remain that just as the suffering created by the tornado or the earthquake is not, morally speaking, violent, given that the tornado and the earthquake are incapable of violent intentions, the suffering created in a just cause is also not violent, given that this suffering is not the primary intent of its perpetrators. This is precisely the kind of argument used by those who attempt to justify violent actions in the name of a higher cause. The ends justify the means because the ends provide the true motive for the action in question; and motive is the determinant of the morality of an act.

The problem with this argument, of course, is that it militates against the goal of the elimination of violence by seeking to justify violence. It does not point the way to a world without terror or war, but seeks instead to justify the existing world order in which terror and war occur. If our goal is the elimination of violence then we must define violence in a way that does not give an opening to such an argument.

I would suggest, at this point, a refinement of my initial definition of violence. A new definition of violence could be the desire or the willingness to bring about injury and any thought, word, or action that arises from this desire or willingness.

I see this revision of my initial definition of violence, based on the meaning of *himsa*, as having a number of advantages.

First, it includes even those violent acts committed, ostensibly, for some purpose other than the mere infliction of the injury which they cause: acts of self defense, of national defense, revolution for social justice, etc. Acts of violence committed even for the noblest of causes are caught in its net.

But it also creates a spectrum, allowing one to make a moral distinction between an act of violence undertaken, say, out of extreme hatred for its intended victim, and one undertaken in the pursuit of a goal that is good in and of itself. There is a difference between a desire to cause injury and a willingness to cause injury in the pursuit of some other goal. This allows us to distinguish, for example, between a person who is abusing a child and another who injures the abuser in order to stop further abuse. But because the distinction is a matter of degree, it also allows us to recognize that both acts are violent, that both acts cause *dukkha*, and that the world we would like to envision would contain neither. This definition, essentially, allows for a kind of "two truths" doctrine, with nonviolence as an absolute in a world of relative violence.[3]

Finally, another advantage of this new definition is that it excludes any actions that bring about injury that the perpetrator neither desires as a primary goal, nor is even willing to countenance, but that nevertheless occurs due to unavoidable circumstances. I am referring here to accidental injuries.

The Jain tradition, of course, argues that there are no unavoidable circumstances, that activity carried out with sufficient care will not cause injury to any being. But this obliterates the distinction between violence and *dukkha* as such. More in keeping with the Buddhist tradition, I wish to preserve a volitional, and so moral, sense of the meaning of violence.

Arguably the greatest weakness of this definition of violence is that it also excludes, besides accidental injury, injury caused by economic and cultural forces that operate beyond the scope of the conscious intentions of human agents. This is what is often referred to as structural violence.

Structural violence is undoubtedly one of the most significant sources of suffering in the world today. The Sanskrit term *himsa*, on which my understanding of violence is based, does not seem to encompass wholly non-volitional forms of violence such as those that the term "structural violence" denotes, violence that is neither intended nor approved by anyone, but that is simply built into the structures of human existence in a particular time and place.

This raises important questions though, and troubling ones for all of us who cannot but participate in the global economy, thereby implicitly supporting the structural violence that it creates. Can violent structures exist in the absence of the volitional choices of the individuals whose repeated choices and actions maintain those structures? Once we become aware of the suffering caused by the structures in which we participate, are we not complicit in it?

With regard to my definition of violence in terms of desire or willingness to cause injury, it seems that structural violence also falls under it to the degree that those who participate in violent structures are aware of the harm that their participation in those structures involves. I may not desire to cause harm to the physical environment or to help fund terrorist organizations or multinational corporations, but every time I put fuel in my automobile I show a willingness to participate in a small way in these harmful activities. I may seek to justify this participation in a variety of ways, like the soldier taking part in violence in a more explicit sense by fighting in what she takes to be a just war.

How so? I may tell myself, for example, that I need to put fuel in my car so I can transport myself to a conference where I am going to speak about nonviolence. But the difference between me and the soldier is only one of degree rather than of kind, at least to the extent that I am aware of the harm my actions help to cause.

The contemplation of structural violence and the degree to which we all acquiesce in its occurrence is sobering, creating an almost Jainesque sense of the nearly superhuman difficulty of truly practicing nonviolence in thought, word, and deed. The contrast between *ahimsa* as an absolute ideal and as a pragmatic reality is most dramatically evident when we look at structural violence.

The Reified Self as the Root of All Violence

Operating with the revised definition of violence just given as the desire or the willingness to bring about injury and any thought, word, or action that arises from this desire or willingness, let us return to the questions with which we began this essay: How does violence arise? And how might a cessation of violence be brought about? What is the path to the elimination of violence? Violence, like every phenomenal experience, involves a subject and an object, a self and an other—in this case, a perpetrator and a victim. At the root of all violence, I wish to argue, is a false separation between these two.

In an essay entitled *In the Name of Identity: Violence and the Need to Belong*, the French-Lebanese, Arab-Christian novelist Amin Maalouf traces the connections between violence and identity. He defines identity straightforwardly by saying, "My identity is what prevents me from being identical to anybody else."[4] He elaborates by explaining that,

> Each individual's identity is made up of a number of elements...Of course, for the great majority these factors include allegiance to a religious tradition; to a nationality—sometimes two; to a profession, an institution, or a particular social milieu. But the list is much longer than that; it is virtually unlimited. A person may feel a more or less strong attachment to a province, a village, a neighbourhood, a clan, a professional team or one connected with sport, a group of friends, a

union, a company, a parish, a community of people with the same passions, the same sexual preferences, the same physical handicaps, or who have to deal with the same kind of pollution or other nuisance. Of course, not all these allegiances are equally strong, at least at any given moment. But none is entirely insignificant, either. All are components of personality–we might almost call them 'genes of the soul' so long as we remember that most of them are not innate. While each of these elements may be found separately in many individuals, the same combination of them is never encountered in different people, and it's this that gives every individual richness and value and makes each human being unique and irreplaceable.[5]

The root of violence, Maalouf argues, is not, as one might expect, and as a Buddhist might suggest, an egotistical desire to assert or to protect our unique, special, individual identities. These he regards, as his language in the quotation just given suggests, as precious, as a source of "richness and value." Difference as such is not the problem. This resonates well with a Whiteheadian process understanding of the self in which the *telos* of the universe is the generation of diverse novel forms of experience. Difference, in such a worldview, is to be celebrated.

The problem, Maalouf says, arises when we define ourselves in terms of just one of our many allegiances. This is a kind of violence to the self, in which we subvert the totality of our complex selves to just one defining allegiance.

Again, this is different from a Buddhist analysis. But I believe the two can be connected in the following way. Both false senses of self–the reified self that is the object of the Buddhist critique, and the exclusive adherence to one allegiance of which Maalouf speaks–are inauthentic forms of self-awareness, reflecting a lack of insight into the true character of self. Both are reinforced through habitual thought patterns. Both are based on fear–or negative desire, as a Buddhist would say–of self-annihilation. Finally, and most significantly, both lead to suffering, including violence.

Maalouf speaks of being asked, as someone who is both Arab and French, which of these two he really is "deep down inside."

For a long time I found this oft-repeated question amusing, but it no longer makes me smile. It seems to reflect a view of humanity which, though it is widespread, is also in my opinion dangerous. It presupposes that 'deep down inside' everyone there is just one affiliation that really matters, a kind of 'fundamental truth' about each individual, an 'essence' determined once and for all at birth, never to change thereafter. As if the rest, all the rest–a person's whole journey through time as a free agent; the beliefs he acquires in the course of that journey; his own individual tastes, sensibilities, and affinities; in short his life itself–counted for nothing. And when, as happens so often nowadays, our contemporaries are exhorted to 'assert their identities,' they are meant to seek within themselves that same alleged fundamental allegiance, which is often religious, national, racial or ethnic, and having located it they are supposed to flaunt it proudly in the face of others. Anyone who claims a more complex identity is marginalized.[6] (Maalouf 2-3)

This, according to Maalouf, is where violence begins: within ourselves, with the suppression of our own inner complexity. From a Buddhist perspective, this is not the ultimate root of violence. But is certainly a possible effect of desire, in this case, the desire to belong.

What are the conditions that make violence possible? Again, violence, like every phenomenal experience, involves a subject and an object, a self and an other. In an essay entitled "War and Warriors: An Overview," Bruce Lincoln argues "that it is only when human actors come to regard others as 'things' that they become capable of employing force, particularly lethal force, against them."[7] If one is to engage in violence against another, one must blind oneself to the ways in which the other is like the self. A necessary condition for violence is the "othering" of the other and the "selfing" of the self.

What does this mean? At the root of all evil, according to the *dharma* traditions of India, is a primordial ignorance or *avidya*. This ignorance manifests, at its most basic level, as a lack of self-knowledge, or of an authentic self-awareness.

The particular form that this ignorance takes and the authentic self-awareness that is its antidote vary from tradition to tradition, depending on the metaphysical and cosmological orientations of each. But all point to an awareness that radically undermines conventional distinctions between self and other. All point to the interdependence and interconnectedness of all beings.

In the *Bhagavad Gita*, for example, Arjuna is cautioned against identifying the self with the physical body, the most obvious distinguishing factor among beings in the material world. The body will perish and pass away, being cast off by the soul like a set of old, worn out clothes.[8] According to the *Gita*, as well as the *Samkhya* and *Yoga* traditions, the body, and indeed all of physical nature, is but the ever-changing play of the three *gunas* of *prakriti*.

Similarly, in the *Chandogya Upanishad*, the doctrine that the body is the self is presented as the doctrine of foolish demons.[9] Ultimately, in the Vedantic tradition, particularly Advaita Vedanta, the self is identified not with the body, but with the *atman*, the universal self, which is ultimately identical with Brahman, the Absolute, Reality as such. Authentic self-awareness therefore consists, broadly speaking, of an awareness not of that which distinguishes us from all other beings, but of that which connects us to all other beings.

In the Jain tradition, the true self, again, is not the body but the soul or *jiva*. Though the *jivas*, according Jainism, are numerically distinct, they possess the same essential nature; and it is the fact that other living beings possess a *jiva* of the same kind as oneself that is the basis for empathy, and for the practice of *ahimsa*, or nonviolence in thought, word, and deed. "To do harm to others is to do harm to oneself. 'Thou art he whom thou intendest to kill! Thou art he whom thou intendest to tyrannize over!' We corrupt ourselves as soon as we intend to corrupt others. We kill ourselves as soon as we intend to kill others."[10] Again, we see an authentic self-awareness as an awareness that connects us in bonds of empathy with other beings.

Finally, in Buddhism, one finds the no self doctrine and the doctrine of *pratityasamutpada* or interdependent arising, according to which, again, the self is not that which finally makes us distinct from all other beings, for no such independent, distinguishing self exists. The idea that there is such a self is the final state of false consciousness that needs to be eliminated in order for *nirvana* to occur.

In the Buddhist tradition an authentic self-awareness is an awareness of perpetually arising and perishing moments of experience. These moments exist interdependently and without any final or ultimate distinction obtaining between self and other. "Self" and "other" are false dichotomizing conceptual constructs.

It is this lack of any ultimate distinction between self and other that is the basis for compassion, for seeing the suffering of the other as one's own; because there is finally, on an ultimate, metaphysical level, no difference between the self and the other. Suffering is suffering and is to be eliminated regardless of where it occurs. So "your" suffering is "mine" and "my" suffering is "yours." We are all suffering together.

True, the Mahayana tradition makes this more explicit than the Theravada, sometimes coming close to an almost Vedantic affirmation of the unity of beings, which one sometimes finds in the Zen tradition, for example. The Mahayana metaphysics of the *alayavijñana* and the *dharmakaya*–which are both principles, among other things, of cosmic unity–allow for such seemingly Vedantic formulations. The ideal of compassion and solidarity in suffering is central, however, to both the Theravada and the Mahayana traditions.

Maalouf draws our attention to the fact that our identities are a complex and ever-changing nexus of allegiances that connect us, in some fashion, with every other being on the planet. Maalouf does not mention Buddhism in his essay, nor is he to my knowledge a scholar of Asian philosophy. But his insight is one which resonates with, and, I think, helps to fill out and complete the Buddhist (and Whiteheadian constructive postmodern) sense of the self as an ever-changing and dependent stream of events with no final defining essence. On a Buddhist analysis, the reification of the self, the attempt to give the self an essence, to make it an "it," a self, in the first place, is the root error that is at the heart of all error, and of all suffering. This error arises from and reinforces desire. This self becomes the object and the subject of desire, of the craving for permanent satisfaction in a world of impermanent events that is the cause of *dukkha*, according to the Second Noble Truth.

Similarly, on Maalouf's analysis, the attempt to define the self–or, to use his term, *identity*–in terms of just one of its many allegiances–usually an ethnic, national, or religious one–is not only a form of violence to the self, but is the shift which enables the objectification of the other that Lincoln affirms to be a necessary condition for the commission of acts of violence against the other. If I identify myself exclusively with my nationality, for example, I blind myself to the host of other allegiances I may share with those who do not share my national allegiance. I distance myself from them, making them "other" and ignoring our shared bonds.

At the same time, Maalouf's emphasis on how the distinctive uniqueness of each being adds richness and value to the universe serves to balance a tendency that one might find in the Asian traditions to emphasize interdependence and unity at the expense of such richness and value. Interdependence and unity need not imply an undifferentiated oneness, such as that affirmed in Advaita Vedanta. Interdependence implies some degree of difference; for two identical entities are not interdependent. If they are identical, they are not two, but one. Dependence is a relation which, as such, can only occur between different entities.

But to affirm a relation is to affirm a simultaneous sameness as well as difference. Two entities are related only if they are, in different respects, both similar and different. Again, two identical entities are not related. They are one. But two utterly dissimilar entities, sharing no common attributes, would be wholly unrelated. According to process thought, as well as Buddhism, no such utterly dissimilar entities exist. To exist is to be related. So an independent entity is a non-entity. If nothing else, two entities share the quality "existence." The fundamental fact of their being, if nothing else, constitutes their relatedness, and vice versa: their relatedness constitutes their existence. So any attempt to conceive of the other as utterly other is rooted in a basic metaphysical error.

Compassionate Violence?

A question, however, still remains. Might even a de-reified self, a being of pure compassion fully cognizant of her relations of dependence upon all beings, still engage in violence, as defined here? Might not such a being still be willing to inflict injury if, by doing so, greater injury would be thereby averted? In the Buddhist tradition, this question arises with respect to the idea of the wrathful bodhisattva. But it is a practical question as well. Is compassionate violence possible?

The Jain tradition, at least on one reading, would be inclined to say "no." Once, Mahatma Gandhi permitted the mercy killing of an injured goat at his Sabarmati Ashram. The animal was in great pain, and Gandhi's rationale was that it was more compassionate to end the animal's suffering than to force it to endure that suffering by not ending its life. This act met with strong condemnation from the Jain community, the rationale being that Gandhi had interfered with the karma of the goat by ending its life "unnaturally."

Such an objection, however, suffers a number of difficulties. It suggests, first of all, that all acts intended to alleviate suffering are inappropriate. If beings suffer because of their karma, because their previous choices determine that such suffering is going to occur, and if any attempt to alleviate such suffering is an attempt to tamper with karma, then no attempt to alleviate suffering should be allowed. But Jains actually go to a great deal of effort to alleviate the suffering of sick and injured animals, short of actually killing them. One could argue that to take a life is always to rob a being of an opportunity for meritorious action and possible liberation from the rebirth process. But if one's argument is that no suffering at all should be ended through outside intervention, but rather allowed to run its karmic course, this would also seem to preclude such interventions as administering medicines, feeding, and so on.

There is a logical problem here as well. The objection of the Jain community was that Gandhi essentially interfered, or sought to interfere, with the karmic process. But, on a Jain understanding, karma cannot be so easily interfered with. It is an inexorable part of the working of the universe. So, if Gandhi had the goat killed, it must have been part of its karmic destiny to be killed at the time that it was. One type of karma, on a Jain understanding, is, indeed, an *ayukarma*, or life span determining karma. If the goat was killed at the age of six years, eight months, three days, fourteen hours, twenty minutes, and fifty-seven seconds–for example–then, in retrospect, we can say that that must have been the life span determined by its *ayukarma*. Gandhi was merely the instrument of the karmic process. Of course, as part of that process, he is also subject to it.

It seems that, from a Jain perspective, properly understood, the problem for Gandhi is not that he tampered with karma. Karma cannot be tampered with, any more than gravity can. The problem for Gandhi is that he engaged in *himsa*, even if it was from a compassionate motive. He was willing to inflict injury on another being, or to permit such injury, since he did not do the deed himself. But to approve of *himsa*, on a Jain understanding, is to engage in it. This is true on my definition of violence as well, as involving either a willingness or a desire to cause injury.

But back to the main question, assuming Gandhi was a pretty advanced being, do we have a case here of violence by someone aware of his relations of mutual dependence with all beings, but who permitted some suffering to prevent even greater suffering?

This question can be seen to suffer from the same defect as the earlier question that required us to make the distinction between a desire and a willingness to do harm. That problem was that such an approach does not point us toward a world without violence, but seeks to justify the existing world order. We also saw that violence on a massive scale could conceivably be justified thereby. If one is willing to approve of violence at all, even in the name of a higher cause then one has not escaped from the cycle of suffering. Harry Truman, it has been argued by some, ordered the bombings of Hiroshima and Nagasaki in order to prevent the more massive loss of (American) life that an invasion of Japan would have involved. But an argument that permits the atomic bombing of entire cities to be justified as an act of compassion is certainly lacking in its ability to point us beyond the existing, violent world order. Once one opens the door to violence it is difficult to conceive of how it might again be closed.

Harry Truman, of course, may be a poor example. Even if one grants the standard argument for the bombing of Hiroshima and Nagasaki–that it was done to prevent even greater suffering–this raises other questions. For example, might yet even more suffering have been averted had the United States demanded less than full, unconditional surrender from the government of Japan? And what of the fact that Truman's act "raised the threshold of conceivable and acceptable violence," making the world more dangerous?[11]

The problem, of course, is that non-omniscient beings cannot foresee all of the possible consequences of either their actions or their inactions. An ostensibly nonviolent act undertaken out of pure compassion could still lead to violent results: saving the life, for example, of someone who goes on to become a mass murderer. Similarly, violent acts can sometimes lead to less suffering than would otherwise have been the case.

This, in part, is why I have chosen to define violence in terms of intentions rather than consequences. In the words of J.R.R. Tolkien, "Even the very wise cannot see all ends."[12] Beings can only act out of the knowledge available to them. The best guide to action for most human beings at most times, then, is to act nonviolently. In the game of predicting the effects of one's actions lies the slippery slope to genocide. To act otherwise is an act of hubris, of "spiritual Titanism," in the terminology of Nicholas F. Gier, of humanity assuming divine prerogatives.[13]

To return to the question "Might even a de-reified self, a being of pure compassion, act violently in order to prevent even greater suffering?" it seems that the logical answer is yes. Such a being will always act to alleviate *dukkha*; for *dukkha* is in its very nature that which is to be alleviated, and causing a relatively small amount of *dukkha* in order to prevent an even greater amount of *dukkha* is, in principle, a perfectly acceptable course of action. Two criteria, however, which human beings are capable of meeting only exceedingly rarely, if ever, are required.

First of all, such an action would seem to require knowledge of the consequences of one's actions bordering on omniscience. This may not, of course, be true in every case. Gandhi was probably correct in his assumption that the sum total of suffering in the universe would be lessened by the death of the goat than in its continued life of pain. But "even the very wise cannot see all ends." Perhaps a cure for the goat's ailment was about to become available. Or perhaps the Jains had a point, and the goat's soul was deprived of a valuable learning experience that Gandhi only postponed. Again, engaging in such calculations can be a slippery slope, but circumstances may also force such calculations upon us.

Secondly, if such a being had a full awareness, as such beings are said to have in many Asian traditions, of the sufferings of all beings, then, in carrying out the act of justified violence in question, our bodhisattva would feel, within its own being, the suffering of its victim as though it were its own. A justified act of violence by such a being could be compared to amputating one's own limb. Such an act, though justified, would still be tragic, and would be felt as such in its full intensity.

Given these criteria, it seems that the recommended course for the vast majority of human beings the vast majority of the time is nonviolence. We are not omniscient, or even nearly omniscient, so it is hard for us to tell if our violent acts really are going to minimize suffering in the end. We are also not omniconscious. As embodied beings, we generally lack the empathy to truly feel the sufferings of others as our own. Inasmuch as we lack these two characteristics, violence, for us, is to cause what should not be caused.

This is not to say that there may not be, as even Gandhi affirmed, those very rare occasions when violence is a necessary evil. We are not, so long as we are in the relative world of time and space, in *nirvana*. But *ahimsa* should always be our absolute ideal.

Conclusion

Violence, then, is the desire or the willingness to bring about injury and any thought, word, or action that arises from this desire or willingness, and at least one condition for the occurrence of violence is a sense of separation, of alienation, between the self, the perpetrator of violence, and the other, the victim. A vast host of factors, it seems, far too many to address in an essay of reasonable length, can produce this alienation. A variety of pathological forms of socialization and of institutionalized ignorance are responsible for much of the violence that occurs in our world today: socialization into gender roles which alienate men from women, creating the conditions for spousal abuse, socialization into ethnic stereotypes, creating the conditions for ethnic violence, socialization into nationalism, creating the conditions for international warfare, socialization into religious bigotry, creating the conditions for interreligious conflict, as well as the whole variety of individual, personal psychopathologies and defense mechanisms that alienate us from one another as individuals, causing conflict in the workplace, within families, among friends, or among perfect strangers.

At its most basic, however, this alienation is the result of a cognitive error, of *avidya*, of a mistaken sense of identity, or misidentification of the self with just one of its complex multitude of shifting components at the expense of other allegiances which, if we acknowledged them, would connect us with our potential victims and produce the realization that this is not an other. This is a fellow being, with feelings and aspirations not unlike my own, who, like me, adds richness and value to the universe.

What is the path to the elimination of violence? If a necessary condition for violence is, indeed, the kind of alienation I have described, based on an inauthentic self-awareness, then at least one condition for the elimination of violence is an authentic self-awareness, a realization of one's interconnectedness with and dependence upon all other beings.

A seemingly simple solution, but one that will require forms of socialization, as well as cultural and material conditions, radically different from those that now obtain.

In the meantime, it seems, the best path available to us is to reduce our participation in violence as much as humanly possible, support structures that reduce suffering, and act with compassion.

Notes

1. John Koller and Patricia Joyce Koller, *Asian Philosophies* (Third Edition) (Upper Saddle River, NJ: Prentice Hall, 1998), 151-152.
2. Douglas Allen, personal communication, May 23, 2004.
3. The two truths doctrine, found in the Hindu, Buddhist, and Jain traditions (in the works, respectively, of Shankara, Nagarjuna, and Kundakunda) essentially postulates a realm of ultimate truth–corresponding to the realm of nirvana in the Buddhist tradition– and a relative world of conventional truths, in which human beings normally operate. Gandhi invokes a similar distinction between nonviolence as an absolute and the realm of pragmatic action, in which the best we can hope for, normally, is to be *minimally* violent. I thank Doug Allen for pointing out the resonances of my definition of violence with the idea of the two truths (personal communication, May 23, 2004).

4. Amin Maalouf, *In the Name of Identity: Violence and the Need to Belong*, Barbara Bray, trans. (New York: Arcade Publishing, 2000), 10.

5. Ibid, 10-11.

6. Ibid, 2-3.

7. Bruce Lincoln, *Death, War, and Sacrifice: Studies in Ideology and Practice* (Chicago: University of Chicago Press, 1991), 144.

8. *Bhagavad Gita* 2:11.

9. *Chandogya Upanishad* 8.7-12.

10. Christopher Key Chapple, *Nonviolence to Animals, Earth, and Self in Asian Traditions* (Albany: State University of New York Press, 1993), 4.

11. Douglas Allen, personal communication, May 23, 2004.

12. J.R.R. Tolkien, *The Lord of the Rings* (Collectors's Edition). (Boston: Houghton Mifflin Company, 1965), 69.

13. Nicholas F. Gier, *Spiritual Titanism: Indian, Chinese, and Western Perspectives* (Albany: State University of New York Press, 2000).

11

Loneliness: A Common Fate for Philosophy and Terrorism?

Vance Cope-Kasten

Both philosophy and terrorism are tightly connected to loneliness in many ways. By exploring these connections, I hope to show that while philosophy and terrorism do share a common fate in terms of increasing vulnerability to loneliness, terrorism's connections are deeper and more recalcitrant, while, of the two, only philosophy has the ability to overcome or ameliorate the loneliness that comes with its territory.

After briefly delineating loneliness, I will first describe some of its key connections to philosophy, taking my cues from both Western and Chinese philosophical traditions. Then I will consider how terrorism and loneliness are connected and consider the problems for terrorism in overcoming that loneliness. Finally, I will sketch the outlook for philosophy to overcome the loneliness with which it is entangled.

Loneliness: A Modest Conception

In the past three decades, there has been a mushrooming of interest in loneliness, especially in American psychology. From that work, I propose to extract a basic, almost common sense conceptualization of loneliness. "Loneliness" will be taken to be an emotional state in which one feels that they have fewer and/or less satisfactory relationships with others than they desire, a state that is permeated with a negative affective quality. This negative affective quality can range from "an exceedingly unpleasant and driving experience"[1] to sadness and self-pity, to the persistent feeling of emptiness or hollowness that seems to be the lot of those psychologists label "the chronically lonely." And "less satisfactory relationships" in this definition refers to the kinds and degrees of mutually considerate intimacies present in the relationships. "Considerate" means here attempting to be aware of and to respond positively to the feelings, desires, and needs of others. That the mutual intimacies which mark the opposite of loneliness must be in this sense considerate is an addition to the standard characterizations, one due to reflecting on how some kinds of terrorism bring about intimacies that only intensify loneliness.

Philosophy and the Production of Loneliness

Much philosophical activity begins with the perception that things somehow don't make rational sense. This perception inevitably involves some sort of disconnect with the uninterrupted flow of lived experience. And this disconnect, in turn, is the breeding ground for the loneliness characteristic of philosophy. In a minimal kind of way, philosophizing is inevitably lonely, for if one is attempting to get things to make more sense, one's relationships with those things, with "others" conceived as broadly as possible, are not as satisfactory as one desires. And, indeed, understanding involves a kind of considerate intimacy.

In addition, and to get closer to our more common and meatier concerns about loneliness, the impulse to philosophy invariably disrupts relationships with others. Those relationships may continue, but even then some aspect of those relationships becomes an object for the philosopher's thought, and those relationships are thus no longer free-flowing interactions with the other. Then, too, philosophy's tendency to abstraction requires the draining of some elements of awareness that are characteristic of intimacies. The flow of philosophical interaction can be, at best, but a part of the free flow of intimate interaction.[2]

This inevitable interruption of free-flowing interaction becomes much sharper, of course, where philosophizing employs the direct use of argumentation, of reasoned criticism of existing ideas and reasoned defense of one's own. The term "argument" itself is hard to separate from its connotations of antagonism, as anyone knows who has ever tried to teach logic to beginning philosophy students. The students' resisting instincts seem right here, for the term "argument" is not just one which involves an ambiguity of totally unrelated meanings. Even in creating arguments for one's own ideas, one is engaging in a dispute with possible opponents, if not actual ones.

That antagonism, however genial and kindly motivated, is disruptive of human relationships is clear. And philosophy East and West thrives on a sense of "reason" in which argumentation has a natural home. Seeing the history of Western philosophy as we do through Hegel's highly antagonistic model of dialectical development, the standard story has philosophy off and running with Anaximander's dissatisfaction with Thales' attempt to make sense of the mystery of change. And while Confucius, like Thales, is not generally presented as developing his ideas as a critical response to some previous philosopher, the very next figure who makes an appearance in the standard story of the history of Chinese philosophy is Mozi, about whom A. C. Graham has this to say: "Since their doctrines are new, the Mohists have to give reasons for them, which they lay out in consecutive essays; this is the beginning of systematic debate in China. It is in the *Mo-Tzu* that we first meet the word *pien* . . . , 'to argue out alternatives', cognate with *pien* . . . ,'to distinguish', which was to become the established term for rational discourse"[3]

There are, furthermore, "Sophists" in both China and Greece who seem to revel in antagonistic reasoning almost for its own sake. And they are not ignored but confronted, often with a not altogether innocent playfulness, by the likes of Socrates or Zhuangzi. Antagonistic argumentation has settled in more deeply in Western philosophy, perhaps because of the speculated connection between rational discourse and political decision-making in the polis[4] and/or the later development of "individualism." But to suggest as Robert Nisbet does in his recent *The Geography of Thought* that this sort of thing pretty much evaporates in China due to an overriding pursuit of harmonious interaction[5] is to ignore, at the very least, the details in how Chinese philosophers sought to establish their vision of harmony.[6]

So it is clear that the practice of philosophy, by its very nature, opens the door to loneliness. Yet it must be noted that it does not necessitate loneliness, as conceived here, except in very attenuated ways. This is because while there is some disruption of relationships with others in philosophizing, it need not be that the disruption leaves those relationships either fewer in number and/or poorer in the degrees and kinds of intimacies that the philosopher desires.

Nonetheless, there are reasons to think that the opening to loneliness that philosophizing presents has either been seized or fallen into to a considerable extent. I would, in the first place, invite you who are reading this to reflect on whether your own philosophizing has been at times a lonely effort in itself and/or a source of loneliness. The perception of philosophers in the West has been of an odd lot, in particular an odd lot of loners, since the time Thales reputedly fell into a well, and certainly since Aristophanes found philosophers floating in balloons, away from human society in their investigations. Though both Confucius and Socrates were married and had children, their families do not seem to have provided a haven from loneliness, and even their relationships with peers and followers are hardly portrayed as permeated by mutually considerate intimacies. The willingness to put up with loneliness seems also to exist in the fondness of Daoist thinkers for the relatively isolated and secluded or, failing that, to be what Don Munro once told me he found an attractive ideal: to be a court hermit, to keep to oneself in the midst of society. Relevant here, finally, is the recurrent thought that significant philosophers are out of joint with their own time. Usually thought to be ahead of their time,[7] Hegel's owl of Minerva image suggests that philosophers are trying to catch up with other developments; the goddess of wisdom's wise bird (philosophy) makes sense of things only when they are over. Either way, ahead of or behind the beat, philosophy isn't quite wholly there.

In addition to these popular perceptions of philosophers as regularly alone and willing to tolerate loneliness, there is the fact that communal living by philosophers has been a relative rarity, at least in the West. There may well be some exceptions, such as the way of the Pythagoreans (a way so different it led historians of philosophy in previous generations to refer to them as a cult) or the genial household of Epicurus, and maybe even the Academy of Plato. Communal living by thinkers in China may offer non-lonely instances, too, though the Hui-Neng's own account of how he received the "Lamp of Transmission" and became the Sixth Patriarch of Chan Buddhism paints a chilling picture of isolation even in that monastic community, a picture that other thinkers in such communities might well recognize.[8]

Finally, it is worth considering the fact that in putting together his anthology of philosophical writing about friendship, *Other Selves*, Michael Pakaluk could find material by widely acknowledged philosophers of the first rank since Cicero and Seneca of Roman times only in the work of Aquinas (in the context of discussing "charity"), of the bachelor but celebrated conversationalist Immanuel Kant, and of that candidate—on the basis of both his writings and his life—for the loneliest of philosophers, Kierkegaard.[9] And Kierkegaard even argues against seeking friendship, while Kant quotes Socrates as saying "My dear friends, there are no friends," implying thereby, Kant says, "that there is no friendship which fully conforms to the Idea of friendship."[10] Having friends is widely considered to be part of a life that is thereby freer of loneliness than it might otherwise have been, both because friendships are relationships of various kinds and degrees of mutually considerate intimacies and because friends can assist in dealing with loneliness resulting from failure or frustration in other relationships. So these less than sanguine views of philosophers might hint at an endemic loneliness for the vocation.

But friendship, too, can lead to loneliness, especially when the friendship breaks off, as when one breaks off critically from another's way of thinking, a common event in the history of philosophy, or when one's friend dies. Even Zhuangzi, whose eponymous work celebrates friendship in wonderful ways, seems to miss his logician friend Huizi, with whom he was often good-naturedly disputing. And Confucius cries out upon the death of the follower he felt was most closely his equal, Yan Hui, "Alas, Heaven has bereft me! Heaven has bereft me!"[11]

Let us conclude this discussion of philosophy and loneliness by briefly considering two of the greatest philosophical icons, Confucius and Socrates. Both are clearly initiators of something new of major significance in their traditions, and so they do not seem to have come from a womb of like-minded thinkers with whom they might have had the kind of relationships characteristic of a non-lonely life. While they are much concerned for others, both are at odds with much of the prevailing thinking in the society around them and of identifiable individuals in that society. Confucius is reported at times to be under threat for his physical safety as a result, though only Socrates seems to have actually been a victim of violence. The disappointment both men must have felt at their efforts for the betterment of society must have led to at least some degree of loneliness, some sense that their relationships with others were fewer and less satisfactory than they would have desired.

Family can be a haven against loneliness, and both Confucius and Socrates were married and had children. Family becomes central to Confucianism, too, of course, yet while historians have it that Confucius' grandson played a role in sustaining and developing his thought, family does not seem to have been a preventative or a cure for Confucius' own possible loneliness. While he married when apparently still quite young,[12] there is no reference at all to his wife in the *Analects*, and though commentators are also generally silent about their relationship, one writes that "(i)t is believed that Confucius did not live with his wife very long, but we do not know if they separated or if he became a widower."[13] In the *Analects*, we find one reference to a daughter, one to a niece, and one to a son, Bo Yu, whom he admonishes to master a couple sections of *The Book of Songs*.[14] Both girls are mentioned in connection with their being given in marriage to people Confucius feels the need to justify, and Bo Yu not only died while Confucius was still alive, but he was said to have been a disappointment to his father.[15]

While Socrates' family (a wife and two young sons) does appear in the early Platonic dialogues, their appearance seems mostly to reveal that they played little functional role in Socrates' own life. He is, after all, seventy, and the one child is described as a "baby."[16] More importantly, he is *not* going to parade them in front of the Athenian jury in a bid for acquittal or leniency, as was apparently customary;[17] he is not going to escape from prison so they he can personally attend to their welfare;[18] and, perhaps most significant symbolically for our concerns, he sends them away from his prison on the day he is to die and sends them away so that he can spend his remain time philosophizing![19]

Philosophy, then, inevitably involves loneliness in the very weak sense that philosophizing presupposes that one's relationships to others, broadly conceived, are not what one desires because they don't fully make sense. In a more robust sense, loneliness is always available to those who philosophize, and evidence from both Western and the Chinese traditions is that philosophers have frequently paid the price, sometimes willingly, to engage in their quest.

Terrorism and the Production and Reduction of Loneliness

The connections between terror and loneliness are, by and large, more direct and straightforward than those between loneliness and philosophy. I will just sketch some of these here, beginning with a focus of the objects of terrorist acts. Then I'll turn to looking at the agents of terror, where the connections to loneliness lead naturally to considerations of the role of terror in overcoming or reducing loneliness.

The central purpose of terrorism would seem to be the achievement of domination of the other by rendering them unable or unwilling to resist whatever the perpetrators want. In some cases of terror, the victims are the same as those the perpetrator seeks to make and keep helpless, as in psychopathic stalking or patriarchal terrorizing of a family. In other cases, especially political terrorism, the actual victims of terrorist acts are used primarily as means to make others unable or unwilling to resist the demands of the perpetrators.

In either case, although terrorism does invariably involve the disruption of human relationships, it does not inevitably involve loneliness even in the very weak sense that philosophy does. There are at least two reasons for this. The first is almost technical in nature. It acknowledges that the atomization of the victims is at the very least very useful for the success of the terrorists, and so this relationship with others is what the perpetrators do desire; hence, given our understanding of loneliness, they won't be any lonelier. To be sure, terrorists probably hope that fear itself drives the victims inward, leaving them less trusting, less inclined to reach out to others, especially if reaching out involves opening up. In addition, the threat of terror tends to narrow the focus of attention to thinking about possible dangers. The likely outcome of all these factors is that those against whom terror is directed are likely to have fewer and less satisfactory relationships with others than they desire or, in short, that they will be more lonely, on top of all their other problems.

The second reason that terrorism does not inevitably lead to loneliness is that the attempt to atomize the victims may backfire. Not only does group identity often intensify amongst the targets of terrorism, but this abstract buffer against loneliness is regularly filled with a real outpouring of concrete acts of mutually considerate intimacies, from the sharing of grief to the sharing of medically-relevant information and skills.

A more direct relationship exists in that the creation of loneliness may be a direct goal of the agents of terror, either for its own sake or for the sake of its effectiveness in making people unable or unwilling to resist. Solitary confinement is a standard "punishment" the world over, no doubt because of the painfulness of the loneliness that goes with it. Solitary confinement, with or without other kinds of torture, could surely be used as an element of terror. Whether banishment, which has similarly evident connections to loneliness, could be considered terror is not so clear, but various ways of driving people from their homes certainly would qualify, and the loneliness which results from the disruption of relationships with others is an all too familiar companion in refugee camps and other places where the dispossessed victims of terrorism find themselves.

Turning now to the agents of terror, it does not seem far-fetched to suggest, in the first place, that loneliness may be a contributing factor in someone's engaging in acts of terror. It is a commonplace that recruitment for terrorist groups finds fertile soil amongst the disaffected. And while loneliness is not commonly mentioned as one of the important disaffections, for the usual analyses are in terms of perceived injustice and the like, loneliness is a major disaffection, and its presence fits very well with our image of likely candidates for terrorist groups.

Furthermore, becoming part of such a group offers much for overcoming loneliness. Intense human relationships involving certain kinds of trust and sharing are vital for the group. And when the others to whom the terrorists feel themselves to be intimately relating are not just some flesh-and-blood individuals, but whole peoples, a semi-divine leader, or a deity, loneliness might well diminish or even disappear.

However, committing acts of terror obviously cuts the agent off from certain kinds of human relationships, mainly those against whom their acts are directed. To be sure, since mutually considerate relationships are not desired by the terrorists with their victims, no loneliness should result from their acts. Yet there is ground for some lingering doubt. We need not pursue here the idea that at some very deep level everyone really desires to have rich and full relationships with all others. More prosaically, we can observe that terrorists are trying to get someone's attention. Terrorism is not just any old murder or genocide. Terrorists desire a relationship of dominance, and so for victims or target group members who refuse to give in, terrorists will be even more lonely.

But even when terrorists succeed in demoralizing and atomizing those whose attention they are seeking to get, the victory, in terms of avoiding loneliness, is likely to be pyrrhic. For to dominate someone whose will is broken, whose character is compressed to little more than seeking to survive, is to be in a relationship which is poor in terms of its possibilities and which is therefore unlikely to satisfy very greatly or for very long; it is to lead, then, to being in a position in which one has fewer and/or less satisfying relationships than they desire or, in other words, to the greater likelihood of increased loneliness.

When terrorist acts fail, then, they likely diminish the loneliness of those they are aimed at in some ways and increase it in others. When they succeed, they most likely increase the loneliness of those they are aimed at, though sometimes just the reverse occurs. And whether they succeed or fail, they are bound in some ways to increase the likelihood of the loneliness for the terrorists themselves, even while diminishing it in others—in joining, planning, and celebrating. At least this seems to be the complex picture on what we may unfortunately have to call an ordinary or empirical level. That terrorists do not seek considerate intimacies with their victims makes it possible to say that at a deeper level, they are inviting loneliness for all affected.

Philosophy and the Reduction of Loneliness

If a philosopher succeeds and is able to make reasoned sense of things, then the universe should no longer seem out of joint in that way that provided a motivation for engaging in philosophy in the first place. For philosophical success understood in this way, the philosopher should feel once again "at home" in the universe and should not be lonely in that minimal kind of way we saw earlier was inevitably connected to philosophy.

When philosophers succeed in this way to their own satisfaction, then imagined opponents cease to exist as opponents. If there were real opponents, though, they might or might not be reconciled. Reconciliation does happen, I think, however much standard philosophical training and practice, at least in the contemporary West, leans against it. When antagonism, even philosophical antagonism, diminishes, relationships are necessarily improved and the conditions for further sharing are created, with the result that loneliness is likely to be diminished. Such beneficial reconciliation might not, of course, occur, with the result that the connections between philosophy and the reduction of loneliness could go in almost any direction.

Philosophers can mistakenly think they have succeeded in their characteristic endeavor. When that happens, the whole range of possible relationships with others could obtain, along with the connections to reducing loneliness. Worth special mention is the relationship between philosophers and their actual opponents. If both believe the philosophical effort has been successful, that should suffice to overcome loneliness, even if this victory is built on an illusion. Overcoming loneliness simply requires that one have the number and nature of satisfying relationships that one desires with others, not that those relationships are built on an adequate understanding of reality. This is partly why loneliness can be a significant motivating factor for joining in terrorist activities. At the same time, it would enable us to see that the closer to the truth one is, the more adequate the way in which things are made sense of, the more stable the achievement of dealing with one's loneliness will be.

This brings me to one particular kind of success at philosophy, a kind relatively unusual within the Western tradition's understanding of itself and yet apparently central to at least the Confucian tradition. Sometimes reality doesn't make sense in the sense that the way things are seems seriously out of joint with the way the philosopher thinks they ought to be. Success in philosophy then permits activism as a legitimately philosophical activity. In the West, it is perhaps Karl Marx who most clearly enunciates this point when he says in the last of his "Theses on Feuerbach" that "[t]he philosophers have only *interpreted* the world in various ways; the point, however, is to *change* it."[20]   This stance may be a significant reason why Marx's status as a philosopher has been so fragile in Western histories of philosophy.

By contrast, the whole point of Confucius' new synthetic vision was to change the world so as to end the chaos in which the world around him had plunged. And the central tensions between Mengzi's Confucianism and that of Xunzi are about how best to attain and sustain a human social order. Furthermore, the concern for proper relationship between thought and action amongst Neo-Confucians from Zhu Xi to Wang Yangming, together with the remarkable social achievements of many of these Confucian philosophers, is ample evidence of the centrality of this kind of attempt to make reasoned sense of things as relevant to success in philosophy in the Confucian tradition. And the connections of this kind of success in philosophy to the reduction of loneliness are many and easy. Suffice it to say that when the world is more harmoniously ordered, the likelihood is increased for people to have the number and kinds of mutually considerate intimacies with others that they desire. But be it also noted, lest this seem too sanguine, that this activist conception of successful philosophy can lead to terrorism, as history has repeatedly shown. To be sure, it need not do so, and it is even rarer, if not unheard of, that terrorism receives any explicit endorsement by a philosopher.[21]   And so the connections of philosophy to loneliness that have been described will require many complications and qualifications, as well as repetitions, none of which we have time for here.

Summary

We have seen that while philosophy inevitably involves a minimal kind of loneliness in a way that terror and terrorism do not, the latter are connected to loneliness in ways that are generally more direct, more powerful, and more intransigent. Terror and philosophy thus share to some extent a common fate because they are intimately connected with loneliness and the possibility of loneliness in many ways, though the differences in these ways are important. We have also seen that the nature of philosophy provides it with significant resources for overcoming the loneliness associated with it, while the practice of terror seems, by contrast, by and large more likely to exacerbate the loneliness with which it is associated. Loneliness is thus a fate of terror that in significant ways are not shared by philosophy.

Notes

1. Harry Stack Sullivan, one of the earliest psychologists explicitly concerned with loneliness, quoted in Robert S. Weiss, *Loneliness: The Experience of Emotional and Social Isolation* (Cambridge: MIT Press, 1973), 15.

2. I owe the idea behind this point to Douglas Allen's very helpful comments.

3. A. C. Graham, *Disputers of the Tao* (La Salle, Ill.: Open Court, 1989), 36. The pronunciation of the two Chinese characters is the same, at least in modern standard Chinese, but the characters are slightly different.

4. See Jean-Pierre Vernant, *The Origins of Greek Thought* (Ithaca: Cornell University Press, 1982), esp. chapter 4.

5. Robert Nisbet, *The Geography of Thought* (New York: The Free Press, 2003). See esp. 166-67.

6. These Whiteheadian "seek simplicity but distrust it" considerations are reinforced and enriched by what Douglas Allen has to say about Indian philosophy: it "…emphasizes inclusiveness and harmony, but it is   extremely argumentative. Indian philosophical systems are forceful and argumentative in trying to destroy the errors and illusions of other systems that are obstacles to true harmony" (personal correspondence).

7. I owe this observation to Peimin Ni.

8. See Hui-Neng, *The Platform Sutra*, section 4-11, in John M. Koller and Patricia Koller, *A Sourcebook in Asian Philosophy* (New York: Macmillan, 1991), 509-511.

9. Michael Pakaluk,   *Other Selves* (Indianapolis: Hackett, 1991). Seneca and Cicero, like the few medievals who consider the topic, lean heavily on Aristotle's extensive discussion of friendship in Books 8 and 9 of the *Nicomachean Ethics*. Aristotle argues for the importance of friendship in the good life, for which philosophy is also important. This important role of friendship, however, is reserved for only one of the three kinds of friendship that Aristotle identifies.

10. Kant, "Lecture on Friendship," in Pakaluk, 212.

11. Confucius, *Analects*, 11.9.

12. F. C. Hsu, *Confucianism* (Pondicherry, India: Sri Aurobindo International Centre of Education, 1966), 16.

13. Betty Kelen, *Confucius In Life and Legend* (New York: Thomas Nelson, 1971), 34. In addition, many commentators note that Confucius' father, K'ung Shu-liang Ho, was quite a bit older than his mother and died when Confucius was very young. His mother, though devoted, was at best tolerated by the family, and the boy grew up in poverty. A story famous enough to be repeated was that while his mother would not tell him where his father was buried, when she died the teenaged son found the paternal grave and buried his mother next to her husband. In addition, he, like Socrates, was apparently quite ugly. (See Kilen, 33.) As these accounts seem speculative, it does not seem out of place to speculate that an often lonely childhood and adolescence was easily available to Confucius.

14. *Analects* 5.l, 5.2, and 17.10.

15. Herlee Creel, *Confucius: The Man and the Myth* (New York: The John Day Co., 1949), 25, 52.

16. Plato, *Phaedo*, 60a. Socrates' wife, then, is most likely no more than half his age. And while we at least are given her name, in contrast to Confucius' wife, Xanthippe has the reputation of being something of a shrew.

17. Plato, *Apology*, 34c-e.

18. Plato, *Crito*, 54a

19. Plato, *Phaedo*, 60a.

20. Karl Marx, "Theses on Feuerbach," in Robert C. Tucker, *The Marx-Engels Reader*, 2nd ed. (New York: W. W. Norton, 1978), 145.

21. Machiavelli and various Marxists (neo-Marxists, quasi-Marxists, such as Georges Sorel and Franz Fanon) come to mind in the West, while Li Si and other Qin Legalists form an early and recurring Chinese tradition.

12

Gender, Violence, and the Other

Joanne D. Birdwhistell

Matters of Gender and Violence

When we speak of gender, we are referring to behavior and to patterns of behavior that are culturally categorized, typically on a scale that places feminine at one end and masculine at the other. The cultural coding of gender varies from one society to another, for different societies may perceive similar kinds of behavior as more masculine, more feminine, or as some other type, such as transgendered. Cultures themselves also change, with the result that new categories and ways of thinking emerge. For instance, a kind of behavior most closely associated with the feminine may become associated with the masculine, and vice versa.

The ontology of a gender system can be understood as consisting of certain kinds of behavior and all the cultural "rules" for exhibiting and interpreting the behavior. Thus, a gender system is a kind of language in which there are actions, as well as words, and rules (often unspoken) for engaging in certain actions, as well as grammar. Just as nonliterate people learn to speak their language without ever studying its grammar in a formal way, so one learns the gender code of one's society without formal instruction in school. One result of the lack of explicit teaching of gender is that people can function successfully in society with varying levels of awareness of how its components are coded. People can and do participate in ongoing cultural systems in which the meanings of actions are a matter of social convention and are not freely or arbitrarily determined by individual participants.

Our knowledge about gender in ancient China comes primarily from visual art and literary, philosophical, and historical texts. While the ancient texts have in the past not been read from the perspective of gender, it is possible to do so, since these texts portray many kinds of behavior. We see gender in action in visual portrayals, in descriptions of people, in images and symbols, and in performances in stories. By praising and denouncing specific actions and characteristics of men and women in specific roles in society, the art and texts illustrate numerous examples of the cultural meanings of behavior considered feminine or masculine or other.

With these ideas in mind, my aim here is to examine aspects of the gender code assumed by Mencian thinking. While much can be learned from the text *Mencius* itself, that investigation is the subject of a separate research project. The Odes (*Shijing*) is, however, another ancient text that provides information about Mencian assumptions regarding gender. The Odes serve as an important source of authority for ideas in *Mencius*, and passages from the Odes are often cited to reinforce, restate, or summarize a philosophical point. (There are thirty-six such references.) Many views stated in prose form within an argument in *Mencius* appear in the Odes in a poem describing the qualities of a person or event. *Mencius* thus puts certain ideas (that are found in the Odes in verse form) into prose form and locates them within an explicit position regarding values.

Before we turn to my analysis, a few comments are needed on how gender is related to the topic of terror, which belongs to the theme of this volume, "comparative philosophy in times of terror." Terror involves uncontrollable violence, and such violence comes in many forms, such as psychological and social violence, physical and military violence. Violence includes economic exploitation, social discrimination, political tyranny, and rape. The fact that one kind of violence may be more visible than another kind does not lessen the destructiveness or presence of that which is more hidden. In many cases visibility does not correlate with personal or social impact. In addition, the pulse of violence can vary greatly. It can be a steady state in which a person or a group lives everyday, that is, a systemic violence embedded in the various cultural systems of a society, and it can be sporadic or episodic, occurring unpredictably or with somewhat predictable frequency.

In patriarchal and hierarchical societies, those who are "others" live constantly in conditions of violence and terror, even though these conditions are ordinarily not perceived as such by those in the subject position. I characterize this state of existence as one of terror because those who are "other" know that violence can be experienced unexpectedly as well as continually. It is a state of violence because those who are "other" are prevented from having access to those things that their society values most. Such things may be tangible, like certain kinds of food and clothing, or intangible, like certain occupations, having a choice in certain matters, or being treated in certain ways by others. Coercion rather than consent is involved, although the more subtle forms of coercion may appear to be consent. Violence toward an "other," whether a person or a group, is often considered justified, moreover, because these "others," including those who participate in the social order seemingly willingly, are seen as somehow destructive of the type of social order that those who are subjects want to maintain.

We can see assumptions about gender depicted in many ancient Chinese texts. Mencian thought during the Warring States period, for instance, openly recognized certain groups and people as "others" or non-subjects. The most notable fall into four categories: first, ethnic groups who are thought of as barbarians; second, rulers, officials, and political advisors (or philosophers) who do not accept the Confucian-Mencian views and values; third, women of all types; and fourth, the natural environment in its "wild" condition. To illustrate briefly, if we use the natural environment as one example of an "other," we see that the rivers and land represent what is chaotic and so must be controlled and ordered. Since these natural phenomena are seen as inherently chaotic, because of their constant overflowing or abundant flourishing, they can never be entirely self-ordering. Thus, a certain amount of continual destruction, violence, or force directed against the natural environment is deemed acceptable and even necessary for the sake of social order. In contrast to ideas in *Zhuangzi*, an ancient Daoist text, Confucian-Mencian thinking does not try to see, or accept the possibility of seeing, the world from the viewpoint of any of these "others," who, if they could, would undoubtedly tell a very different story about what the world is like.

Returning to some fundamental assumptions of Mencian thinking, let us now consider how both the subject and the "other" belong to the gender system of ancient Chinese philosophy. Implicitly constructed from the perspective of elite males, as is the later, highly systematized *yinyang* thinking, this earlier gender order associates some kinds of behavior with women and other kinds with men. In the Odes as well as in *Mencius* there appears only a little formal instruction on how to exhibit and understand behavior, for the "rules" are more performed than they are told. Nonetheless, this gender code links subjects and various "others" together in a network of mutually reinforcing threads.

We should note further that historically the Chinese, like many cultures worldwide did not make a distinction between female and feminine or between male and masculine. The distinction between sex and gender began to be made during the Enlightenment (eighteenth-century) in Europe, but it was not widely discussed and accepted until the twentieth century. Although the Chinese have been influenced in modern times by many aspects of Western culture, contemporary scholars do not completely agree on the extent to which the Chinese now endorse the sex and gender distinction, a distinction grounded after all in Enlightenment assumptions about the world and reality. It is accepted, however, that the ancient Chinese employed a single term (*nü*) in many senses, including girl, woman, female, and feminine.

The *yinyang* system, which became dominant in China about four hundred years after Mencius, categorizes the world in terms of a range of behavior bounded by two, mutually-related and interacting "poles" that are termed *yin* and *yang*. Since this is a cosmic system of correlations, everything in the cosmos is classified as *yin*, *yang*, or some degree of both. *Yin* is associated with such things as water, moon, wet, dark, and female, while *yang* is associated with such complementary things as land, sun, dry, light, and male. In contrast to most interpretations, my claim here is that it is a coercive system, for there is no alternative to it, there is no way out of it, and it supports and is realized in a social-political system that ultimately allows only one subject, the elite man.

Although I would argue that many of the poems are compatible with Mencian assumptions, given the lack of any major gender contradictions in the Odes, here I draw on only those poems cited in *Mencius*. In each instance of appealing to the Odes, *Mencius* only quotes a few lines, never an entire ode. Still, it is not unreasonable to assume that the compilers and readers of *Mencius* were familiar with all or most of the stanzas of those particular odes. Thus I am assuming that the entire ode is either potentially relevant as a general source of authority for Mencian ideas or it expresses ideas that are congenial with Mencian views. Since *Mencius* appealed to the Odes for different reasons, I do not claim that the ideas of a particular ode are relevant only in the Mencian passage in which it is cited. Rather, these odes as a whole reveal a pattern of assumptions, as the discussion below will indicate.[1]

Characteristics of the Subject Position

Tian (Heaven)[2]

The subject position is occupied by two kinds of entities—*tian*, which I shall translate here as Heaven, and a few elite men, who are seen as heroes and leaders of the ancient Zhou people. Heaven and these elite men have similar gender characteristics, for both have primarily masculine traits combined with some feminine traits (keeping in mind that in this ancient world masculine and male are interchangeable as are feminine and female). As subjects, they have the capability to absorb aspects of the "other," but this capability is theirs alone and is not possessed by the other.

The references to Heaven are numerous and so provide ample examples of behavior that can be understood from the perspective of gender. First, Heaven's behavior has a spatial and visual dimension. It, or he, is depicted as vast, distant, wide, and high. In addition, Heaven is bright and glorious. His height, vastness, and brightness should not be taken to imply inactivity, however, for Heaven is active and has great power.[3]

From the way that Heaven exercises power, it is clear that Heaven is in charge and is superior to all other beings. Heaven is described as purposive, as mighty, and as a ruler. He is a god, an august god on high, a shining power. At times, he is swift and terrible in his actions, and he causes humans to have an immense terror of him. He can become enraged and vicious and so bring about calamities, hardships, and turmoil. He can depise men and so punish them and put curses on them. He brings agony, death, destruction of the king, and agricultural ruin. Rather than providing aid, for example, at times he abandoned the state of Zhou, leaving the people to death, disorder, famine, hunger, and drought. In sum, these characteristics emphasize superiority, forceful and powerful behavior, the power to make judgments and initiate corresponding action, and as such they embody masculine behavior.

Heaven also has changes and has other sides, which lead to his being called father and mother. At times, he protects the people from war and sickness, he guides them, and he blesses them. He is described as having nurtured Jiang Yuan, the ancestral mother, and as having given birth to the Zhou people. Heaven had especially high regard for Kings Wen and Wu. He blessed and received sacrifices from King Wen and other rulers, whom he commanded to engage in war. He also received sacrifices from Liu the Duke, the ancient ancestor who brought the Zhou people to Bin (Shaanxi area), and he created Zhong Shan Fu, a high officer of Zhou, to guard the Zhou ruler. Heaven is said to act according to the values manifested in the customs and rules of the Zhou people. He makes earthly counterparts and gives his charge to them, of whom the first was King Ji (Wang Ji), the father of King Wen. His charge is hard-to-keep, however, and is not permanent.

In sum, these characteristics reflect behavior that is more fluid in gender terms, suggesting the possibility of a range of gendered behavior. To give birth, nurture, and protect are certainly female-gendered traits, all initially associated with mothers. At the other end of the scale, to rule, to command, and to give and take away the authority to rule on earth characterize male-gendered behavior, most typified by a leader with the power to enforce his commands. In between, we find behavior that suggests authority but without the use of heavy force. To guide and bless are examples, and perhaps also the act of receiving sacrifices. An element of concern or kindness appears to be present in these kinds of behavior. However, since Heaven's behavior is overwhelmingly masculine in terms of its context, actions, and power, it seems clear that Heaven here is an elite male. Heaven's feminine behavior represents an appropriation, incorporation, and transformation of female-gendered behavior by an elite male, not the elevation of elite females. A woman gives birth to and nurtures only a single infant, whereas Heaven gives birth to and nourishes a whole people, the people of Zhou. By transforming a familial activity into a political activity, Heaven is considered much greater.

Elite Men of the Zhou

In addition to Heaven, elite men occupy the subject position. They are the ones who initiate action, and their actions take place within their realm of responsibility, the political realm. Like Heaven's, their behavior is primarily masculine, but it also includes certain feminine traits. With these elite men, it becomes clear that a new kind of power, a moral power, is established through their display of female-gendered behavior, which is signaled by their obedience to a higher power (Heaven). This group consists of Zhou legendary rulers, ancient kings, and high officers.

A number of legendary and historical men are named, the most famous of which are Hou Ji (or Lord Millet), the son of Jiang Yuan (the ancestral mother); Yü, the ancient sage ruler; Liu the Duke, the ancestor who brought the Zhou people to Bin; Dan-fu the duke, father of Wang Ji and grandfather of King Wen; Wang Ji (King Ji); King Wen; King Wu; and Zhong Shan Fu. In addition, there are two types of subjects who are unnamed. One is a moral man (often a ruler), and the other is a nonmoral man. These men all had strength and military power, which they used successfully. For instance, Yü forced the Feng River to flow inside a channel, Liu the Duke led the Zhou people to Bin, and Dan-fu the duke led them to the Mt. Qi area. The latter also drove away and conquered barbarian tribes and rebel groups. Wang Ji extended the area under Zhou rule. King Wen followed with many more military victories and further expansion of territory. Most notably, he and his descendants conquered the sons and grandsons of the Shang dynasty. His son, King Wu, completed this great military and political effort. Lastly, there is Zhong Shan Fu, a great military officer who continued his ancestors' work by helping to maintain Zhou control.

While this masculine behavior of force and military might is glorified, it actually is not the primary focus of how these men are depicted here. Rather, their accompanying social actions loom more important. Such actions are, in particular, those that create human civilization and a social order and that reflect obedience to Heaven's commands.[4]

First, there are the activities that make agriculture possible. These include Hou Ji's teaching the people how to farm and the laying out of the boundaries of agricultural fields by both Liu the Duke and Dan-fu the duke. Like Yü's control of the flooding waters, their actions of cutting down trees, clearing the land, marking boundaries, and building walls demonstrate control over land that is considered wild. Since land division contributes to the production of taxes as well as food, it is a critical foundational activity for the building of a state.

Other activities are important too. They have houses and a capital city built. Acknowledging their inferior position in regard to Heaven and the powerful spirits, these elite men perform sacrificial rituals to God or Heaven, to the Zhou ancestors, and to spirits of the land. Kings Wen and Wu and Zhong Shan

Fu are praised for continuing the old ways, values, and teachings that had brought success and peace to their ancestors. These later leaders are known for their obedience to Heaven and so are models for others. Their demeanor is described in such terms as friendly, accommodating, careful, shining, glorious, diligent, respectful, reverent, mild, care taking, good, dignified, gentle, kind, and protective. It is suggested that they are especially gifted, blessed by Heaven, and able to make their inner virtuous power shine forth.

If we consider the gender associations of these actions and descriptions, we see that almost all are explicitly or implicitly associated in some way with women and so also with female-gendered behavior. For instance, women and agriculture are culturally transcoded through such activities as birth and nurturing. This association is reinforced with the establishing of boundaries--marking off fields and keeping functions of men and women separate. Establishing boundaries also enables the one in the subject position to have control over those who are other, whether that "other" is flooding water, wild land, barbarians, or females. This kind of control is ultimately coerced. Showing reverence and respect in sacrificial rituals means, in part, that one is acknowledging one's inferior position in relation to a superior force and moral power, especially that of Heaven or God. In the social order, women as wives are typically the ones in the inferior position, which they embody by behaving in ways that are judged gentle, mild, dignified, obedient, kind, respectful, and protective. Finally, the notion of being blessed and of having an inner power that one can make shine forth, illustrated in one's glorious political and military achievements, is not too far removed from the inner power of a woman to give birth to an infant.

Thus we see that, like Heaven, the elite men (mostly rulers) embody some female-gendered traits along with their male-gendered traits, and again this phenomenon is not kind to actual women. Rather, it coerces them into a position of an "other," which is a position of inferiority, characterized by a lack of self-ordering and the lack of a voice. These two traits, the inability to order and regulate oneself properly and voicelessness, are endemic to the conditions of those people and things that cannot be in the subject position in this gender order. This exclusion results in a world of difference existing between female-gendered traits exhibited by elite men and similar traits exhibited by those who are other. Although the actions may seem similar, their meanings are simply not the same.

Characteristics of the "Other" Position

The World of Nature

Turning now to those who are not in the subject position, those whose behavior (broadly conceived) renders them objects or "other" in some way, we see that there are various types of entities fitting this category. Some belong to the natural world, in distinction to the human realm, and others are humans. With the exception of time, which is marked off as seasons, and certain stars in the sky, all these entities of nature are associated with the earth--its land, rivers, and animals. Although they are "other" and not subjects in the ancient Hua (or Chinese) gender order, they are subjects in suppressed, rival gender orders. These other orders do not, however, have a voice here. First, I shall examine the natural world and then the various categories of humans in relation to gender.[5]

In the few references to animals, birds, and fish in their natural states, we see that they are often thought of as flourishing and abundant. Even more often, however, they are mentioned in contexts of their use to humans. They are objects. For instance, bulls and sheep are sacrificed, trees and plants are cut down and cleared away to set up agricultural fields, the Feng River is forced into a channel made by Yü, various plants and animals are eaten or used for making silk or fur robes, horses are yoked to hunting chariots, wild animals are hunted for food, grasslands are simply sites where hunting occurs, and time (which is measured in months and seasons) is the set of conditions in which farming and related activities occur. It is stated explicitly that the various stars in the sky, to which names are given, cannot weave, be yoked to a cart, sift grain, or scoop wine, and so they cannot be used by humans.

A few conflicting views seem also to be expressed. For instance, one view suggests that fish have feelings, for it is claimed that the fish in the pond are also unhappy. This unhappiness does not arise from their own circumstances, however, for it is suggested that the fish's unhappiness simply reflects the feelings of the people. Given the blatant use, control, and destruction of entities in nature, there clearly exists an assumption that the land, birds, and animals do not suffer from what humans do to them, thus suggesting that things in nature lack feelings or that humans are indifferent to their feelings. Some birds, like the kite-owl, are said to be wicked and destructive, whereas the spirit of the fields has sacred, creative power. In sum, nature in its many forms is seen as a type of object to be used by human beings, and even when it is accorded some kind of feeling or power, that feeling and power are evaluated from a human viewpoint.

Humans

There are several types of legendary and historical humans who are categorized as "other," and the following discussion presents them in order of their status vis-a-vis society.

First are the elite women who are named. (There is not sufficient space here to address the issue of names and naming, but it is tremendously important.) In chronological order, these women are: Jiang Yuan, the ancestral

mother of the Zhou; Lady Jiang of Zhou, the wife of Dan-fu and mother of
Wang Ji; Tai-ren, the wife of Wang Ji and mother of King Wen; Tai-si, the wife
of King Wen and mother of King Wu; and Lady Bao Si, consort of King You
and destroyer of the majestic capital of Zhou. Gender characteristics variously
ascribed to these women include giving birth, being married to (or being a consort of) one of the rulers, having flawless power, being well loved, and having
great dignity. In terms of cultural associations, we should note that one of these
women, Tai-ren (mother of King Wen) came from a Shang lineage, the rulers
conquered by the Zhou, and that another woman (Lady Bao Si) was considered
so sexually unrestrained that her evil behavior helped to destroy Zhou power.[6]

Second, there are three unnamed women.[7] One is a lady from Qi on her
way to be married, aware that she ought to obey the marriage-related norms and
not let her fancy roam anymore. This ode draws a comparison between a man's
taking a wife and the fact that there are proper ways to plant hemp and cut fire-
wood. The second woman is "our mother," who had only grief and care, but
was wise and kind. Still, although she had seven sons, her heart could not be
soothed by them. The third is a young woman who is sad and sorrowful but not
supported by her brothers in her anguish. These examples make it clear that
feminine behavior primarily concerns activities relating to marriage, having
children, sexuality, taking an inferior position, a life of suffering, and the condition of having no voice.

The non-Zhou peoples, who live in the Zhou frontier area, constitute a
third subordinate group. Although they are named in some way, they also occupy a position of "other" by virtue of being outside the Zhou culturally and
geographically and by being defeated in some way by the Zhou. Thus we see
that the Mi dared to revolt and actually invaded some areas of Zhou territory,
but were unable to take any strategic hills or places with water. Chong, a forti-
fied city, was destroyed and its people defeated. The Kun tribes were driven
away from their land by Dan-fu the duke, who also conquered the peoples of Yu
and Rui after they rebelled.[8]

A fourth group consists of the defeated Yin-Shang people, who were conquered by the Zhou.[9] The point is made that they brought shame on their ancestors by losing Heaven's mandate to the Zhou. They are especially criticized by
King Wen as violent men, as slaughterers, and as having an arrogant spirit. They
are disorderly and support brigands and thieves. They confuse the accumulation
of resentment with inward power, which they do not make shine brightly. They
do not follow the old ways and so will be destroyed like the Xia. Although the
Yin-Shang are not Zhou people, the Zhou elite have close relations with some of
the Yin-Shang and so the latter are particularly condemned for their bad and
shameful behavior, which has led them to be destroyed. It should be noted that
disorderly and shameful behavior is often depicted as feminine traits, linked to a
lack of self-control.

The people make up the fifth group belonging to the category of "other."[10] Although they work hard, the credit for prosperity is given to the ruler. At best, their lives consist of farming and providing food for others, but they often suffer the hardships of drought and famine. They are believed to need guidance, because they lack the ability to regulate their behavior properly. In terms of gender, the people's behavior is feminine, for they serve the elite, they follow and obey, and they have no voice to represent their viewpoints. The fact that their work is primarily agricultural further associates them with female-gendered behavior.

Concluding Comments

Although the Odes does not present any finely worked out theory regarding gender, it does illustrate gender practices that are consistent and fairly well codified. Similar views also appear in *Mencius*, in that certain kinds of behavior are viewed as male (or masculine) and other kinds as female (or feminine) and only certain elite men have the power to embody both. The gender consistency in the types of behavior exhibited in the Odes and in *Mencius* indicates the existence of an implicit, if not explicit, social ordering on the basis of gender. The violence and terror that maintain this order are more immediately apparent on the macro level, such as in the violence against non-Zhou peoples, but careful examination reveals their existence in the lives of Zhou women, the people of Zhou, and nonhuman living things too. Coercion without consent, a refusal to recognize the legitimacy of the perspectives of other groups, the voicelessness of those who are other, and the assumption of their inability to order themselves are four primary features of this social system. A fifth feature, existing here only implicitly but explicitly important later in *Mencius* and in the *yinyang* system, is that of maintaining difference. The requirement of maintaining recognized differences in behavior ensures the perpetuation of higher and lower status positions and so also violence and terror. The power to blur different types of gendered behavior resides only with the superior, namely, one who is in the subject position.

Notes

1. All references to the Odes and to *Mencius* are from the following translations: Arthur Waley, trans., and Joseph R. Allen, ed. and trans., *The Book of Songs (Shijing)* (New York: Grove Press, 1996); and D. C. Lau, trans., *Mencius* (London and New York: Penguin Books, 1970). The intent of my references to the Odes in this paper is to note gendered behavior that appears only in those individual odes from which *Mencius* par-

tially quotes. My aim is to be sufficiently informative but not to be exhaustive in citing from the Odes.

2. *Tian*, translated here as Heaven, is an extremely complex concept and has no single meaning. Its meanings evolved over time, and it retained its earlier senses even as it developed new meanings. It has been translated, for instance, as God, Heaven, Lord, the skies, (social and environmental) conditions, and Nature. To cite a few of its meanings, some consider it an anthropomorphic deity, others regard it as an impersonal ultimate power, and still others think of it as nature, as opposed to human society. Here, Heaven clearly has anthropomorphic characteristics and is a very powerful deity.

3. For characteristics of Heaven, see the following Odes, which are cited by their are conventional Mao number, then by the chapter in which they are quoted in *Mencius*, and then by the page number in Lau's translation. For example, Mao 198/1A/55 refers to Ode, Mao number 198, *Mencius*, Chapter 1A, Lau translation, p. 55. Mao 198/1A/55; Mao 272/1B/ 62; Mao 241/1B/62; Mao 192/1B/65; Mao 244/2A/80; Mao 235/2A/81; Mao 235/3A/99, Mao 235/4A/119; Mao 235/4A/120; Mao 300/3A/104; Mao 300/3B/115; Mao 254/4A/118; Mao 255/4A/119; Mao 257/4A/121; Mao 257/4A/122; Mao 258/5A/142; Mao 243/5A/142; Mao 260/6A/163; Mao 197/6B/172.

4. For references to the varied behavior of these men, see Mao 300/3A/104; Mao 300/3B/115; Mao 244/2A/80; Mao 250/1B/66; Mao 237/1B/66; Mao 237/7B/197; Mao 241/1B/62; Mao 240/1A/56; Mao 272/1B/62; Mao 241/1B/62; Mao 244/2A/80; Mao 235/2A/81; Mao 235/3A/99; Mao 235/4A/119; Mao 235/4A/120; Mao 255/4A/119; Mao 244/2A/80; Mao 260/6A/163; Mao 212/3A/98; Mao 249/4A/117; Mao 249/4A/117; Mao 257/4A/121; Mao 257/4A/122; Mao 205/5A/142; Mao 243/5A/142; Mao 247/6A/169; Mao 198/1A/55; Mao 192/1B/65; Mao 101/5A/139; Mao 197/6B/172.

5. For references to the natural world, see Mao 242/1A/50; Mao 197/6B/172; Mao 272/1B/62; Mao 154/3A/97; Mao 212/3A/98; Mao 179/3B/107/ Mao 203/5B/158; Mao 241/1B/62; Mao 237/1B/66; Mao 237/1B/66; Mao 237/7B/197; Mao 192/1B/65; Mao 237/1B/66; Mao 244/2A/80; Mao 257/4A/121; Mao 257/4A/122; Mao 154/3A/97; Mao 212/3A/98.

6. For references to named elite women, see Mao 300/3A/104; Mao 300/3B/115; Mao 240/1A/56; Mao 237/1B/66; Mao 237/7B/197; Mao 240/1A/56; Mao 192/1B/65.

7. For unnamed women, see Mao 101/5A/139; Mao 32/6B/173; Mao 26/7B/197.

8. See Mao 241/1B/62; Mao 237/1B/66; Mao 237/7B/197.

9. See Mao 235/2A/81; Mao 235/3A/99; Mao 235/4A/119; Mao 235/4A/120; Mao 255/4A/119.

10. See Mao 250/1B/66; Mao 154/3A/97; Mao 254/4A/118; Mao 257/4A/121; Mao 257/4A/122; Mao 154/3A/97; Mao 212/3A/98; Mao 260/6A/163.

13

Confucian Perspectives on War and Terrorism

Kirill O. Thompson

"War is always a losing proposition"
(Sun Wu)

Confucian thought was conceived and incubated during centuries of imperial breakup. The eastern Zhou court was in decline, and her power and prestige were slipping during Confucius' lifetime (Spring and Autumn period, 722-481 BCE). Meanwhile, the states and principalities comprising the empire increasingly asserted themselves and struggled to extend land and power during the lifetimes of Confucius' followers Mencius and Xunzi (Warring States period, 480-221 BCE). To hold their seats at court, early Confucians had to grasp military arts and warfare. Han dynasty court bibliographies reveal that more treatises on warfare were written during the Warring States period than all the Confucian classics combined. Thus, while attributing the cohesion of the realm to the ritual propriety and ethical probity of the central court, Confucians still grasped the need to comprehend the military arts and to be willing to take up arms when necessary. From the beginning, they understood that the *wen* of culture had to be supported and complemented by the *wu* of martial attainments. Indeed, the "Six Arts" of Confucian cultivation included archery and charioteering as attainments of a worthy noble.

Confucians as Guardians of Noble Tradition

As guardians of ritual culture and executors of order, Confucians tended to speak little of military arts and war. Insisting that peoples and states gravitate toward rulers and regimes renowned for ritual propriety and ethical rule, they viewed the rampant interstate wars of their time as Pyrrhic if not self-defeating. They thought that, by making power and greed motives for taking military action, such wars lead to endless warfare that despoils the land and devastates the common people. Consequently, they legitimated war only in the form of punitive action initiated by the highest-level authority, the emperor.

This position landed the early Confucians in paradox because they, at the same time, glorified several noble founding emperors of the Shang (c. 1766-1027 BCE) and Zhou (c. 1027-256 BCE) dynasties for deposing corrupt, despotic emperors of preceding dynasties, thus implicitly condoning military action from below and outside the established regime. Moreover, these Sage kings had risen to power militarily and not by cultural and moral preeminence, only later assuming the mantle of culture. Mencius responded to this paradox by redefining a "corrupt, despotic" emperor as a "mere fellow" who had lost the mandate of heaven (i.e., the hearts of the people), and who thus deserved to be deposed by the noble-minded rebels. Inevitably, this was a teaching that later rulers often proscribed and had censored from the *Mencius* (1A:8).

From early in the Han (c. 206 BCE) until the end of Imperial China in 1911, Confucians continued to ponder warfare, particularly at times when the central plains lay in barbarian hands, as did Zhu Xi during the Southern Song (1127-1279), and when dealing with frontier tribes, as did Wang Shouren during the Ming (1368-1644). Generally, however, the later Imperial court held absolute power, and the Confucian legitimization of punitive action initiated by the highest-level authority just served to strengthen the imperial hand. Even today, China adopts this sort of imperialist rationale for its draconian treatment of "separatist elements" in Tibet and Xinjiang.

Confucius: Activist for Noble Classical Tradition

Confucius (551-479 BCE), the paradigmatic scholar-teacher, was trained in the martial skills befitting a noble of his times. A keen archer and adept charioteer (9.2), Confucius esteemed valor and honored knights willing to risk their lives in the face of danger (14.12). Nonetheless, he placed priority on ritual conduct, just rule and upright human relationships; for example, he said he had learned how to arrange ritual vessels but never how to arrange military formations (15.1). He insisted that when the *Dao* (Way; proper order) is practiced in the empire, ritual propriety, music and punitive campaigns are initiated by the Emperor; but, when the *Dao* is not practiced, these activities are conducted by lords, ministers or stewards (16.2), a potentially unstable state of affairs.

Confucius identified the common people as the most important element in a state and considered grain distribution and popular trust more indispensable to state security than military arms (12.7). This in mind, he saw a lesson in the fact that, whereas two heroic warriors of antiquity had died miserably, Yu and Ji, two humble tillers of the land, had survived to ascend the throne (14.5). Admitting that states at times had to defend themselves, he still regarded sending untrained people to battle as needlessly "forsaking them" (13.30). Confucius identified war as a matter of grave concern to be handed with circumspection and foresight (7.3).

Confucius embraced the ideal that only the Emperor had the authority to launch military campaigns because history had taught him that states within the realm, even those claiming good intentions, frequently resorted to war when they were having internal problems (16.1). Moreover, blind to the cost of war in lives and resources, they engaged in military assaults to enlarge their land, triggering chain reactions of interstate aggression. From this perspective, Confucius respected the diplomatic efforts of prime minister Guan Zhong (d. 685 BCE) to dissuade ruling nobles from fighting each other. The Master praised his "humanity" for these efforts to avert the squandering of lives and resources (14.16).

Mencius: Defender of Confucius' Ideals

Mencius (c. 372-289 BCE) lived in a more warlike age than Confucius, the vanishing imperial court now had little real or moral power. He expanded on Confucius' views on military arts and war in response to the worsening situation as well as to counter rival political and philosophical views. Strongly opposed to the wars of conquest that typified his age, Mencius delineated Confucius' notion of justifiable military action as that initiated by the Emperor. At the same time, he set forth conditions under which a bad emperor himself may be overthrown and replaced.

Arguing that a state's eminence and influence sprang more from just rule, ritual propriety and fair distribution than from its military strength, Mencius disparaged advisors and ministers who emphasized state wealth and power, particularly those who stressed military power as an instrument of internal control and external expansion. A case in point was minister Ranyou, a former student of Confucius who catered to the Ji clan's greed for wealth and land in his counsel. Mencius concluded a tirade against ministers like Ranyou by saying, "When they contend for land by waging war, the carnage fills the cities. This is what is called teaching the land to devour human flesh—death is too good for such people. Thus, those (ministers) who are skilled at waging war should suffer the harshest punishment, those who forge alliances among the feudal lords should suffer the next, and those who open up the frontiers for homesteading should be next" (4A.14). To Mencius, military experts were the worst of criminals, for their teachings led to suffering, destruction and death.

Ultimately, Mencius' teachings on war seemed to be directed to another age, when a wise emperor would be in place to run the Empire and initiate just punitive campaigns. His teachings offered little guidance for times when, in the absence of a viable central court, wars were waged between contending states with impunity. Even during the preceding Spring and Autumn period, none of the wars were, in Mencius' view, just, though some wars were less unjust than others (7B.2). In discussing a state whose ruler deserved to be deposed, Mencius said the neighboring state's intent on deposing him was not itself morally qualified (2B.8). But, given his strict criteria, no state at the time was morally qualified to initiate a war.

Rival Views on War

During the chaotic Warring States period (c. 403-221 BCE), military power and prowess were absolutely vital to a state's survival. Thus, Mencius' philosophical rival Mozi (490-303 BCE), who taught practicality and economy, was an expert on defensive war. Mozi argued that war is evil for the death, damage and cost it wreaks, so states should not attack each other. He promoted defensive readiness as the best means of deterring war, thus ensuring the safety of the people and survival of one's state. The Legalists (*Fajia*) taught ways to concentrate political, economic and military power in the hands of the ruler. Finally, Militarists (*Bingjia*), such as Sun Wu (Sunzi fl. 475 BCE) and Sun Bin (c. 380-316 BCE), were experts not only on strategy and tactics but on raising and training a lethal fighting force. It must be added that expert Militarists were also most cautionary, stressing that war is costly and the outcome not assured, that the war best won is the war that need not be fought at all, and that the best military deployment is just to threaten and deter the enemy in the larger field of interstate diplomacy and relations (Ames 1993 111f, 1996 153, 2003 125).

Xunzi: Adding Teeth to the Confucian View of War

Xunzi (c. 312-238 BCE) lived in an even more lethal age, when there was no central court and interstate conflict grew more large-scale and vicious. Eager to know the secrets of bolstering and extending their power, kings and ministers solicited "expert" advice wherever they could find it, and a hundred schools of thought rose in contention. In this free market of ideas and debate, Xunzi was pressed to argue for the continued viability of Confucianism. He ramified the notion of ritual action with penal regulations, and argued that the possibility of individual excellence and humaneness depended on rigorous training in ritual conduct and instruction in *bona fide* Chinese classics. He also encouraged an activist government that would ensure public trust and order by taking such measures as standardizing weights and measures and even regulating word meanings and language use.

Xunzi devoted a lengthy essay specifically to "Military Affairs" (ch. 15), countering the emphasis of more realistic thinkers and advisors on economic and military power for bolstering the regime and strengthening the state. Xunzi insisted that it was the eminence of a just, ritually proper ruler and the vitality of his state that attracted the favor and allegiance of peoples and rulers.

Xunzi did not linger at the level of generality; his essay included a debate with a militarist named Linwu that got into examples and specifics. Following militarists like Sun Wu and Sun Bin, Linwu identified timeliness, geography, enemy movements and rapid actions as decisive military matters; Xunzi countered by insisting that, more basically, the king needed a loyal and unified people who were steadfast and well-trained. Linwu then listed measures for power and advantage, stealth and deception, secret movements and sudden attacks, to which Xunzi countered by asserting that such measures work only against ambitious feudal lords, not true kings: since the true king enjoys the allegiance of his and neighboring peoples, people willingly provide him with intelligence about enemy movements and actions. Moreover, his troops are well-trained and the chain of command clear, so his forces can meet any threat, and his commanders can counter trickery. By the same token, whereas the justice and propriety of a true king win him the allegiance of the people, the selfishness of the rival lords earn them dissatisfaction and rancor. When Linwu suggested that lords and commanders win the loyalty of their troops by sharing the spoils of war, Xunzi replied that such material rewards only inspire selfishness and the profit motive; they don't inspire the unconditional loyalty that is forged in honorable relations with a just lord or commander.

Xunzi held that the good reputation of the true king and his generals influences even enemy troops, for all know their motives for fighting: to resist those who would harm the people, and to oppose significant wrongs. Consequently, the true king receives a godlike respect from his troops when he enters their military encampment. His noble demeanor inspires and transforms his officers and troops. At root, the principles of noble political rule hold equally for military command. Xunzi rounded out his argument by reaffirming that military affairs are ancillary to more basic concerns of rulership: even if a king wants to annex a neighboring state, displaying excellent domestic rulership is more effective than using military force or economic power. Excellent rulership draws neighboring people (and feudal lords) to what they perceive to be a worthy king, whereas military force is costly, violent and weakens the king and use of economic power depletes the king's reserves. Furthermore, holding another state is significantly more difficult and costly than annexing it. The best way to gain the allegiance of another state is not by force but by excellence: the king's honor and ritual propriety make the neighboring lords willingly submissive while his fair administration makes their people feel secure.

Xunzi upheld the noble aspirations and demands of upright Confucian rulership while answering more pragmatic, hard-headed thinkers and advisors in those chaotic times. Significantly, while contextualizing the role of the military in state politics and society, he delineated the traits of the true king and went beyond Confucius and Mencius by describing the effective general and offering practical advice on military training, command, intelligence, planning, and action. Moreover, with the central court in shambles, Xunzi sought to make state kings aspire to be true kings in the hope that the best among them would eventually prevail and forge a new empire based on the noble traditions as distilled, preserved and transmitted by Confucian teachers such as himself.

Evolution of Confucianism

Confucianism gradually asserted itself as the school of classical learning and administration during the Han dynasty (206 BCE–220 CE). Conservators of ancient traditions and ministers of humane order, Confucians confined themselves to the humanities and public affairs, and did not pay particular heed to martial matters. A new form of Confucianism arose in the Northern Song (960-1127) that revived Confucius' original focus on self-cultivation. War and military affairs remained secondary to their sense of pressing ethical and philosophical concerns. One of the founders of Neo-Confucianism, Zhang Zai (1020-77), in youth loved to discuss military matters and sought to make a name for himself for this attainment; but, at the age of 18, when he posed a military question to scholar-minister Fan Zhongyuan (989-1052), Fan asked him how a student of the Confucian Way could concern himself with military matters and told him to devote himself to the transmission contained in the *Doctrine of the Mean* (Zhongyong). This exchange established a trend among Neo-Confucians to confine their study efforts to their school texts, the classics and the *Four Books* (*Great Learning, Mencius, Analects, Doctrine of the Mean*).

Zhu Xi: Synthesizer of Neo-Confucianism

The greatest Neo-Confucian, Zhu Xi (1130-1200), distinguished himself by mastering all of the Chinese humanities, as well as some science and medicine. Zhu's studies included military strategy and tactics and military history, which he sought to master in contemplating ways that imperial forces might wrest the central plains back from Jurchen control. Unlike ordinary Confucian scholars who believed that those conversant in humanity (*ren*) and appropriateness (*yi*) shouldn't concern themselves with military and financial matters, Zhu asserted that it was precisely those conversant in humanity and appropriateness, who were most responsible to master military and financial matters. Following Confucius, Zhu believed that military affairs and finance were of secondary importance for a state's security and power, but he insisted that military affairs and war be managed by men of courage and integrity. And military deployments and actions must be just those authorized by the emperor as punitive actions.

Zhu drew lessons from history in considering possible military responses to the Jurchen presence on the ancestral Chinese plains. In 1162, the imperial court faced the dilemma of whether to prosecute a war (for which the cost of victory would be eventual defeat) or negotiate a treaty (that would yield internal dissent). Zhu's solution was to neither fight nor sue for a peace treaty, but to maintain the status quo while the newly installed emperor took time to be groomed for leadership, improve his administration, and strengthen the realm. On this premise, the regime would grow stronger and nurture its readiness so that when the opportunity arose to recover the central plains, the emperor could mount a military campaign. As it turned out, the court negotiated with the Jurchens, but without strengthening the empire, which led to a stalemate that lasted until the Mongol invasion in the mid-13th century.

Wang Shouren: Neo-Confucian Scholar and Military Commander

Ming dynasty Neo-Confucian master Wang Shouren (Yangming 1472-1529) championed the notions that "knowledge and action form a unity" and that people possess an inborn capacity to know the good, and the ability to act on this knowledge. Thus, he sought to revive Confucius' spirit of activism at a time when Confucian scholars mostly were pedants. In response to imperial concerns about the problem of tribal banditry on the frontier, Wang wrote a celebrated memorial outlining measures to meet the crisis (Chan 1963, 284-92). While premising his view on classical Confucian ideas, Wang drew freely from *Sunzi's Art of Warfare* in making his case, in this way reestablishing the Confucian correlation of *wen* and *wu*.

Nearly twenty years later, Wang was appointed governor of a southern border area, responsible to pacify the region. On arriving in Jiangxi in 1517, he set to work recruiting able-bodied fighters, reorganizing the armies, instituting a ten-family joint-registration system and restoring social order. Fighting soon broke out, but Wang subdued the rebellion quickly. He secured social order by rehabilitating the old bandits and improving the local economy. Several months later rebellions broke out in surrounding areas, but Wang suppressed them all within six months and quickly improved social order by setting up schools and local administrations. Wang's greatest challenge occurred in 1519 when Prince Ning, a nephew of the emperor, assembled an army to take the capital and establish a new dynasty. Facing Ning's well-entrenched army, Wang used deft political and military maneuvers to subdue the rebellion and capture the prince in just ten days.

Zheng He: Adventurer and Master of Espionage

Also notable in this regard was a Chinese adventurer during the early Ming dynasty, Zheng He (1371-1435). Zheng led seven grand sea expeditions to Southeast Asia, India and Africa, once rounding the southern tip of Africa. Before undertaking these voyages, he had been charged with pacifying some of the marauding tribes on the western frontier. He used stealth and wit rather than force in carrying out his missions. His favored technique was to infiltrate a band of hostiles, ingratiating himself with them until he gained their trust. Then, he would sow seeds of mistrust among them and secretly kill their leader, so they would quarrel and fight each other, thus neutralizing their threat. Zheng displayed less interest in civilizing the tribesmen than did Wang Shouren.

Confucian Root of True Power: Civilized, Noble Rule

In summary, as conservators of ritual culture and executors of order, Confucians spoke little of war or the military arts. They distrusted the use of force of arms, except as a measure of last resort, ideally in the form of punitive action initiated at the highest level of the realm. The early Confucians, in particular, believed that the realm would grow and flourish naturally under the auspices of wise and noble rulers, who would attract people from outside the realm to join or pay tribute. In addition, Chinese civilization generally was centered on the fertile heartland, so it tended to be a stay-at-home culture, not given to launching far-flung crusades. Moreover, lacking conceptual and religious universalism, the Chinese had little penchant for evangelism or exporting their culture to challenge other traditions. Their cultural experience bears the stamp of accommodation, making their civilization porous and long enduring. In short, traditional Chinese, the Confucians in particular, generally did not feel the need to force their beliefs and traditions on others outside the realm militarily.

Confucian Leadership Ideals

While concerned about war and military arts, the Confucians were keen to see interstate conflicts settled by diplomacy and negotiation. They had witnessed the unspeakable death and destruction wrought by war, and knew that military adventures and war should be measures of last resort; hence, the prestige and power Confucius, Mencius and Xunzi accorded to rulers who stood on ritual conduct, ethical relations, fair distribution, and, most importantly, to rulers who cared for the common people.

Bound up with this ritual, ethical orientation was the perceived need for effective, positive communication between leaders and the people as well as among officials and among the people themselves. Indeed, this ritual, ethical orientation itself was intended to enhance communications by encouraging people, including rulers, to display sincerity and seriousness in dealing with others. For Confucians, communication was not just a matter of words, or even of icons and symbols; they saw it as a total process of conveying thoughts, feelings and intentions through one's overall behavior and conduct, even one's dress and demeanor. Education thus involved cultivating the whole person, including ritual attunement and respect toward others. As Confucius said, one cultivates humanity by mastering the (ego)self and practicing ritual conduct (12.1).

The cultivation/learning process was especially broad-based for prospective early Chinese rulers who would have to deal with a variety of peoples reflecting a range of cultures and values. The problem of leading diverse peoples was a real one in early China, where the various states had different customs. While the emperor and his court followed a preferred elite code and set of rituals, he and his officials still had to deal with subject-kin from various locales with an eye to their different practices. Even as culture and language throughout China gradually became more homogenous through unified political control and written language and the dissemination of Confucianism, Chinese officialdom constantly still had to deal with outside countries and tribes, some tributary and some not.

These considerations, I think, underscore the fact that effective communication skills were an essential element in the early Confucian notion of leadership. Who did the Confucians regard as the greatest kings and emperors of early China? Who was the king without a throne? Including emperors Yu, Yao and Shun, the Duke of Zhou, kings Wen and Wu, and Confucius, these were the called "Sage kings" and the "Sage". They tended to be dynastic founders or innovators rather than just keepers of the order (Confucius was a moral, cultural innovator). Since they occupied themselves with conquering, establishing or reforming a dynasty, they had to be artisans of effective communication in order to attract followers, persuade people, win support and cooperation, issue commands, etc., so everyone would cooperate and meet challenges together. For his part, Confucius effectively communicated to his students and those he counseled, not just in pungent sayings using novel value ideas, but also in unfailingly scrupulous, circumspect conduct. The voice and figure of Confucius in *Analects* continue to "speak" to readers across the centuries.

Let's consider the Classical Chinese word for Sage (*sheng*) or Sage king (*shengwang*), one of the few terms used in common by most of the early schools of thought in China. *Sheng* is homophonous with the word for "sound" or "voice" (*sheng*), and the character graph resembles that for "listen" (*ting*). Looking at the character, one is initially impressed by the image of an ear and a mouth over a person, suggesting that the person listens and speaks, with the connotation of listening before speaking. Roger Ames emphasizes that the character displays an ear (*er*) listening on left and the act of illustrating, manifesting, expressing (*cheng*) on the right, such that the sage is a virtuoso at communicating—heeding the views of others and weaving and expressing their summation (1998 62f; 1987 256ff.). This emphasis would make sense in the context of early China where the king or emperor sought to harmonize, lead and direct lords and peoples with differing dialects, values and customs. Leading willingly submissive subjects by respectful ritual and reasonable persuasion would be easier and less costly than forcibly compelling them to follow. In sum, the character graph for Sage gives the impression of a distinguished personage who listens to various views and considerations, the most reasonable of which he would express in policy. All of these highly developed communication skills would facilitate official dealings with problems and discord among peoples within and without the realm.

Does this account of the sage exaggerate her communicativeness and flexibility? Is this consistent with the vaunted all-knowingness of the sage? In view of the fact that the paramount sage, Confucius, busied himself with learning well into old age and could always learn something from the people around him, the all-knowingness of the sage had more to do with perspicacity and responsiveness than in knowing all the facts *per se*. Hence, the hallmark of the Chinese sage, enlightenment, was manifested in perspicacity of discernment and aptness of response. The observations, responses and deeds of the sage were enlightened and transforming. At the same time, this did not mean complete flexibility: her immersion in and commitment to the Way and noble values would condition her perception and conduct. Notably, to the extent this commitment was expressed in a firm attachment to specific policies, Mencius took this as a potential limitation of sages.

For Mencius, the wisdom of Confucius surpassed the discernment of the sages in that he was sensitive and responsive to subtle changes in time and circumstance, whereas they had to stick to their plan. Ordained the sage of timeliness, Confucius notably could modify his approach flexibly to fit specific situations and achieve optimal outcomes. Hence, Mencius likened the "wise" person to the skilled archer who can make adjustments for adverse conditions, such as wind and distance, to hit the mark, that is, to do what is most apt and appropriate, all things considered (5B.1). To underscore his flexibility, we recall Confucius' refusal "to entertain conjectures or insist on certainty; [or] . . . to be inflexible or to be egotistical" (IX.4). He had "no preconceptions about the permissible and the impermissible" (XVIII.8).

Confucian Views and War and Terrorism in the
Contemporary World

How would Confucius and his followers view the world and the phenomena of war and terrorism early in the twenty-first century today? First, I would like to observe that Confucius and Mencius' views appear to be more suggestive regarding the role of the United Nations, while the later Confucian perspectives are more suggestive regarding international relations. That is, whereas Confucius and Mencius saw their emperor as leading and shepherding the whole world (*tianxia*) as rather loose confederation of states with common allegiances and goals, later Confucians saw their empire more as one socio-political entity among others.

I believe the early Confucians would have been taken with and celebrated the United Nations, with its mission and operations based on the UN Charter as a covenant among member nations dedicated to equality, peace and security among all nations in the world. The UN would express their ideals for the Chinese regime and empire as a harmonious confederation covering "all under heaven" (*tianxia*). In fact, drawing on classical Confucian ideals, Kang Yuwei (1858-1927) prescribed a world of Great Unity (*Datong*) in which sovereignty would be circumscribed and peoples would care for each other across borders.

Although the early Confucians would be unacquainted with the democratic formation of the UN bodies and decision-making processes, they had the similar idea of consensus and would be impressed by the probity, seriousness and idealism of UN proceedings generally. At the same time, they would tend to doubt the probity of individual (or small groups of) member nations taking military action, unless mandated by the Security Council to do so. (Admittedly, the Security Council has been hostage to political or economic concerns of some of its powerful members.) Their deep-seated distrust of individual (or small groups of) nations initiating military action on their own would move them to suggest a strengthening of UN bylaws to prevent this sort of unilateral action. Additionally, they would recommend greater allocations of resources for UN peace-brokering and peace-keeping, for example, so the UN could offer to substitute things/matters over which countries or peoples were fighting, or develop a certain area in such a way that two contending groups could utilize it together.

Finally, they would suggest seeking ways to enhance and deepen communications among peoples through shared humane values. To this end, they would recommend devoting more resources to cultivating culture and values among peoples and leaders so as to strengthen people's self and mutual respect and tolerance. Importantly, Confucians would promote cultural learning in the form of a self-cultivation that would refine people's habitual thought above the bottom line thinking stressed in modern economic and management culture that focuses on tangible gain and loss, the very sort of consideration that lies behind so many conflicts. As Confucius affirmed, the gentleman is one who is conversant with appropriateness, whereas the small man is conversant with profit (4.16, 4.10).

Rising public ethical concerns have influenced the operation of another global organization, this one intended to avert trade conflicts by setting guidelines for fair trade among nations. That is the World Trade Organization. In a recent study, *One World: The Ethics of Globalization,* Peter Singer shows how the WTO, to which member states surrender some of their economic sovereignty, is being nudged away from treating just tariff (profit) issues as sacrosanct and decisive to addressing issues that most (non-economist) people regard as more basic, such as working conditions, pay rates, environmental impact, and the like. That is, people generally want the WTO to broaden its narrow tariff criteria into a wider set of ethical criteria, especially as global trade has an increasing impact on, not only people's livelihood, but on culture, lifestyle, and the environment.

In summary, the early Confucians would advocate a strengthened UN that is more active in brokering and creating the conditions for peace. And, as for dealing with recalcitrant countries, the Confucians would insist that the Security Council, like sage emperors of old, initiate decisive action to deal with them, still using a carrot and stick approach, while discouraging individual (or small groups of) countries from vigilante-like going it alone. In addition, these eminent Confucians maintained a certain integrity and devotion to truth. Regarding the pretexts and claims offered by states for making war, they would insist on the Security Council's reaching a level of certainty about such claims before authorizing military action. In the 2002-03 Iraq crisis, the UN Security Council did display such probity, but the US & the UK were impatient to wage war, and started the attack before the truth of their claims could be confirmed, or disconfirmed.

The Confucian lessons for nation states, strong nations in particular, are strategic and tactical. According to Xunzi, for a great nation (and leader) to become eminent, it needs to exhibit the characteristics of good rule, good economy and fair distribution, as well as an orderly society; such a nation will certainly attract states and peoples wishing to emulate it. Surrounding smaller states will be willingly submissive in order to develop and participate in her viable institutions and good practices. Under such circumstances, a strong state would exert a benign influence over other states. Given such willing cooperation, the great country wouldn't need to conquer or buy out the smaller countries.

Daodejing ch. 61 expresses the underlying symbiosis of this sort of asymmetrical interstate relationship in terms poetic and profound. In the translation of Ames & Hall (2003, 172):

> A great state is like the lower reaches of water's downward flow.
> It is the female of the world....
> In the intercourse of the world,
> The female is always able to use her equilibrium (*jing*) to best the male,
> It is this equilibrium that properly puts her underneath....
> Hence, if the great state can get underneath the small state,
> It can rule the small state;
> If the small state is able to get underneath the large state,
> It can get to be ruled by the large state....
> Now, the great state wants no more than to win over the other state and

      tend to it,
While the small state wants no more than to offer the great state its services.
If they are both getting what they want in the relationship,
Then it is fitting for the great state to take the lower position.

When armed conflict becomes inevitable, the good leader will continue to dispose herself with honor and always make her war aims clear and plausible. Generally, her punitive strikes would be to avenge injustices or crimes against people, property or lands. Under such circumstances, her military campaigns would be broadly understood and supported. I would add that the case for starting a war has to be transparent and obvious, and leaves no room for doubt. Wise leaders know that peddling false or undemonstrated reasons as justifications for military actions can backfire, especially as military campaigns grow more costly. Like gossip, such falsehoods have a way of taking on a life of their own, and inevitably lead to questions of the real motive for going to war.

Wang Shouren provides instructive guidance for stronger countries taking on smaller countries or tribes. The stronger countries typically see themselves as putting down troublemakers that are disturbing their society and economy, and prefer to unleash overwhelming force in order to snuff out the problem. Wang's lesson to them is based on the Confucian complements of *wen* (culture) and *wu* (martial spirit): recognize, first and foremost, that those frontier peoples are human beings, too, with life aspirations for themselves and their children, just as "we" have. While it might be incumbent on the large country to flex its muscles and demonstrate its superior force to make an impression, the ruler's main concern ultimately should be, rather than shock and awe, to demonstrate to them her respect for them and her willingness to offer them a way to participate in his socio-economic system, such that they needn't engage in the disruptive activities that disturb the large country. Here again, all the aforementioned effective communication skills of enlightened leadership would come into play.

I believe that this sort of approach is also suggestive for the treatment of ethnic minority groups dwelling within a country. If we are distressed by the actions taken by a cruel government and concerned about the minority people under its rule, it is incumbent on us to open the doors of diplomacy first, to initiate communications, to engage them, to show them our strengths perhaps, and offer them better ways. Use respect and persuasion to draw them out, to initiate intercourse. They will perhaps change as they see the advantages of becoming more interactive and integrated into the global systems and networks. (This strategy of engagement has been working with China and Vietnam. Why not try it with Cuba?)

Conclusion: Facing Terrorism

As to the problem of terrorism, the vital Confucian prescription would involve a combination of Zheng He's approach of infiltrating and sabotaging marauding groups from within together with Wang Shouren's *wen-wu* approach of subduing and then integrating marginal groups into the larger economy and society. Launching full-scale military assaults into hostile areas is usually costly, uncertain and likely to cause collateral damage and arouse resentment, thus feeding further terrorism. Moreover, any armed invasion would best be followed up by humble support in reconstruction. It would be far better, initially, to try to engage a threatening terrorist group covertly, while working quietly to understand the local peoples generally and identify the roots of their resentment and hostility. Inquiring into and understanding the local conditions and culture, we should make suitable initiatives to improve the economy and open up the culture of the region. Such efforts might seem to be slow and costly, but the costs of such peaceful efforts would be hundreds, perhaps thousands, of times less than war costs, and they would offer innumerable other dividends. While active terrorist groups that have already perpetrated terrorist acts mostly would have to be forcibly neutralized, other groups that are less active or in formative stages generally would be capable of reform. Only the most extreme, irrational and violent groups should be dealt with decisively at the outset; many groups have legitimate grievances and should be understood, appreciated and responded to humanely. And those with simple misunderstandings should be approached and communicated with. Oftentimes, our inability to appreciate their grievances reflects our own obtuseness as much as their unreasonableness. Ruling groups, the elite, particularly in large, powerful countries need to learn to listen, to heed and then to respond humanely and reasonably.

Ultimately, Confucian values are premised on the principle of mutual respect and tolerance (as reflected in Confucius's negative formulation of the Golden Rule) and dedicated to communication and deeper mutual understanding (the character graph for Sage depicts and ear and a mouth over a person). Confucius himself grew up in a society shaped by several distinct dynasties comprised of the diverse cultures of numerous states with distinct dialects and customs. He already knew a world fractured by strife and in need of a tolerant, flexible confederative framework that would allow effective communication in diversity, a world much like the one in which we find ourselves today. The dynamic, vibrant harmony of Confucianism is, after all, premised on interactive diversity in various forms.

Select Bibliography

Ames, Roger, and David Hall. *Daodejing: A Philosophical Translation*. New York: Ballantine Books, 2003.
Ames, Roger, and David Hall. *Focusing the Familiar: A Translation and Philosophical Interpretation of the Zhongyong*. Honolulu: University of Hawaii Press, 2001.
_____, and Henry Rosemont. *The Analects of Confucius: A Philosophical Translation*.   New York, Ballantine Books, 1998.
_____, and D.C. Lau. *Sun Pin: The Art of Warfare*. New York: Ballantine Books, 1996.
_____, and David Hall. *Thinking through Confucius*. Albany: SUNY Press, 1987.
_____. *Sun-Tzu: The Art of Warfare*. New York: Ballantine Books, 1993.
Chan, Wing-Tsit. *Reflections on Things at Hand: The Neo-Confucian Anthology Compiled by Chu Hsi*. New York and London: Columbia University Press, 1967.

_____. *Instructions for Practical Living and other Neo-Confucian Writings by Wang Yang-ming.* New York and London: Columbia University Press, 1963.

Hsu, C. *Ancient China in Transition: An Analysis of Social Mobility, 722-222 B.C.* Stanford: Stanford University Press, 1965.

Dubs, Homer. *Hsun Tzu(Xunzi): Works from the Chinese.* London: Probsthain, 1928.

Lau, D.C. *Confucius: The Analects.* Hong Kong: Chinese University Press, 1992.

_____. *Mencius.* 2 vols. Hong Kong: Chinese University Press, 1984.

Loewe, Michael., and Shaugnessy, Edward. *The Cambridge History of Ancient China: From the Origins to 221 B.C.* Cambridge: Cambridge University Press, 1999.

McKnight, B. "Chu Hsi (Zhu Xi) and his World." *Chu Hsi and Neo-Confucianism.* Ed. Wing-Tsit Chan. Honolulu: Hawaii University Press, 1986.

Schirokauer, Conrad. *A Brief History of Chinese Civilization.* San Diego: Harcourt Brace, 1991.

_____. "Chu Hsi's (Zhu Xi) Political Career: A Study in Ambivalence." *Confucian Personalities.* Eds. Arthur Wright and Dennis Twitchert. Stanford: Stanford University Press, 1962.

Singer, Peter. *One World: The Ethics of Globalization.* New Haven & London: Yale University Press, 2002.

Veblen, Thorstein. *An Inquiry into the Nature of Peace and the Terms of Its Perpetuation.* New York and London: Macmillan, 1917.

Watson, Burton. *Hsun Tzu (Xunzi): Basic Writings.* New York and London: Columbia University Press, 1964.

14

Great Teacher and Great Soul: Ueshiba and Gandhi on Personal Violence

C. Wesley DeMarco

It is not easy to speak of martial arts or martial artists in the same breath as Gandhiji. Nevertheless the founder of Aikido, Morihei Ueshiba (1883-1969), regarded his martial art as a practice of nonviolent conflict resolution and came to speak with increasing frequency of nonviolence.[1] Aikido (the Japanese term means something like 'the way of harmonizing spirit'[2]) is a martial art that is, in the founder's words, "[A]n expression of ultimate harmony and absolute peace."[3] That is because it cultivates tranquility in the soul of the practitioner, peaceable and harmonious relationships with other people, and—when push comes to shove—ways of handling personal violence without injuring the assailant. Ueshiba even declares, in a renowned and at first blush incredible formulation, that Aikido is "the martial art of love."

Ueshiba's talk of nonviolence and nonresistance invites a comparison with Gandhi's way. After highlighting some key similarities and differences, I want to ask whether Ueshiba's art is or could be Gandhian. The answer is complex. I shall argue that while their ideas of nonviolence and nonresistance are disparate, Aikido and satyagraha[4] are companionable practices in the sense that a Gandhian need not become an Aikidoist and an Aikidoist need not be a Gandhian, but an Aikidoist may consistently be a Gandhian and a Gandhian may consistently practice Aikido. Beyond this, each may assist the other with indeterminacies in its own practice. I shall suggest that there is a moral indeterminacy in Gandhian thought and practice regarding personal violence; Aikido may prove useful in addressing it. And Gandhians offer something very important to Aikidoists, because anyone who pursues Aikido as a way of peace must face two hard questions that Gandhians have but Aikidoists have not yet learned to face. In fine, it would be good to rouse discussion between Gandhians and Aikidoists not only because of their fascinating resonances,[5] but because each way of peace leaves some issues hanging that the other may help address.

I

Morihei Ueshiba, known to Aikidoists as 'O-Sensei' or 'great teacher,' declares, "Nonviolence is the true practice of Aikido....Aikido is nonviolence."[6] He proclaims that Aikido is "a way to promote love and goodness among humankind" (32-3). Morihei came to consider Aikido the "art of peace," the motor and model of a serene and harmonious life. He writes, "The practice of Aikido is...a belief in the ultimate power of nonviolence" (44, translation modified).[7] He continues, "It can never be violent....The purpose of Aikido is to teach people how not to be violent, and lead them to a higher path. It is a means of establishing universal peace" (33).

The core practice of Aikido is a martial art based on a form of ju-jutsu. But in Aikido there are no attacks;[8] its practitioners train hard for a purely defensive response to violence.[9] Moreover this defensive response is smooth—even gentle—and above all calculated to avoid harm. "When the techniques are applied by Aikidoists who have achieved a certain degree of mastery in the art, they will leave no serious injury in their wake."[10] Aikido's central techniques turn on a radical and practical form of nonresistance. The most aggressive assaults are not opposed. There is no clash of powers. Force is not met with counterforce. The standard response is rather to blend with the thrust of an attack and smoothly redirect it so that it is defused without injury to the assailant or defender. There are all sorts of interesting subtleties in such responses that are the stuff of instructional manuals and are not germane here; suffice it to say that training this sort of responsiveness is difficult for a host of technical and psychological reasons. Aikido training is not training in 'fighting'.[11] The point is to avoid hostilities and end a fight without fighting back. For this reason Aikidoists do not combat or even contest.[12] The point is to bring a violent confrontation to a peaceful resolution without harm to the defender or the attacker. An accomplished Aikidoist will never even engage an attacker, in the sense that she will not play his game and will not respond in kind.

Westbrook and assert that it is the ethical message that "gives Aikido its unmistakable identity and qualifies it as a superior method of integration and development". They continue, "It is the ultimate motivation of the art...[to] to bring order where there is disorder, to integrate where there is separation, to reconcile where there is strife."[13] Setting aside Westbrook's and Ratti's claims about Aikido's superiority, I want to concur that it is the ethical intent of Aikido that makes it unique. This is not the often-repeated claim that the study of martial art—at least an "Asian" martial art[14]—will almost inevitably make one less violent because it promotes self-control and confidence and so on. It is true that many traditional arts will teach one never to attack first and will encourage self-control and a noble bearing. For some, training may even be cathartic. But this is a weaker claim than that made on behalf of Aikido. Though the study of a traditional art of attack and defense may raise the threshold of response, once a response is engaged, someone who is trained to strike or kick or otherwise fight back will tend to respond as she is trained to respond. Ueshiba says, "To injure an opponent is to injure yourself. To control aggression without inflicting injury is the art of peace," i.e., is Aikido (67).

Aikido is not, however, the only martial art that can defuse attacks without inflicting injury. Other 'soft style' martial arts can handle full-bore aggressive assaults without harming the attacker in the process. For instance, it is said that the taiji master Yang Lu-Chan (1799-1872), called 'Undefeatable Yang,' never hurt anyone in his many challenge matches. Robert W. Smith remarks of the twentieth century taiji master Zheng Manqing, "[H]e would permit you to use anything short of a hammer and would defeat you without hurting you" (42).[15] Such skill is commonly praised in these traditions as something desirable. However, I know of no style of taiji or related arts that makes this ethical intention a central purpose of training. With Aikido, the ethical intention is a central purpose and it is one that is proclaimed and trained from the beginning. If it were not, the moral point could be lost or indefinitely deferred; moreover, it could easily be marginalized by being regarded as merely a side-effect of a certain level of skill. I want to argue that it is important to put the ethical purpose front and center. A practitioner of Ueshiba Aikido will sincerely desire to defend herself without harming others and will train with this purpose in view.

To bring this desire to fruition, the practitioner must be, as Westbrook and Ratti assert, "Well on the way toward integration of mind and body, of physical means and ethical motives."[16] There are two reasons why the ethical purpose of Ueshiba Aikido requires this integration of mind and body. For one thing, it is needed merely to perform a technique successfully at a level that will work most of the time in most real-world situations. But there is another reason. No punch hits as hard as unforgiving tarmac clouts a body thrown overpoweringly to the ground. Many Aikido throws can result in serious injury. Indeed Aikido schools are said to have the highest injury rates of any style of martial arts. This seems paradoxical.

Aikido owes its technical content primarily to *Daito-ryu aiki-jutsu*, though there were other influences on its development.[17] Hence in reference to its techniques Aikido is a form of jujutsu, one known for its beautiful flowing circular movements. There are numerous styles of jujutsu. Cutting across them all is the distinction between (i) approaches that use muscular force efficiently—principles of leverage and limb-opposition and so on—to maneuver an assailant's body, (ii) approaches that make more subtle use of the assailant's own force so that it can be redirected, and (iii) approaches that make such full use of the attacker's momentum and intent that they require minimal movement or effort on the part of the recipient.[18] This third is the level of *aiki*. Though this is the technical center of Aikido, it does not yet give voice to Aikido's ethical purpose. Aiki-jutsu may be soft or hard, may use large or small circles in its responsive movements, but need not respect the opponent or refrain from injuring him. That is an additional imperative that does not flow automatically from the mastery of technique.

Though Ueshiba spoke of "divine techniques that do not kill"[19] and often enjoined his students to submit their movements and wills to the techniques, it is not the techniques that injure or do not injure. It is the practitioner who injures or does not injure in the application of his techniques. This point is particularly pertinent to Aikido since the difference between a controlled take-down and a slam-dunk throw is slight. In fact it may be two inches difference in direction of pitch or a few ounces of additional force or a last-minute return arc of circular motion. With throws (where a hard slam is possible) and locks (where a joint break is possible), there is always a choice between a calm and continuously monitored control and a pulse of violent intent.

It is part of martial arts lore that the true master acts so much without calculation or forethought that she is not really responsible for the violent consequences of her actions. One hears for instance that it is the sword and not the swordsman that kills. This is sometimes held to be a consequence of *mushin* or the state of no-mind.[20] In a famous story, Nobunaga destroys the Tendai monastery along with thousands of monks and asserts, "I am not the destroyer of this monastery. The destroyer of the monastery is the monastery itself".[21] Howsoever 'Zen' this sounds, the Aikidoist should regard it as sophistry of the most pernicious sort. O-Sensei would have none of it. In Ueshiba Aikido, the practitioner is constantly reminded "[Y]ou must be responsible for not inflicting unnecessary damage upon your attacker".[22] A clear locus of responsibility is recognized in Aikido theory and practice. Even where there is 'no-mind,' there is a locus of action and choice that may move for well or ill. Ueshiba led the technical art of aiki-jutsu onto an ethical path that stresses both the responsibility of the practitioner and the moral standing of the assailant. In so doing he transmuted the principles of *aiki* into first principles capable of shaping a whole way of life. That is the point of calling Aikido a 'd̲' (Chinese *dao*) or way.

II

Whether in moral or political life, there are no *techniques* that are intrinsically and essentially nonviolent. In politics, the point applies to the use of boycotts, embargoes, mass marches, and so on. More than one boycott has resulted in layoffs that have adversely affected lives. More than one embargo has left hungry people in their wake. More than once Gandhi called off a march because there was good reason to suspect harms to people or property would occur. Nevertheless, in the personal as in the political case, there are techniques that can be turned to a nonviolent use and techniques that cannot.[23] It is up to the practitioner first to choose methods that are actually effective; second, to select those effective methods that are open to nonviolent use; and third, to use those methods in a nonviolent way in practice. All three points are essential to Ueshiba Aikido. All three resonate with Gandhian political action.

First, Gandhians are not idealists in any sense that excludes realism about power and violence. They want effective means of disposing of brutality and promoting peace and justice. Means that are moral but ineffectual are not of interest. Second, some but not all effective methods are inherently violent. The trend in self-defense—at least in Europe and the States—is toward the most aggressive methods. Headbutts, knee and elbow strikes, eye gouges and various menus of 'dirty' moves are routinely taught and used. The words "savage" and "devastating" and "vicious" have become the most hackneyed terms in martial arts advertising, where they are used as badges of realism and effectiveness and indicators of product desirability. Even though it is being practiced in politics, pre-emptive violence is not overtly encouraged in personal self-defense, at least in Europe and the States (because of legal restrictions on levels of response and jurisdictionally variable definitions of 'reasonable force' and 'excessive force' and so on). But the trend in martial arts circles is to approve if not recommend all-out, no-holds-barred vicious aggression once one is threatened—or at least feels threatened.

There are, however, methods of dealing with aggression that are effective (point one, above) and can be turned to nonviolent use (point 2). All Aikido techniques fall into this category. Again I want to stress the wrinkle that many of these same techniques can be quite devastating if inconsiderately applied. No technique is inherently nonviolent; it is the practitioner's use that is violent or nonviolent. The hard tarmac that ends an uncontrolled throw is far nastier than most any human fist. An Aikido practitioner must learn how to use all her moves nonviolently while keeping them effective. This is difficult, but it is possible. Because it is possible, it is imperative.

So far I have been arguing that Aikido offers techniques that can be effective and that may be used nonviolently (that is, without significant injury to the defender or the assailant), though their nonviolent use depends upon the ethical intent of the practitioner. It is this intent that is dear to Ueshiba Aikido. Moreover, this intent ought to be explicit from the outset and part of the student's training from the start. This distinction in Aikido training and practice reflects a familiar distinction in political nonviolence: that between tactical or strategic nonviolence and principled nonviolence.

'Violent' and 'nonviolent' are not two mutually exclusive categories: there is a continuous series of possibilities, and sometimes it is hard to tell where to draw the line. In any case the course of ongoing events must be continuously monitored to see where these lines arise and might be crossed. An embargo could be part of a siege with consequences of the most drastic affliction and human suffering. Or it might be applied with sensitivity to its effects on a targeted populace, so that blocks are adjusted or even removed if things get too rough. Even a 'nonviolent' application may nevertheless be merely tactical, simply an expedient. Strikes, boycotts, marches, work stoppages, and the whole gamut of strategies may be employed merely because members of some group believe them to be their only effective recourse, not because they are found to be a more moral recourse that is adopted from principle.

Similarly, Aikido is studied and used most often not by individuals who are committed to some quasi-religious 'way of peace' but individuals who simply want something effective. It is studied for instance by law enforcement personnel, corrections officers, and security staff in hospitals and mental health facilities who are under special constraints and must exercise extraordinary care with their populations. It is always the practitioner's responsibility to make the choice for a controlled, nonviolent response to aggression and to use a technique in a way that bears out this choice. But this may be a more limited choice made for special purposes (special populations, particular tasks), or it may be part of a large choice of an integrated way of life. This would be a decision to pursue the Aikido way of peace as a 'd_' or way of being. This may sound Gandhian; but it is not quite so.

Nonresistance (*muteiko*) is a key principle of Aikido.[24] Morihei sometimes goes so far as to identify them, saying, "Aikido is the principle of nonresistance. Because it is nonresistant, it is victorious from the beginning" (66). Gandhi also makes nonresistance a central part of his teaching. But Ueshiba's concept and practice of nonresistance is not equivalent to Gandhi's. The point can best be illustrated with a story. Renjiro Shirata, a senior student of Morihei, once was lecturing on *muteiko*. Without warning, a champion sumo wrestler wishing to challenge Shirata jumped up from the crowd and rushed at him, bellowing, "Nonresist this!" Shirata smoothly evaded the charge, pinned the wrestler to the ground in a flash, and then said with a chuckle, "See? No one can resist nonresistance!"[25]

Though the idea of Aikido was forged in the fires of a truly pure heart, the practice is still in its technical core a kind of jujutsu. And Gandhi explicitly says that satyagraha "needs no jiu-jitsu."[26] This is not what Gandhian nonresistance amounts to.[27] On the political stage, the employment of ju-jutsu in a satyagraha campaign would appear bizarre and ultimately out of place. Imagine, for instance, a satyagraha campaign facing resistance from the oppressor group. As the agents of the oppressors violently assail the protestors, the recipients calmly guide their attackers to the ground over and over again, tossing them gently aside as wave after wave advances upon them. Supposing such a response to be possible—and so far as I know Ueshiba didn't envision organized armies of Aikidoka—it would be a nonviolent response in just about anyone's definition of the term. However, it is not an example of Gandhian nonresistance. It does not seem to suit the Gandhian purpose, which involves transformative suffering as an integral component.

There are three aspects to this Gandhian purpose. An act of suffering experienced in the service of a just cause is purification to the practitioner, is aimed at the conversion of the oppressor, and is calculated to be visible to third parties (peoples outside of the struggle, observers, nations aligned or nonaligned and so forth) who might in one way or another be moved and so come to be persuaded of the justice of the cause. While Ueshiba is clear about the purificational aspect of Aikido,[28] he is not at all clear whether Aikido would exhibit the second or third of these three aspects of the Gandhian purpose. I shall discuss them below. For now, let me simply state that because it is doubtful whether Aikido exhibits all three aspects, it is doubtful whether it could serve the essentially Gandhian politico-moral purpose. For this reason alone, Ueshiba's way of peace should not be identified with Gandhi's.

Nevertheless there is a gap in received Gandhian teaching when it comes to personal violence. Curiously, there is a gap here for precisely the same reasons that Aikidoesque strategies and Ueshiban nonresistance seem out of place on a Gandhian political stage.

Consider the extreme, but by no means uncommon, case where one individual assaults another in some back alley unobserved by any third party. If the recipient responds in the way counseled by Gandhi—covering the head and dropping to the ground—and lets herself be battered, does it serve any of the three purposes of Gandhian suffering? It may serve her self-purification (if she survives, and if she can handle the psychological consequences of assault, rape or what have you), but it is unlikely to serve the conversion of the assailant and by hypothesis it cannot affect any third parties. If it is true that an individual responding in the same way in this more private or personal situation will not have the same effect, then there may be a problem with so responding. And if there is a problem, then it looks as if there is a lack in received Gandhian teaching.

III

This is such a sensitive issue, I want to be clear at the outset about two points. First, I mean to compare the Aikidoist who is devoted to Ueshiba's way with the Satyagrahi devoted vocationally to Gandhi's way. Plainly, most people who study Aikido are not really interested in the rigors and moral purism of Ueshiba Aikido; most people who have borrowed leaves from the Mahatma's works do not commit themselves vocationally to satyagraha. Nevertheless, it is important to be clear about the pure cases not only for their own sake but because these are the ideal types from which the rest of us will take our bearings in our less stringent espousals and more painless adaptations.

Second, I want to be clear that the apparently submissive sort of response to personal violence sketched above does not in the least exhaust the resources of Gandhian thought and action.[29] It not my aspiration to canvass these resources, since I wish to focus specifically upon the issue of personal violence, but it should go without saying that nonresistance does not reduce to lifeless responses such as falling down and hoping that one's own suffering will inspire an assailant to change his ways. Gandhi's analysis of the tangle of social conditions that foster violence, and his positive recommendations for constructive development are more incisive and more practical than commonly admitted. However, once all of the recommendations for analysis and social formation are taken into account, it is still the case that when one is assaulted, the Mahatma enjoined his satyagrahis to refrain from fighting back. It is in these moments that he unreservedly counseled the acceptance of suffering, unto death if need be.

Gandhians I know tend to assimilate personal violence to one of two situations. They may take the circumstance of personal violence as a political situation in miniature. This would imply that the recipient of violence (I hesitate to say 'victim,' since victimhood is an attitude) should behave as would the member of an organized political campaign. Or they may cite stories such as the rogue tiger that Gandhi admitted could be shot—as a last resort, and with regret—if lives were at stake.

Though Gandhi was, more than most, alive to the realization that the personal is political *and* the political is personal, it is surely not mandatory to treat every encounter with a street thug or drunken brawler or rapist as if it were part of a political campaign. And though there are cases of a criminally insane person on a killing spree who may need to be shot if he cannot be quickly enough restrained, these cases are few and they make a bad model for the standard self-defense situation. So far, I have heard from Gandhians too little about the middle ground between on the one hand suffering injury or death while keeping the courage of one's conviction, and on the other hand responding regretfully but violently. The first option assimilates personal violence too hastily to systematic political or institutional violence and the second tempts us to dehumanize every assailant. Aikido explores this middle ground, and so extends to the Gandhian a fresh area of study and practice.

Regarding the personal dimension, Morihei would agree with Mohan's claim that "the best and most lasting self-defense is self-purification" (50). He would agree with satyagraha's imperative of nonretaliation (56) as well as its demand for the continuous cleansing of the adherent (218). Morihei would en-thusiastically agree that there is an absolute need for absolute calmness under fire (56). He would well understand the "cool courage" of which Gandhi speaks (57-8)[30] that permits one to face pain and affliction and death. Ueshiba would agree with Gandhi every adherent must dwell upon death and must always be ready to face death (229). For he too counseled the *memento mori*, a constant mindfulness of death and a continual preparation for it. But though he enjoined his followers to avoid killing, Ueshiba did not recommend such a quick readi-ness to accept death. That is because there are ways of defending oneself (and, perhaps, third parties) without killing others. Even if we accept that a readiness to accept death and suffering has its place in an organized campaign, it has far less of a place in personal situations of assault and battery.

It should be plain by now that Aikido embodies a different understanding of nonviolence in general and nonresistance in particular. In the situation of per-sonal violence, it does not fight back, but is less passive. Again, let me be clear. Gandhian nonresistance is not reducible to a merely 'passive resistance.' Satya-graha is not passive and it is not resistance. It is proactive, organized nonresis-tance. It answers political violence and injustice with mobilized noncompliance calculated to make the hidden visible and make unjust power impotent. It dwells on relationships and builds communities. Nevertheless, in response to personal violence *at the flashpoint of physical assault*, during a campaign or apart from it, Gandhi does counsel a noncompliance that is, while not submissive, radically passive. This is clear from the ways satyagrahis are trained to respond to people wielding clubs and so on: they are to suffer the blows in the name of peace, cov-ering their heads, perhaps falling to the ground, but offering no active response whatsoever.

It is also clear from Gandhi's occasional remarks on "hooliganism." When Mohan was asked about hooliganism, he replied, "Satyagraha brigades should be organized in every village and in every block".[31] Now this is exactly the right answer. It gestures toward an active, social and organizational effort in response to personal violence that corresponds to constructive programs on the political side. But when it comes to face-to-face encounters at the flashpoint of violence, Mohan insists that solitary satyagrahis should rather be prepared—as always—to lay down their lives rather than fight back. He is unequivocal about this. "To lay down one's life, *even alone*, for what one considers to be right, is the very core of Satyagraha" (380, emphasis added). Though there is the constructive and positive answer of social organization, in a situation of personal threat, *suffering* is, Gandhi confesses, his "only answer" (269) to thuggery. This is, mainly if not exclusively, because it remains his conviction that the sight of this suffering will "melt the heart of the aggressor" (362). Mohan summarizes his teaching on this specific point simply and eloquently. "[T]o die without killing. I know no other way" (51).

Ueshiba Aikido offers another way. In the conviction that a Gandhian may respond as an Aikidoist in situations of personal violence while remaining true to her core principles, I recommend Aikido for situations of personal violence. Aikido training should be a welcome supplement, not only because it fills a need, but because it might re-institute some of the rigor of satyagraha discipline as found in the old handbooks, a rigor that seems to have been mostly lost among Gandhians who seem nowadays to train not for physical violence but mainly for verbal assaults. My suggestion is that a Gandhian need not, but may, without contravening her principles, study and employ Aikido in situations of personal violence or third-party defense.[32]

IV

I suggested above that those who see the roots of personal violence in the larger human environment, but fail to appreciate that at its center is a face-to-face encounter with aggression that the Gandhian must always be prepared to endure without riposte, miss something at the ethical heart of the Mahatma's teaching. On the other hand, those who see in Gandhian teaching only the satyagrahi's yielding and suffering, even if they appreciate its purposes of personal purification and the conversion of violators and third parties, neglect its larger background. Gandhi did not neglect that background in all its complexities, either in his diagnosis of the causes of violence or in his proposed preventatives. The whole issue of the background of violence—with its social, political, economic, ideological, and other roots—is far more ambiguous in Ueshiba, however.

The main influence on Aikido's spiritual development was Onisaburo De-guchi, longtime leader of the Omoto-Kyo sect, though the militant social activist and environmentalist Kumagusu Minakata (1867-1941) was also an early influence. Omoto-Kyo, part nature religion and part radical social movement, was solidly pacifist in outlook. Its founder was Nao Deguchi (1836-1918). Nao, who came from desperately poor straits, wrote, "Do away with emperors, kings, and artificial government; establish true equality; abolish capitalism; live in God's heart, simply and purely!" (8). Onisaburo was Nao's son-in-law, and an early environmentalist and social activist. He wrote, "There is nothing in the world more harmful than war and more foolish than armament. The real fight is not against foreign adversaries but against those here at home who suppress our freedom, trample on our human rights, crush peace, and destroy our culture for the sake of profit."[33] A key belief of the Omoto-Kyo sect is that "art is religion," the idea that the practice of an art can be a religious practice. That idea, extended into *martial* art, became one of the two taproots of Ueshiba Aikido. The other root is the ethical vision of which I have spoken.

Ueshiba wrote, "The way of a warrior...is to stop trouble before it starts."[34] Aikido excels at blending with an attack—or now we may say, with a threatening situation—and defusing it.[35] On or off the mat, Aikido is about personal relationships. But large-scale political organization and social development are also ways of stopping trouble before it starts. Does Aikido neglect this dimension?

Ueshiba was personally concerned with social transformation from an early age. He never tired of asserting his conviction that the practice of Aikido could change social relations and thereby could actually transform the world. Morihei writes that Aikido is "a way to promote love and goodness among human-kind...a means of establishing universal peace" (32-33). The idea seems to be that by exhibiting a way of handling violence peaceably, Aikido could somehow serve as a model for others. The most natural interpretation of this idea is that Aikido can show others that a peaceable way is possible in the large (in social and political life) because it is actual in the small ('on the mat' or 'on the street'). Still, in this interpretation, Aikido *per se* remains on the side of the small and personal, on the side of the flesh-to-flesh encounter. While political activism was always part of Morihei's life, it did not carry over to become an essential ingredient in the practice of Aikido.

Admittedly Ueshiba often spoke in the first person plural to say, "Instead of foolishly waging war, we will wage peace....We will train to prevent war, to abolish nuclear weapons, to protect the environment, and to serve society."[36] But these activities remain in a sort of limbo, since on the one hand they are recommended, obviously endorsed by the founder, and yet on the other hand they are not really made part and parcel of the practice he bequeathed. If Gandhi is right about the causes of violence and its preventative remedies, then Aikido cannot have the full transformative effect the founder intended without them. I invite Aikidoists devoted to O-Sensei's way to consider Gandhi's more comprehensive vision on this point.

V

I want finally to consider two moral problems that are not familiar enough to Aikidoists, though they are quite familiar to Gandhians. They are especially acute in the matter of personal violence, and therefore are particularly intense for Aikidoists training it as a way of peace. The first concerns the beginning Aikido student primarily; the second is pertinent to all practitioners of the art.

Call the first moral difficulty the 'stopgap' problem. How is a student who trains Aikido as a way of peace to handle personal violence before her mastery is sufficient to deal with a realistic range of real challenges in the appropriate way? If she needs effective self-defense, should she train effective but violent techniques—which are typically much easier to apply—in tandem with Aikido practice? Is it not probable that allowing oneself stopgaps will make their use more likely? (There is an analog here of the 'paradox of deterrence' in international affairs.) And even if allowing oneself stopgaps did not make their use more likely, will the time spent training these more violent responses not take time away from Aikido training? Even if it did not take appreciable time away from Aikido training, does not the mere fact that one allows oneself stopgaps tend to soften the imperative to peaceable means and therefore tend to defer, perhaps indefinitely, the goal of Aikido as a way of peace?

This leads directly to a second question, pertinent to the adept as well as the student facing the stopgap problem.[37] Call this the dilemma of defeat. Is a commitment to Aikido as a way of peace and harmony a commitment to accept defeat if violence cannot be handled according to its precepts? This question must be faced squarely, because self-preservation is a strong motive and it is tempting to seek to prevail even after all peaceable means have been exhausted. When the practitioner cannot handle a particular adversary in a principled way, but might prevail by violent means, must she then choose defeat, injury, even death? Is this really the course blazed by principle?

Gandhi enjoins satyagrahis to be ready to admit defeat if a campaign cannot proceed in a nonviolent manner. As we have seen, the devotee is enjoined to endure suffering and even death; similarly, she might need to accept that a campaign has failed and desist from pressing on. Satyagrahis must put the commitment to *ahimsa* above success. That is easy to say and incredibly difficult to practice. It is part of the practice of preparation for dying of which the Mahatma spoke so often and so eloquently. Aikidoists have not faced this problem so squarely. Each Aikidoist must ask if her commitment to Aikido as a way of peace is so strong that she will refrain from injurious methods of self-defense even if the consequence is accepting defeat—and therefore injury or perhaps even death.

The obvious response is that if one seeks to use peaceable means that is all well and good, but if those means fail in the course of some actual attack then plainly one may and indeed must do what he can to survive. Is it not simply realistic to admit that anyone will do what she needs to do to prevail, and utterly idealistic to suppose that anyone would accept defeat, injury, or death in the name of some fuzzy moral ideal? This seemingly commonsensical response is too hasty. Warriors, historically, are trained to believe—and in the thick of things have shown that they can believe—that death is not the ultimate evil. Dishonor, for instance, is worse than death. Ought a devotee of Ueshiba's way of peace pledge a similar troth? Ought she to regard stepping outside her 'way of peace' a dishonor of such magnitude that she would face serious injury or even death rather than resort to injurious means?

Perhaps the question forces the issue; one might argue that an Aikidoist really does not need to face this question head on. It is standardly avoided by saying, 'I do not know how I would go; I would have to be in the situation; it is not a matter upon which I must pledge my honor in advance.' That common response is a dodge. It is unacceptable precisely because Aikidoists are to train seriously for such eventualities. Of course one who makes such an ultimate pledge may fail and resort to fisticuffs (or biting, gouging, tearing, etc.) in some actual situation, but the fact that one might fail to live up to a pledge is not a reason for avoiding it, much less for dodging the question. One should not train as if the question were open. Rather, one should train with purpose, admitting that one might fail, but not using that admission as an excuse for avoiding the issue or lightening the exercise. The issue is whether as a matter of principle and commitment and training one will stake one's honor on the point—come what may. This most testing sort of personal moral commitment cannot be settled by appeal to universal duties or cultural standards. And yet without it, it seems as if a commitment to Ueshiba Aikido as a way of peace would be less than a total commitment.

I remarked above that Ueshiba Aikido puts a nonviolent ethical intent front and center, and places the responsibility for executing this intent squarely upon the practitioner. Though the founder and his successors have provided students with methods of handling violence that are effective and capable of being used nonviolently, it is up to the Aikidoist to use them in a nonviolent way. Why would anyone want to take up such a difficult path? It plainly is a sort of special calling to which not all are summoned—though unless some few people are actually heeding the call and shouldering this austere responsibility, the very idea of Aikido would pale. One can be an appreciator and even to some extent a follower of Ueshiba without pursuing his 'way of peace' to the *ne plus ultra*, just as one can be an appreciator and even to some extent a follower of Gandhi without being a radical pacifist. But we need devotees. Without some actual practitioners in the world willing to stake their lives upon it, the idea is in each case left merely abstract and the movements, utopian.

VI

I began by comparing Ueshiba Aikido with Gandhian practice and then argued that Ueshiba's 'way of peace' is not exactly Gandhian. Nevertheless it is a companionable practice. It is companionable in the sense that a Gandhian may train in Aikido while remaining true to her principles (indeed I have recommended it for situations of personal violence) and in the sense that an Aikidoist can be a Gandhian, though to be so, she must face two moral questions of supreme difficulty. I shall close by considering two final points of comparison that are perhaps of more interest to the moralist but are nonetheless subtle and important.

Ueshiba repeatedly focused on the moral standing of the attacker. It may seem a refinement that only a moralist could love, but this is a significant shift in focus. Other martial arts such as taiji praise the man able to handle an attacker without harming him. But it is the skill of the martial artist that is in the focus of commendation. In the case of the adept who happens to be able to deal with violence in some unimpairing way, it is his own talent and proficiency that is made pivotal. The focus is on the superiority of the defender. For Ueshiba, on the other hand, the focus is not upon the defender and his superiority or skill but upon the other. He seemed to recommend caring for the other, even a violent other aiming to impair. This is why Ueshiba called Aikido the "martial art of love." He asserts of Aikido, "Its base is love..." (31). Obviously the practitioner will focus upon herself in an art that is technically demanding and that calls explicitly for not just daily training but for ritual purification. However the motive and focus in actual application is upon the other; the reason for the ethical stand of Aikido is care for the other. This shift from a focus on the practitioner's superiority to care for the other is subtle, but makes all the moral difference in the world. Ueshiba was not ashamed to claim this was 'love of the enemy' made practical and effective. Gandhi shares this concern and this focus on the other.

There is a second ethically significant concern that is not so obviously shared. Gandhi repeatedly emphasized that the nonviolent encounter with violence should be a transformative encounter.[38] The conversion of the oppressor is a paramount consideration in the Gandhian way of peace. Gandhi writes, "The Satyagrahi's object is to convert, not to coerce, the wrongdoer" (87). Organized nonviolent movement is designed to transform political structures and social relationships and the suffering of the oppressed is made visible to 'change the heart' of those who control or benefit from those structures and relationships. It is not clear whether conversion is a focus for Aikido.

Ueshiba declared, "If your heart is large enough to envelop your adversaries, you can see right through their petty mindedness and avoid their attacks. And once you envelop them, you will be able to guide them along a path indicated to you by heaven and earth" (74). There is little in Ueshiba's writings, however, that speaks to the question of whether the conversion of a particular assailant is part of the purpose of handling him in the Aikido way. He does say that Aikido "consists in defeating your adversaries spiritually by making them realize the folly of their actions."[39] Making another realize the folly of his actions is a species of conversion, to be sure. But these passages are not unambiguous. Other Aikidoists also graze the issue. Mary Heiny, for instance, says "My point of view had to be . . . to teach that aggression was self-destructive...[to show an attacker that] aggression opens you up to your own self-destruction".[40] On the other hand, O-Sensei writes in his memoirs, "The only opponent is within. Aikido is not for correcting others; it is for correcting your own mind."[41]

The issue is whether there is supposed to be something about a violent man's being handled the Aikido that should sway him from his ferocity, something parallel to the transformative effect of Gandhian suffering in the name of a just cause. In other words, is it part of Aikido's purpose—part of its professed 'love for the enemy'—to sway a violator from his violence *in and through* his being handled in Aikido's peaceable way? I have not found unequivocal statements of the question or the answer. A concern for the transformation of the practitioner is explicitly part of Ueshiba's larger program, and, I believe, a concern with transformation of the violator is a natural implication of the care for the other that is already part of his vision. Aikidoists should ponder this further.

Though Ueshiba and Gandhi both speak of peace and love, nonresistance and nonviolence, I have argued it is hasty to suppose Aikido is Gandhian. Nevertheless Aikidoists must face two hard questions about their level of commitment to their path of peace, and one way of answering these questions leads straight to the Mahatma. Gandhians must revisit the question of personal violence, and one way of answering this question leads straight to O-Sensei. So we may say that one construal of satyagraha leads to Aikido as a legitimate way of dealing with personal violence, and one construal of Aikido leads ultimately to a Gandhian pacifism. If Aikido and satyagraha are companionable in these respects, there surely ought to be more dialog between these two great "ways of peace." There might then be a larger chorus of voices joining with Ueshiba when he avows, "We have no enemies in Aikido, none of us are strangers. Every day, let's train to make the world a little more peaceful" (26).[42]

Notes

1. It is good to say at the outset that Ueshiba never called himself a pacifist. This may have been due to his friendship with and loyalty to many friends in the military and police. Ueshiba served in WWI but he opposed WWII and withdrew from service. By the time of the Second World War he was a prominent public person and his nonparticipation was quiet. His private and personal noncompliance stood in marked contrast to the response of his spiritual mentor Onasiburo Daguchi who spoke out loudly against the war and even risked charges of treason by praying for Japanese defeat. I say just a bit more about the evolution of Ueshiba's ideas about peace in due course, though that history is not my focus.

2. 'Spirit' translates 'ki' (from the Chinese 'qi'). The word 'spirit' can mislead both because there are other Japanese terms that more directly render 'spirit' and moreover because we tend to contrast spirit with matter, while in the traditional cosmologies, matter is a sort of condensation of ki and not ontologically other than it. This is not the place for a discourse on ki, but one can hardly talk about any 'internal' martial art—much less Aikido which defines itself in reference to it—without a few words. Ki is understood to be the common root of vitality, sentience, and physical energy. It is experienced inwardly as a circulating calm; it seeks a point of rest in every interaction and follows a path of least effort in every movement, and therefore appears paradigmatically in balance of forces and harmony of relationships. By following ki's own path, one is brought into harmony with others and their movements and intentions; by being in harmony with others, one is brought into harmony with oneself. I elaborate on these and other points in "The Experience of Qi" in preparation.

3. John Stevens, *The Art of Peace* (Boston: Shambhala, 2002), 33. Unless otherwise indicated, all Ueshiba references are to *The Art of Peace*.

4. Satyagraha is best left untranslated. Etymologically, it means something like a steadfast holding to the truth of being (*Sat*). It is often rendered 'truth-force.' In the strict or narrow sense of the term, satyagraha is the practice of an adept in the Gandhian way of nonviolence, the special proficiency of a special calling. In the broad sense, satyagraha is the generic name for a Gandhian way. Not everyone who practices satyagraha in the broad sense—who participates in a satyagraha campaign for instance—is a satyagrahi in the narrow or strict sense.

5. The idea of satyagraha that is action which flows from the moral truth of nonviolence is the practical expression of what we know experientially as the truth of being. Ueshiba (late in life, at least) and Gandhi both believed that violence is unethical but also untruthful. John Stevens, Ueshiba translator and biographer, goes so far as to assert the following in *The Philosophy of Aikido* (Bunkyo-ku, Japan: Kodansha International Limited, 2001), 18: "Aikido ethics revolve around one principle: *makoto*. The literal meaning of *makoto* is 'true acts,' and the word denotes 'sincerity that is natural, spontaneous—free of duplicity and artifice'." Violent, untruthful acts are an obstacle to personal realization and a block to our understanding reality. If so, then arts such as taiji or Cheng Hsin that are technically similar to Aikido and also claim to provide insight into reality—*without*

cleaving to nonviolence—will miss something essential in their ontology. This is an intriguing and controversial point of metaphysics I discuss elsewhere.

6. Ueshiba quoted by Stevens in *The Shambhala Guide to Aikido* (Boston: Shambhala Press, 1996), 101.

7. Biographer and intrepid Aikidoist John Stevens uses the phrase "art of peace" to translate 'Aikido.' This act of overtranslation has point, since it emphasizes that Aikido is not supposed to be just one more martial art, not even one more special school of jujutsu, though this is typically what one learns in the schools.

8. "In Aikido, we never attack. An attack is proof that one is out of control. Never run away from any kind of challenge, but do not try to suppress or control an opponent unnaturally. Let attackers come any way they like and then blend with them....Redirect each attack and get firmly behind it" (80, translation modified).

9. Even this generalization has exceptions, since some schools stress *atemi* (strikes or feints of strikes) more than others. When I speak of 'Ueshiba Aikido' I do not intend to isolate one style in particular but to refer to any art that keeps central the ethical intent of the founder.

10. Adele Westbrook and Oscar Ratti, *Aikido and the Dynamic Sphere* (Boston: Tuttle, 2001), 19.

11. Alan Bäck and Daeshik Kim ("Pacifism and the Eastern Martial Arts" *Philosophy East and West* 32, No. 2 (1982): 177-86) claim that everyone except the radical pacifist has a *prima facie duty* to learn how to fight, and even a pacifist really should learn how to fight even if she has no duty to do so. They offer three reasons why a pacifist should study an "Asian martial art." (See note 14, below.) First, the study of an "Asian martial art" cultivates a state of no-mind in which he can "divorce himself from violence" [184]. (See note 18, below.) Second, the pacifist who learns how to fight needs to do so to confront "the violent part of his nature" even if he does not engage others in violent exchange. Third, "[A] system that promotes the development of self-control in violent situations is...one that the absolute pacifist should learn" (184-85). Bäck and Kim conclude that "the duty of knowing how to fight is important morally, without qualification" (186). Aikidoists seek to face violent situations but train not to fight. If Aikido is a practicable response to violence, then the argument of Bäck and Kim rests on a false presupposition. That one ought to learn to deal with real violence does not imply that one ought to learn to fight.

12. One student of Ueshiba, Kenji Tomiki, introduced friendly Aikido contests on the model of Judo competition (Tomiki was also a student of Kano, the founder of Judo). Ueshiba strongly disapproved and virtually disowned the man. Traditional Aikido dojos do not allow competition, though most practice some sort of free play (*randori*) and situations of unexpected attack that call for spontaneous adjustments and improvisation (*takemusu aiki*).

13. Westbrook and Ratti, *Aikido*, 360-61. There is no unanimity about this claim that the ethical aim is part of the essence of Aikido as the founder came to conceive it. Some books on Aikido will pay lip service to it, but that is about all; many do not mention it. The popular book by Ueshiba's son and successor Kisshōmaru, *The Spirit of Aikido* (New York: Kodansha, 1984), does not discuss ethics at all.

14. Bäck and Kim, "Pacifism and the Eastern Martial Arts," limit their claims to "Asian martial arts," but this is suspect. Consider the inconclusive but highly suggestive results reported by Geoffrey Wingard, "Aggressive Discourse in the Martial Arts: An Ethnographic Survey" *Journal of Asian Martial Arts* 11, No. 1 (2002): 53-57. In one week of submissions to an on-line 'Martial Arts' forum, practitioners of "traditional" arts made 12% of statements deemed "derogatory" and 73% of statements classified as "inclusive"; practitioners of "nontraditional" arts were responsible for 27% of inclusive statements, 88% of derogatory statements, and 100% of the statements deemed "threatening." While the samples are quite small and the statistical method rudimentary, this seminal study is quite suggestive. Notice that Wingard's 'traditional/nontraditional' distinction cuts across Bäck and Kim's 'Asian/Western' dichotomy. Pentjak Silat and Muay Thai are examples of Asian arts that have the essential features—and, one supposes, the consequences for discourse and action—of Wingard's aggressive "nontraditional" arts. If so, then the study of some "Asian martial arts" may have ill effects on the behavior of the practitioner, and Bäck and Kim and others cannot use the ethnic demarcation as a line of ethical distinction.

15. "A master passes: A tribute to Cheng Man-ch'ing" *Shr Jung Newsletter* 1, No. 1 (1975): 2-7, cited in "Fifty Years in the Fighting Arts: An Interview with Robert W. Smith, *Journal of Asian Martial Arts* 10, No. 1 (2001): 36-73, 42. This is undoubtedly an understatement, since taiji stylists like others train to respond to people attacking with bottles, pipes, batons, and so on.

16. Westbrook and Ratti, *Aikido*, 34.

17. The Daito style was due to Sokaku Takeda, a fierce and bloody character who lived in constant fear of those who sought revenge on him for murdered friends or family. Takeda's astonishing martial skill is legendary, as are his carrying of weapons, his constant nighttime shifting of his bed roll to foil nocturnal attackers, and so on. Ueshiba studied with Takeda for several years before gradually distancing himself from the master of Daito-Ryu. It is fascinating that the technical roots of Ueshiba's "art of peace" are in this violent man and his school; it is as if Gandhi learned his principles of strategy from the most vicious of guerillas.

18. This three-level distinction is common in *Daito* circles. The clearest exposition I have seen is by Tony Annesi, "Three Levels of Aiki" (video, Bushido-Kai productions, 1995).

19. Stevens, *Shambhala Guide to Aikido* (Boston: Shambhala Publications, 1996), 14. This is a common sentiment. Cf. *The Art of Peace*, 32: "In Aikido…we try to completely avoid killing, even of the most evil person."

20. Responding to the conference version of this paper, Keiko Takioto Miller raised the issue of *mushin*. Kenneth Inada invoked *wu wei*. Both seemed to want to suggest that the ethical consequences I extol flow from these states. But this is not my experience. It also flies in the face of history. The bloodiest of samurai were capable of *mushin*. The same Daoists who were adept in *wu wei* were sharply rebuked by Zhu Xi for their immorality. No, these states are, for better or worse, morally neutral. I frankly suspect the belief that these would solve all the moral problems is part of a larger conviction that *wu wei* or *mushin* involve a sort of magic whose invocation can make all moral or metaphysical troubles vanish.

21. Cited by Bäck and Kim, "Pacifism and the Eastern Martial Arts," 184.

22. Westbrook and Ratti, *Aikido*, 20.

23. It should be said that there is honest dispute among martial artists about which techniques are more humane. Paul Vunak, well-known Jeet Kune Do stylist, Navy Seal trainer, and darling of the headbutt crowd, argues that an eye strike (a fast fingertip flick, not a deep gouge) followed by a few quick strikes is far *more* humane than a throw. Is the use of pain-compliance morally problematic even when no significant injury accrues? (After all, the pain may linger for days....) Why is a takedown less 'violent' than a few well-placed punches? These are legitimate questions that have their political parallel in issues about the consequences of 'surgical' military strikes as against embargoes and the like.

24. If it is too hasty to identify Morihei's nonresistance with Gandhi's, it is all the hastier to identify Aikido's 'turning' with the Christian's 'turning the other cheek.' The literal meaning of that Christian text is far closer to the Gandhian practice of accepting blows and suffering injury in the name of a higher moral cause. The Aikidoist's references to 'turning' are, focally, to the 'irimi/tenkan' or 'irimi/kaiten' movement by which an attack is avoided and the practitioner is positioned to neutralize. Stevens, (*The Philosophy of Aikido*, 24) too glibly assimilates the Aikidost's 'turning' to the Christian's.

25. Reported by Stevens, *The Art of Peace*, 14.

26. Mahatma Gandhi, *Nonviolent Resistance (Satyagraha)*, ed. Bharatan Kumarappa (New York: Schocken, 1961), 52.

27. I hope to have made this assertion plausible, despite the fact that analysts of nonviolent tactics, notably Gene Sharp, frequently compare them to ju-jutsu.

28. *Misogi* is ritual purification and renewal in Aikido practice. It helps one contact the true emptiness that is manifest physically in *sumikiri*, which Stevens renders as "perfect clarity of body and mind" (*The Philosophy of Aikido*, 52).

29. Thanks to Doug Allen for suggesting I make this point more explicit than it was in the draft.

30. "And just as we need...cool courage...we need perfect discipline and training in voluntary obedience to be able to offer civil disobedience" (54). Civil Disobedience is the active expression of *ahimsa par excellence*.

31. Mohan writes, "Surely a few hundred men and women giving themselves deliberately to mob fury will be any day a [better and] braver method of dealing with such madness than the display and use of the police and the military" (86). The brigades were to be constituted according to the *satya* principle of moral membership, so that "only those are eligible who believe in *ahimsa* and *satya*" (381).

32. I have mentioned, but have not broached, the matter of third-party defense. The use of Aikido to defend third parties under duress is something that Aikidoists have hardly explored at all. Some practitioners of Hapkido, a comprehensive Korean art influenced in part by Aikido, have begun to do so. The investigation of Aikido interventions to aid third parties is, I think, an important task for the future.

33. Cited in Stevens, *The Philosophy of Aikido*, 66.

34. Stevens, *The Philosophy of Aikido*, 69.

35. Morihei liked to say that for an Aikidoist, a fight is 'over before it has begun.' The meaning of this aphorism continues to be pondered and debated by Aikidoists. It

may refer, for instance, to the ability of an adept to sense an intent to attack and respond to it before that intent blooms in the mind and body of the assailant. In its ethical meaning, it may refer to the fact that it takes two to fight and if one is always prepared to defuse an attack, no fight can ever even begin to get started. This is Ueshiba's vision of the Aikidoist: a person in whose sphere of influence attackers virtually neutralize themselves and violence simply dissolves.

36. Stevens, *The Philosophy of Aikido*, 70.

37. The dilemma of defeat is germane to most high-level practitioners. There may be exceptions. Morihei himself is credited with astonishing abilities. This small man could throw and pin huge sumo wrestlers with no apparent effort. He could not be budged by the strongest of men. When asked by a large Nepalese wrestler for the secret of his technique, Ueshiba replied, "I am one with the universe. Who can lift that?" (20). He is reputed to have twice arranged to face a firing squad with live ammo, and both times evaded the bullets. (Stevens claims there is documentation of this because waivers had to be signed.) Though he attributed his powers to a 'divine spirit,' he did not claim this to be an exclusive possession. "The divine spirit is always present within me—and you too, if you delve deeply inside…I am just obeying its commands and letting the awesome power of nature flow through me" (25).

38. Thanks to Bart Grusalski of the Pacific Center for Sustainable Living for suggesting I say more about conversion and transformation.

39. Stevens, *The Philosophy of Aikido*, 69.

40.Mary Heiny, "The Principles of Aikido," video, Arete Press 2001.

41. Cited by Heckler, *The Anatomy of Change* (Boulder: Shambhala, 1984), 135.

42. Thanks to the Society for Asian and Comparative Philosophy for the invitation to deliver a version of this paper at the conference "Comparative Philosophy in Times of Terror" and to conference participants for excellent discussion. Thanks to Doug Allen for extensive comments on the draft, supererogatory editing and some sage advice.

15

Himsa and *Ahimsa* in the Martial Arts

Judy D. Saltzman

The martial arts in their true and original spirit are a way of peace. From the softest Tai Chi or the large circles of Aikido to the tough linear movements of Shotokan, or the flowing hard style of Kenpo, they seek to empower the practitioner with serenity and self-control. The way of the martial arts is called *budo*. Its two Japanese Kanji characters originally meant "to stop clashing weapons" (*bu*) and "the way of the Tao" (*do*). Together they can mean "the Way of brave and enlightened activity."[1] *Budo* also advocates being at harmony with the environment and to be content in the presence of others. It further insists that one not to be a threat and to be tranquil, even if threatened. Philosophically, the martial arts are based on the Buddhist ideal of renunciation of the ego, and the following of the effortless, but powerful way of the Tao.

However, an epitome of Budo can also be found in the *Bhagavad Gita* in which *himsa*, or the use of violence or doing harm is demanded of Arjuna by the incarnate deity Krishna. *Himsa* must be used because it is the last resort and the cause is righteous, even if it is against Arjuna's own relatives and friends. The Gita has been interpreted by Gandhi and others to justify *ahimsa*, non-violent action or force. In Gandhi's view the Gita is a metaphor of a spiritual war against one's own violent and lazy tendencies. He enjoins *ahimsa* against *himsa*. In no case does Gandhi advocate passively "taking it" and accepting injustice. This essay will argue that the true spirit of Budo is much like Gandhi's spirit: the effort in all cases to settle a problem through *ahimsa* and peacefully. The martial artist uses *himsa* only when absolutely necessary, and then in a controlled way that will end the fight. Although Gandhi said he would never use violence (*himsa*), I want to argue that the martial arts is in the spirit of Gandhi and in the tradition of Mahayana Buddhism—a golden mean between reckless violence and passively accepting defeat by doing nothing.

The martial arts always teaches one to do something, even if it is finding "action in inaction" and "inaction in action" (the *wu wei* of Taoism). What is meant by this paradoxical idea is that a martial artist can stop a fight or an altercation simply by knowledge of her/his skill and an attitude, and thus have taken a kind of action without effort. Cleveland Amory, founder of The Fund for Animals, reported an example of this. He mentions that the group was protesting the slaughter of wild birds and other animals in rural New York. When some of the hunters approached them with hostility, Amory's bodyguard, a small Asian man who was a black belt in Chenkido, met the hunters halfway. Amory describes the incident in this way: "Primo moved forward just one step. 'Stop,' he said quietly...Equally the men stopped in their tracks. They had just decided upon closer inspection, that there was something about him that made it clear to them that to do anything more was not going to be either profitable or healthy."[2] The little man faced down three much larger men with no weapon himself. Here was a perfect *ahimsa* solution to potential terror and violence. Martial arts training can lead one to this ideal solution more often than otherwise. However, if *himsa* is a last resort, and one must harm the attacker in defense, the martial artist is prepared.

Whether the martial art involves weapons or empty hands, they are methods of empowerment for peace and inner tranquility. For this reason, I want to consider the issue of terror through intimidation and personal assault and a remedy: empowerment through *budo*. These ideas are especially offered for those who feel themselves weaker in society: women, racial minorities in certain areas, homosexuals and children. Terror, although in no means as constant and pervasive as in larger cities, is very real in pleasant San Luis Obispo County where I live. In the last fourteen years, a woman from Cal Poly and one from nearby Cuesta College have been murdered. A third disappeared in 1990 and has never been seen since. Several of my male students and one homosexual colleague have told me about being accosted and badly beaten on the streets of our nice town,. I know children who have been cruelly molested. There are many people in similar situations.

The first point of development in training is mental attitude. A classical example of negative attitude is in the *Bhagavad Gita*. The warrior Prince Arjuna has entirely the wrong mind set. He is depressed because he is fearful of killing family and friends, even in a just cause. However, serious students of the *Gita* know that these people and the "killing" simply represent the evil, passive, indolent nature, which must be overcome. The most difficult task of all is to slay even good men, such as Bhisma and Drona because they are serving the wrong cause. The Samurai in Japan had to perform these kinds of duties regularly. Analogized to the contemporary martial arts, the first step must be overcoming the snide comments from friends, such as, to a man or a woman, "I had better be careful around you!" or to a woman, "Why would a woman of any femininity want to study fighting? Worst of all, "What's the matter honey, can't you get a man?" Once these "friendly" efforts to keep one among the unaccomplished and the mediocre who do not wish to develop themselves are overcome, one can start training in one of these world's best aerobic exercises and methods of personal fulfillment. Self-defense is only an application. Getting rid of the victim mentality and perceiving the difference between real and imaginary threats are essential. This beginning is simple, but the end results can be dramatic. Some of the heroes on United Airlines Flight 93 on September 11, 2001, which crashed in Pennsylvania, rather than submit to terrorists were martial artists.[3]

Aside from general terrorism, there is the whole issue of self-defense for women. My mother used to say, "What can a woman do alone?" "Do not go out at night; do not go to unknown or to dark places, do not take risks!" But then she would say, I know you are athletic, but isn't taking karate being a little too different?" Sexist women and men might think that women need to remain passive and defenseless, because they lack ability or will lose their sacred "femininity" and capacity to love in the process. A case in point is Theodore Roszak's ideas about men and women's roles. Although he gives an excellent analysis of feminism, he implies that, by learning an art such as karate, women want to become "brutes and bastards" like men. Roszak wrote: "Perhaps the historical purpose will be to shatter the sexual stereotypes at the expense of the compassionate virtues, leaving us all, men and women alike, with the nobler task still to achieve. Gandhi's hope: all power renounced but that of love." [4]

Daly's critique is as follows:

> Rosak apparently does not perceive the connection between women's learning karate and the overcoming of the dichotomy between power and love. As long as love is assigned to one sex and power to the other, the ontological union of love, power and justice—Gandhi's dream—will be unrealizable. Learning karate is not an act of violence but of prevention of violence, for it is directed to removing potential victims from a rapist world that requires for its perpetuation a caste of people educated to be victims. Male liberation cannot happen with this de-victimization. But perhaps in the long run this is what even male feminist's fear, for as Marcuse says of our society in another context: "the real spectre is liberation."[5]

Supporting Daly's idea, Professor Daniel Bolelli, a Kung Fu practitioner, writes powerfully about the importance of martial arts for women:

> Thanks to the martial arts, women have the occasion to come in contact with their long repressed yang energy and physical power without having to turn into androgynous steroid fed machines. Becoming able to trust one's ability to defend oneself and fight, and

taking one a role other than the prey or victim, pushes fear away. When you know that you can flatten to the ground stronger, bigger men, something inside can afford to relax for the moment in which you know the real measure of your power. You don't have to put on a show to prove your worth. If you know how to fight, peace is a choice. In this way a woman can stop seeing herself as weak and defenseless in both body and character.[6]

I agree with Bolelli that women can develop an inner power. The first step to their liberation is to identify the nature of the oppressor. What are the characteristics of the terrorist that the potential victim faces? In many cases the individual terrorist of a woman, a weaker man, or a child, acts in a similar manner to the international terrorist, but on a less grandiose scale. The terrorist proceeds with stealth and deceit, and is treacherous, giving no warning. There is no honor or honesty to this kind of predator. The victim of choice may be a relative, a friend, a child, or a non-combatant in a war situation. Men previously known to the victim perform most sexual assaults. There is always an element of fanaticism, such as revealed by the following statements told to me by people who have interviewed known rapists: "She deserved it because of the way she dresses!" Or "A man just can't stop if he is having sex, even if a woman can."

One might say that the international terrorist who commits suicide for his/her cause might be acting unselfishly, as opposed to a rapist who acts for a different motive. However, the similarity between the individual predator and the political terrorist is that they are both acting for a limited concept of themselves: my gratification, my family, my tribe, my nation, and my religious ideology. They both attempt to instill extreme fear in order to terrorize their victim and to make him/her act against their own interests. The rapist or murderer who grabs someone and says, "If you scream, I'll kill you," is trying to get the victim to do precisely the opposite of what might help him/her: attract attention; take action. My martial arts teacher says: "Do something; it is much better than nothing." The ultimate goal of the individual predator or political terrorist is the "Stockholm Syndrome," or getting one to sympathize, or even to share the power objective. "Because you have excited me, don't you really want to be raped?" or "Since your people killed one of my family members, is it not just that I kill you?" What these examples show is that the terrorist never acts for humanity as a whole. Although he or she may be courageous enough to sacrifice life in the case of the suicide bomber, or bold enough, in the case of the rapist, to take what he wants, there is the inevitable cowardice of attacking those who are unsuspecting and weaker: a girl walking home from school, a smaller man coming out of a bar, a bus, a busy airport, a Passover dinner, or Muslims praying in their mosque.

The martial artist must learn to deal with all these by refusing to be a defenseless victim. Vigilance may lead to a pre-emptive action. This move can be non-violent, if done in time. Once when I was a young graduate student in Berkeley, I realized that I was being followed on Telegraph Avenue. I began to be concerned as the street became less populated. I finally spun on my heel, and told the startled young man who had a very guilty expression: "I know you are following me. Stop it now!" He turned away. I circled through a market for sometime and established that the coast was clear before I went home. The attitude of watchfulness against the terror of sexual harassment or robbery is universally applicable. I am grateful to the nice guys on the beach who asked me if I were being bothered by some men hanging around where I was sun bathing. The report of suspicious activity in an airport, the offer to walk a friend home, can stop a potential tragedy.

The efforts of women to pre-emptily protect themselves are many and varied. Mine is the martial arts, but another's may be different, although they both involve a watchful attitude. My own example is an experience I had in a very large supermarket around midnight. I was in the checkout line in a virtually deserted store. The grocery clerk had to leave for a few minutes. I suddenly became aware that the two men behind me were very intoxicated. They started to make comments, gestures and noises. One started to extend his hand toward my rear end. I had been grabbed there and in other places in the past. I was tired and in a bad mood. As the man moved in, I slowly lowered my center of gravity and formed a fist which they could not see. One touch and he was going down! Then I remembered the story about a martial art's master who had been able to defeat an opponent with a single look. I turned and gave them the dirtiest look I know. They both took three steps backward, and the situation was diffused. I had read about the art of Aikido that "Aiki is the art of defeating your opponent by a single glance."[7] It is necessary to develop *kime* (focus) to do this.

Another example of a resourceful woman is from a friend who is a professional actress and storyteller, and therefore a careful observer of people. She observed a "bag lady" in New York, skillfully wending her way down the street with a shopping cart holding her belongings pulled by a team of five dogs. The dogs looked well fed and cared for. Although obviously homeless, the woman held her head high. My friend thought, "How brilliant! This lady has the dogs not only to relieve her from pushing the cart, but also to protect her since she was alone and when she slept in the park at night . they were also warm bodies from the cold. People who had sympathy for animals would give her money to feed the potentially starving dogs as well. She had intelligently insulated herself from the terror of bullies and attackers, as well as the economic violence of her situation."[8]

The notion of preconceived defense is universally applicable, although pre-emptive action is not always as universally advisable. For example, a martial artist might take away a knife, gun or club, if someone is a threat. He or she would block or counter attack, if a man or a woman tries to grab or hit. However, not threatening or striking first is a matter of *budo* principle. However, although the attitude of vigilance is advisable in international politics, the taking away of weapons by pre-emptive military action is not always the solution. What can be done about any terrorist threat, individually or internationally, varies with the situation. Offering to meet the terrorist's goals, if possible, without violence, defense by *ahimsa*, is ideal and best. In the case of a fanatic, or a person intent on doing harm, it may not be possible.

In the case of the martial arts, whether one should take pre-emptive action or not, often depends on a quick judgment. In the international arena, it may depend on long and careful study. The martial arts will not solve the problem of international terrorism.. Nevertheless, it offers a philosophy for dealing with it. Morihei Ueshiba, the founder of Aikido, established the International Aikido Foundation to promote peace and good will through *budo*. He is quoted as saying: "In Aikido we never attack. If you want to strike first to gain advantage over someone, that is a proof your training is insufficient. Let your partner attack, and use his aggression against him. Do not cower from an attack. Control it before it begins."[9] In the case of international terrorism, those who would prevent it also need to take control by obtaining a thorough knowledge of the strength and motives of the aggressors, not by striking first on the basis of incomplete intelligence and faulty assumptions.

Sensei Morihei Ueshiba is an inspiration to anyone who wants to study the martial arts, or to fight terrorism. His is a consummate philosophy applicable to all the martial arts. He is the founder as well as supreme practitioner of Aikido, the school of the harmony of the way. Born in 1883 in rural Japan, he became a practitioner of Shingon Buddhism in his youth, and later joined a group called Omoto-Kyo. The Shino prophetess Nao who claimed that god Konjin spoke through her had inspired this sect. Her disciple Onisaburo preached the doctrine of non-violence, peace and the imminent descent of Shambala. Morihei studied with Onisaburo for sometime. Because he was extremely tough and trained in the hard styles of the martial arts, he accompanied Onisaburo to Mongolia as his body guard. There he had an overwhelming experience of enlightenment. This supreme moment led him to the philosophy that a true martial art must be totally defensive and in harmony with the universe. Thereafter, he developed Aikido, which is large circle jiu-jitsu, combined with other arts.

Devastated by World War II, he realized that the way the Japanese military used martial arts was not true *budo*. He told his students: "Even in war, the taking of human life is to be avoided as much as possible. It is always a sin to kill. Give your opponents every chance to make peace."[10] On another occasion he told his son: "Reckless fools, ignorant of statesmanship dominate the military and religious ideas. They slaughter innocent citizens indiscriminately and destroy everything in their path. They live in total contradiction to the will of the gods, and will surely come to a sorry end. True *budo* is to nourish life and foster peace, love and respect, not to blast the world to pieces with weapons."[11] Ueshiba's employment *of budo* for nondestructive purposes is an inspiration for peace, but it is also a philosophy of defense against terrorism. Although I practice Kenpo, not Aikido, what Ueshiba Sensei and my teacher have taught me is to be alert, really alert. Because he was so alert, Morihei was often able to verbally preempt opponents who planned to attack him. He said that some of his amazing feats, such as being able to dodge bullets, were because no one could hurt him until his time on earth had been accomplished. He said that to defeat an opponent was to reharmonize him. His last words were, "Aikido is the entire world."[12]

In Aikido as in other martial arts, the primary aim of *budo* is mental serenity and strength. In his book *On the Warrior's Path,* Daniel Bolelli wrote about the ancient symbolism in the martial arts: the Warrior, the Dragon and the Princess. The Warrior has the courage to fight, and the Princess has the serenity and wisdom to live. With some exceptions,[13] the Warrior never fights in an unjust cause, unlike the simple soldier who just takes orders. The Warrior is also not afraid of being afraid. He or she learns to overcome fear by challenging its energy. Ueshiba said, "The way of the warrior is the creation of harmony."[14] Bolelli goes on to explain that many martial artists were and are also painters, poets, calligraphers, teachers, doctors, healers, and artists of various types. This is the Princess in them, the balance between the Yin and the Yang. However, the Warrior must ultimately face the Dragon which can take the form of an unjust system of social advancement, a dysfunctional family, a negative relationship which drains energy, as well as an attacker.

In this context, I would like to discuss the hero of women and the disadvantaged who try to overcome obstacles by the martial arts: Wing Chun. She was a woman who had the courage to fight the Dragon over three hundred years ago in China. The system now called Wing Chun originated with the Buddhist nun Ng Mui, a master of Shaolin kung fu exercise and its attendant fighting art, Kenpo "the law of the fist." The style was passed on secretly through various students. Later it became known for Yim Wing Chun, Master Ng Mui's first disciple. A native of Canton, Wing Chun was a brilliant, athletic girl. Her mother died shortly after her betrothal to Leung Bok Chau, a salt merchant. Unfortunately, about the same time, her father Yim Yee, was wrongfully accused of a crime. Rather than risk the vicissitudes of an unjust system, Yim and his daughter fled to the Tai Leung Mountain near the border of Szechuan and Yunan Provinces. There they opened a bean curd shop.

Meanwhile, Kung Fu and Kenpo had become very popular in the Buddhist monasteries during the reign of emperor K'anshsi of the Ching Dynasty (1662-1722). The southern monastery, Siu Lam, aroused the suspicions of this Manchu government. They thought that insurrection was brewing there, but their troops were unsuccessful in attacking the monastery. Money and other incentives persuaded a treacherous monk, Ma Ning Yee, to set fire to Siu Lam. When it burned down, the Abbess, Master Ng Mui, and several abbots had to go their separate way. Ng Mui took refuge in the White Crane Temple near Mt. Tai Leung. There she met Wing Chun and her father from whom she bought bean curd.

At fifteen Wing Chun had become very beautiful. Being a poor girl, she attracted the attention of a local bully who tried to force her to marry him. Master Ng Mui observed his aggressive behavior and felt sorry for Wing Chung. She began to teach her fighting techniques. Finally, Wing Chun followed Ng Mui into the mountains where she trained day and night for an undisclosed period of time. Upon her return, she challenged the bully to fight and beat him up. Her teacher, Master Ng Mui, then chose to travel, but she made Wing Chun promise to follow the Kung Fu tradition very strictly, and to help overthrow the Manchu government in favor of the Ming Dynasty. She was also admonished to continue to develop the fighting art, after she married. She was obedient, and taught kung fu to her husband, Leung Bok Chau. He taught the art that became known by his wife's name to a whole line of successors . Among others, the six and one-half feet bow techniques were incorporated. The line of succession remained unbroken down to Grandmaster Yip Man of Hong Kong and his son Master Yip Chun.[15]

What I have learned from the story of Wing Chun and from the practice of Kenpo Karate is to be alert, and to do everything that can be done in any situation. In any circumstance, I ask myself, have I avoided a dangerous situation? If I have to be in one, have I done all I can to protect myself and others for whom I am responsible? If so, then I relax. This enables me to handle the problem in a more efficient way, if one arises. I am learning from Kenpo how half asleep most of us are much of the time. Often we do not hear what is said. Many of us are unaware of our surroundings and the people there. These are vital factors in self defense.

In conclusion, I would like to discuss the idea that a real *budo* practitioner against terror and for self-development follows the Bodhisattva path. The ancient Japanese *Tale of the Secrets of the Old Cat* is a case in point. It tells of a giant rat which was terrorizing a master's house and garden. None of the young cats could get it. The Old Cat, a plain gray male, was brought in. The rat froze, and the Old Cat immediately grabbed it by the neck and gave it to the master. Then the Old Cat was given the place of honor and began to teach the young cats and kittens who were filled with ego about all they had learned. When each spoke, it turned out that every one of them had a pre-conceived idea of how to capture the rat. They had a pattern in their minds about what they would do. The Old Cat instructed them that they need to be prepared, but to get to a place of *mushin* or No Mind. This state involved ultimately "no enemy, no cat, no rat, no self." The Old Cat said: "Because there is a self, there is an enemy. If there is no self, there is no enemy. 'Enemy' is that which is in opposition. The type of opposition that appears external in ying and yang, fire and water. Every object with form has its opposite. When mind has no form, there is nothing to opposite it. When there is no opposition, there is nothing to fight against. This is called 'no enemy, no self'."[16] Even the sword master listened to the instruction of the old Bodhisattva cat. The Old Cat is so successful because he is without ego. Ego can lead to erroneous preconceptions. Instead, he becomes "one with his opponent." He knows the opponent's mind, and therefore just what to do. He succeeded where the younger cats failed.

This example can be applied to us humans in personal and international situations. Do we really know the mind of a potential attacker? Do we retaliate without ego or need of personal gain, but simply to defend ourselves? The answer could certainly be "no" in many instances: we were not watchful for an attack. For example, does a woman walk across a dark bridge alone at night or fail to secure the windows of her apartment? Or there is a huge scramble after the September 11, 2001 attacks to learn about Islam and the Middle East, populated with Muslims who have been criticizing our ignorance for years. We discover that we do not understand these people, "the others" at all. We are anything but one with them.

It can be concluded from this instruction that the best way to fight any kind of terror is calm alertness or *mushin*. This lesson can be learned from all of the martial arts. I know that every time I plan a strategy in a sparring match, it does not work out. However, if I just follow the natural flow of attacks and parries, I get quite a few strikes. Funakoshi Gichin, the Grandmaster of Shotokan Karate, wrote in his Twenty Principles of Karate: "Everything you encounter is an aspect of Karate; find the marvelous truth there."[17] He means that although the physical training is practiced, only the dojo, everything we encounter, requires a reaction. A reaction too soon or off base, preconceived, or too early or too late, can be disastrous. A well-timed reaction coming from *mushin*, can be beneficial. An example of the serene state and openness of mind that Funakoshi achieved can seen in the following incredible feat. Sensei Teruyuki Okazaki describes the following incident when he was invited to strike at the Grandmaster: I charged and punched him. I thought he was on the floor when I felt somebody tapping me on the shoulder. "You need more practice Okazaki!" I don't know how he did it. My classmates said I did a good job, but it was as if my punch went through Master Funakoshi's body."[18]

I am learning much about the Bodhisattva path in my school, Craft Kenpo Karate.[19] The new students, the white belts, are the most important students in the school. Because they are new to training, they must never go uninstructed. In fact, a brown or black belt in our school would be in trouble with Grandmaster Craft, if they practiced their advanced forms and ignored a newcomer needing help. Through this, I have learned that the best way to defeat terror is to empower others who are worthy to learn, but weaker. They first learn that this art is always for the good and to help others. Daniele Bolelli says of this idea:

> The Bodhisattva doesn't have all the answers and is not a raving Messiah coming to save the world. He is a calm warrior, aware of his powers and ready to use them. Some American Indian tribes had a similar idea. They say that it is a warrior's duty to take care of everything and everybody. Just as the Bodhisattvas have achieved awareness allowing them things out of the ordinary, warriors have the strength to do what others cannot. Thus it is their responsibility to share this talent. [20]

I have seen many individuals empowered by the shared talent and helpful attitude of the school to which I belong. All the different types of people have come: (1) the young macho male who already knows "how to fight," but cannot stand to get hit the first time he spars. (These usually do not stay, but some do.) (2) The man who has no self confidence because of a childhood trauma. (3) The smaller guy who has a "little man" complex," but learns too that he is faster and more agile than the bigger men. (4) The girl who has been intimidated by older men and boys or may even have been hurt or molested. (5) People who are looking for a new and different athletic experience for themselves and their children. Of course all these are ideal types. Many who at first could not even stand up straight, make a correct fist, or keep a balanced stance, have been empowered by Kenpo.

Anyone who takes this training seriously must learn to develop *mushin*. It is a state beyond terror and defeat, beyond concern for results. The consequences must be suspended if the action is to be good in itself. In other words, one learns to fight with the right technique and the proper mind, not just to defeat one's opponent. However, if one has these virtues, one will always be victorious, because of doing well in the flow of the fight. This teaching is the same as that of the *Bhagavad Gita*: "Make pleasure and pain, gain and loss, victory and defeat, the same to thee, and then prepare for battle, for thus and thus alone shalt thou in action still be free from sin."[21] This instruction to the warrior Prince Arjuna is simply to act with what *kokoro,* the warrior's heart, striving with all you have, yet letting go the result for personal self. The Kung Fu Meditation says:

> The greatest object
> Of the superior person
> Is to preserve tranquility.
>
> He takes no pleasure
> In winning battles
> For if he did so
> He would finding gratification
> In the pain of others.
>
> He believes
> That he who takes delight
> In the defeat of others
> Does not follow the Tao.
>
> That which is not in the way of the Tao
> Will not endure.[22]

All these teachings of the *Gita,* the Buddha, and the Tao flow together in the practice of the martial arts. This is the power which brings peace.

Notes

1. John Stevens, *Budo Secrets: Teachings of the Martial Arts* (New York: Shambala Press, 2002), ix.

2. Cleveland Amory, *The Best Cat Ever* (New York: Little, Brown & Company, 1993), 79.

3. Charles B. Rubin and William R. Channing, Ima Renda-Tanalai, Thomas Birkland, "Major Terrorist Events and their Outcomes" (1988-2002), March 3, 2003, <www.Colorado.edu/hazard/uplwp99.html >One of the major instigators of counter terrorist measures on this United Airlines flight which went down near Somerset, Pennsylvania on September 11, 2001, was a judo practitioner.

4. Theodore Roszak, "The Hard and the Soft," *Masculine and Feminine,* 103-104, cited by Mary Daly, *Beyond God the Farther* (Boston: Beacon Press, 1973), 171.

5. Daly, *Beyond God the Father,* 171.

6. Daniele Bolelli, *On the Warrior's Path: Philosophy, Fighting and Martial Arts Mythology* (Berkeley: Frog Limited, 2003), 51.

7. Takeda Sogaku, Headmaster of the Daito Ryu Aikijujusu. Major Forrest E. Morgan, *Living the Martial Way* (Fort Lee, New Jersey: Barricade Books, 1992),

8. Erica Lann-Clark, professional actress and storyteller, resident of Soquel, California. Ms. Lann-Clark told me that this character is actually a composite of several such individuals she observed.

9. Moihei Uyeshiba, John Stevens, *Budo Secrets: The Teachings of the Martial Arts* (Shambala: Boston, 1992), 72.

10. *Morihei Ueshiba* , John Stevens, *The Invincible Warrior: A Pictorial Biography of Morihei Uyeshiba, the Founder of Aikido* (Boston: Shambala Press), 65.

11. Morihei Uyeshiba, 65.

12. Morihei Uyeshiba, 72.

13. The samurai who fights a number of the Ronin on the bridge in the film *Chusinguru: The Story of the Forty-seven Ronin,* was sworn to an unjust master. However, the Ronin bow to him when he is dying because of his loyalty, courage and skill.

14. Morihei Uyeshiba, *On the Warrior's Path,: Philosophy, Fighting and Martial Arts Mythology,* 57.

15. Grandmaster Yip Man, *The Origin of Wing Chun,* <http://www/wingchun.com/ history.html > (May,19 1995).

16. John Stevens, *Budo Secrets*, 56.

17. Funakoshi, Gichin, John Stevens, *Budo Secrets*, 25.

18. Teruyuki Okazaki in Jose M. Fragas, *Karate Masters* (Burbank, California: Unique Publications, 2001, 289.

19. Grandmaster Lloyd Craft founded this school in 2000 in Los Osos, California. He teaches the Chinese style of Shaolin Kenpo, as well l as the hybrid style of Kajukenpo from Hawaii. He also teaching the Philippine style of Arnis stick fighting.

20. Daniele Bolelli, 109.

21. *The Bhagavad Gita*, Los Angeles: The Theosophy Company, 1947. Rendered by William Q. Judge.

22. Meditation #25. *Kung Fu Meditations and Chinese Proverbial Wisdom.* Selections adapted by Ellen Kay Hua and Calligraphy by Maky. New York: Bantam Books, 1974.

Index

Abdul-Rahman, Omar, 9
Abouhalima, 5
Absolute Reality, 163
absolute truth, 32–35, 38n12
absolutism, 16
Abu Ghraib prisoner scandal, 22, 23
action, 49, 133, 134, 152
adeês, 47
Adi Granth, 91
aeterna veritas, 80n31
agape, 15
aggression, 213
ahimsa, xiii, 24–25, 164, 220; example of, 230; in martial arts, 229–39
aiki, 212
Aikido, xiii, 209, 229; attack forbidden by, 225n8; competition/friendly play in, 225n12; defense based nature of, 210–11; dilemma of defeat in, 220, 228n37; focus of, 222; Gandhians' incompatibility with, 215; injury rates of, 211; nonresistance in, 214; nonviolence of, 210, 211, 213–14; philosophy of, 210; stopgap problem with, 220; third-party defense in, 227n32; translation of, 225n7; turning in, 227n24; use of, 214. *See*

also Morihei, Ueshiba
Aikidoists, 209–10
al-Ala Mawdudi, Maulana Abu. *See* Mawdudi
alayavijñana, 95, 164
alcohol, 20–21
alertness, 235
Allen, Douglas, ix, 180n6
Ames, Roger, 203
Amory, Cleveland, 230
Analects (Confucius), 175
anatta, 141, 151
anger, 128
anicca, 151
Apology (Aristotle), 41–42
appropriateness *(yi)*, 200
Aquinas, Thomas, 45
arahant, xi, 109–11; framework of, 111; human rights and, 109–10; ideal of, 114; life of, 116; stages to, 111
arahantship, 111, 115
Aristotle, ix–x, 41–42; on action, 49; on courage, 46–47; on death, 46; al-Farabi and, 77n16; on fear, 42, 47–48; on fine, 47; on friendship, 43–44, 180n9; on goodness, 42–43; on illness, 50n8; Plato and, 78n22; on pleasure, 50n1; on revenge, 50n9; on soul, 44, 50n2; on substance, 50n2; on

Philosophy (Cornell University Press, 1991). She is currently writing a book on Mill for the Blackwell Press Great Minds series. She has published articles on environmental ethics, feminist ethics, and Buddhist ethics.

Peter S. Groff is Assistant Professor of Philosophy at Bucknell University. He has published several articles on Nietzsche's thought, co-edited the four-volume *Nietzsche: Critical Assessments* (Routledge 1998), and guest-edited a special comparative issue of the *Journal of Nietzsche Studies* (Autumn 2004). His current work focuses on Nietzsche and Islamic philosophy.

Christopher W. Gowans is Professor of Philosophy at Fordham University in New York City. He works primarily in ethics, with concentrations in Buddhist philosophy, Hellenistic philosophy, Kant, and contemporary moral theory. His publications include *Innocence Lost: An Examination of Inescapable Moral Wrongdoing* (Oxford University Press, 1994) and *The Philosophy of the Buddha* (Routledge, 2003).

Jim Highland, Philosophy, University of Hartford, is currently doing comparative research focusing on ethical and aesthetic themes, especially the role of narratives in how we experience, judge and act in the world. His most recent articles are "Transformative Katharsis: The Significance of Theophrastus' Botanical Works for Interpretations of Dramatic Catharsis," in the *Journal of Aesthetics and Art Criticism* (Spring 2005), and "Transformation to Eternity: Augustine's Conversion to Mindfulness" in *Buddhist Christian Studies* (Fall 2005).

John M. Koller is Professor of Asian and Comparative Philosophy at Rensselaer Polytechnic Institute. A past president of the Society for Asian and Comparative Philosophy, he is author of more than fifty journal articles and book chapters. His three books currently in print are: *A Source Book in Asian Philosophy* (New York: Macmillan & Co., 1991); *Asian Philosophies,* 4 ed. (Englewood Cliffs, NJ: Prentice Hall, 2002); *The Indian Way: An Introduction to the Philosophies and Religions of India,* 2 ed. (Englewood Cliffs, NJ: Pearson Prentice Hall, 2005).

Anna Lännström is Assistant Professor of Philosophy at Stonehill College where she teaches courses on Aristotle, Plato, ethics, and Indian philosophy. Her publications include *Loving the Fine: Goodness and Happiness in Aristotle's Ethics (*University of Notre Dame Press, 2006) and "Am I My Brother's Keeper? An Aristotelian Take on Responsibility for Others" in *Responsibility*, ed. by Barbara Darling Smith (Lexington Books, 2006). She is also the editor of *Promise and Peril: The Paradox of Religion as Resource and Threat* and of *The*

About the Contributors

Douglas Allen, Professor of Philosophy at the University of Maine, is author and editor of many books, most recently *Myth and Religion in Mircea Eliade* (Routledge, 2002). Honored with the Distinguished Maine Professor Award (teaching, research, and service) and the Presidential Research and Creative Achievement Award (outstanding Maine research professor), he has been recipient of Fulbright and Smithsonian grants to India. Doug served as President of the Society for Asian and Comparative Philosophy (2001-2004).

Michael G. Barnhart is a Professor of Philosophy at Kingsborough Community College of the City University of New York. He teaches courses in all areas of philosophy, but his research centers on issues in comparative philosophy and ethics about which he has written numerous articles as well as edited *Varieties of Ethical Reflection: New Directions for Ethics in a Global Context* published by Lexington Books.

Joanne D. Birdwhistell is Professor of Philosophy and Asian Civilization at the Richard Stockton College of New Jersey. Her publications include *Transition to Neo-Confucianism: Shao Yung on Knowledge and Symbols of Reality* (Stanford University Press, 1989) and *Li Yong (1627-1705) and Epistemological Dimensions of Confucian Philosophy* (Stanford University Press, 1996). She has philosophical interests in Daoism and Confucianism and in comparative studies of gender and wilderness.

Vance Cope-Kasten, Professor of Philosophy at Ripon College, is interested in the philosophical significance of loneliness and is currently researching what might be learned about that from the treatment of loneliness in Asian thought. He is the author of "Meeting Chinese Philosophy," which appeared in *An Introduction To Chinese Culture Through the Family*, edited by Howard Giskin and Bettye S. Walsh (SUNY, 2001).

C. Wesley DeMarco teaches at Clark University and Assumption College. He advocates a "Neo-Socratic" philosophy that offers a fresh approach to metaphysics, ethics, and philosophy of symbol. Wes was awarded the Aristotle prize by the Metaphysical Society of America in 1997 for "Modality and Mental Illness." He is a published poet and amateur composer and musician.

Wendy Donner is Professor of Philosophy at Carleton University, Ottawa, Canada. She is the author of *The Liberal Self: John Stuart Mill's Moral and Political*

Stranger's Religion: Fascination and Fear (University of Notre Dame Press, 2003 and 2004 respectively).

Jeffery D. Long is Assistant Professor of Religious Studies at Elizabethtown College in Elizabethtown, Pennsylvania. He is the author of *A Vision for Hinduism: Beyond Hindu Nationalism* and has published in *The Journal of Religion, Science and Spirit, Creative Transformations,* and several edited volumes. He has presented papers for the American Academy of Religion, Association for Asian Studies, and Society for Asian and Comparative Philosophy. His primary areas of expertise are Indian philosophy (classical and contemporary), Hinduism, Jainism, and process thought.

Judy D, Saltzman, Professor Emerita of Philosophy at California Polytechnic State University, San Luis Obispo, earned a Ph.D. in religious studies from the University of California, Santa Barbara. She is the author of *Paul Natorp's Philosophy of Religion with the Marburg Neo-Kantian Tradition* and a number of articles on the philosophy of religion. She is a black belt in the martial art of Shaolin Kenp.

Sor-hoon Tan is Associate Professor of Philosophy at the National University of Singapore. She is author of *Confucian Democracy: A Deweyan Reconstruction,* and editor of *Challenging Citizenship: Group Membership and Cultural Identity in a Global Age.* She co-edited *The Moral Circle and the Self* and *Filial Piety in Chinese Thought and History.* Her articles have appeared in journals including *Philosophy East and West, Journal of Chinese Philosophy, International Philosophical Quarterly,* and *Metaphilosophy.*

Kirill O. Thompson teaches at National Taiwan University. Specialized in Zhu Xi, his interests span the spectrum of Chinese thought. His scholarly papers in Chinese philosophy have appeared in books and periodicals for two decades. Recent projects include an English translation of Qian Mu's study of Zhu Xi into English, as well as an inquiry into Thorstein Veblen's critical approach to socio-economics.